RELATIONAL TREATMENT OF TRAUMA

Relational Treatment of Trauma: Stories of loss and hope is the culmination of over 35 years of psychotherapy with children and adults, many of whom have suffered the effects of physical, emotional, or sexual abuse. It addresses a gap in the literature on the treatment of trauma and chronic loss that is a ubiquitous part of life in foster care. While "trauma informed care" has received considerable attention recently, there is little that focuses on the consequences of repeated, unexpected, and unexplained or unexplainable losses of caregivers. *Relational Treatment of Trauma* explores the ways in which those experiences arise in the therapeutic relationship and shows how to help clients build the trust necessary for establishing healthier, more satisfying and hopeful relationships.

Toni Heineman introduces and reinforces the concept of the relationship as the most powerful agent of therapeutic change. She highlights the ways in which clinicians can build and sustain a relationship with clients whose experience of trauma can make them wary of trusting, which she illustrates throughout the book with compelling case vignettes.

The book will be essential reading for psychoanalysts, clinical psychologists, social workers, psychiatrists, and family therapists working with children who have been affected by abuse; and it will be valuable to clinicians in the early part of their career, who are working for the first time with children suffering from abuse.

Dr. Heineman has practised in San Francisco working with children, adults, and families for over 35 years. She is the founder and executive director of A Home Within. Dr. Heineman presents and publishes widely.

Relational Perspectives Book Series
Lewis Aron & Adrienne Harris
Series Co-Editors

Steven Kuchuck & Eyal Rozmarin
Associate Editors

The Relational Perspectives Book Series (RPBS) publishes books that grow out of or contribute to the relational tradition in contemporary psychoanalysis. The term *relational psychoanalysis* was first used by Greenberg and Mitchell[1] to bridge the traditions of interpersonal relations, as developed within interpersonal psychoanalysis and object relations, as developed within contemporary British theory. But, under the seminal work of the late Stephen Mitchell, the term *relational psychoanalysis* grew and began to accrue to itself many other influences and developments. Various tributaries – interpersonal psychoanalysis, object relations theory, self psychology, empirical infancy research, and elements of contemporary Freudian and Kleinian thought – flow into this tradition, which understands relational configurations between self and others, both real and fantasied, as the primary subject of psychoanalytic investigation.

We refer to the relational tradition, rather than to a relational school, to highlight that we are identifying a trend, a tendency within contemporary psychoanalysis, not a more formally organized or coherent school or system of beliefs. Our use of the term *relational* signifies a dimension of theory and practice that has become salient across the wide spectrum of contemporary psychoanalysis. Now under the editorial supervision of Lewis Aron and Adrienne Harris with the assistance of Associate Editors Steven Kuchuck and Eyal Rozmarin, the Relational Perspectives Book Series originated in 1990 under the editorial eye of the late Stephen A. Mitchell. Mitchell was the most prolific and influential of the originators of the relational tradition. He was committed to dialogue among psychoanalysts and he abhorred the authoritarianism that dictated adherence to a rigid set of beliefs or technical restrictions. He championed open discussion, comparative and integrative approaches, and he promoted new voices across the generations.

Included in the Relational Perspectives Book Series are authors and works that come from within the relational tradition, extend and develop the tradition, as well as works that critique relational approaches or compare and contrast it with alternative points of view. The series includes our most distinguished senior psychoanalysts, along with younger contributors who bring fresh vision.

1 Greenberg, J. & Mitchell, S. (1983). *Object relations in psychoanalytic theory.* Cambridge, MA: Harvard University Press.

Vol. 1
CONVERSING WITH UNCERTAINTY
Practicing Psychotherapy in a Hospital Setting
Rita Wiley McCleary

Vol. 2
AFFECT IN PSYCHOANALYSIS
A Clinical Synthesis
Charles Spezzano

Vol. 3
THE ANALYST IN THE INNER CITY
Race, Class, and Culture
through a Psychoanalytic Lens
Neil Altman

Vol. 4
A MEETING OF MINDS
Mutuality in Psychoanalysis
Lewis Aron

Vol. 5
HOLDING AND PSYCHOANALYSIS
A Relational Perspective
Joyce A. Slochower

Vol. 6
THE THERAPIST AS A PERSON
Life Crises, Life Choices, Life Experiences,
and Their Effects on Treatment
Barbara Gerson (ed.)

Vol. 7
SOUL ON THE COUCH
Spirituality, Religion, and Morality in
Contemporary Psychoanalysis
Charles Spezzano & Gerald J. Gargiulo (eds.)

Vol. 8
UNFORMULATED EXPERIENCE
From Dissociation to Imagination in
Psychoanalysis
Donnel B. Stern

Vol. 9
INFLUENCE AND AUTONOMY IN
PSYCHOANALYSIS
Stephen A. Mitchell

Vol. 10
FAIRBAIRN, THEN AND NOW
Neil J. Skolnick & David E. Scharff (eds.)

Vol. 11
BUILDING BRIDGES
Negotiation of Paradox in Psychoanalysis
Stuart A. Pizer

Vol. 12
RELATIONAL PERSPECTIVES
ON THE BODY
Lewis Aron & Frances Sommer Anderson (eds.)

Vol. 13
SEDUCTION, SURRENDER, AND
TRANSFORMATION
Emotional Engagement in the Analytic Process
Karen Maroda

Vol. 14
RELATIONAL PSYCHOANALYSIS
The Emergence of a Tradition
Stephen A. Mitchell & Lewis Aron (eds.)

Vol. 15
THE COLLAPSE OF THE SELF AND ITS
THERAPEUTIC RESTORATION
Rochelle G. K. Kainer

Vol. 16
PSYCHOANALYTIC PARTICIPATION
Action, Interaction, and Integration
Kenneth A. Frank

Vol. 17
THE REPRODUCTION OF EVIL
A Clinical and Cultural Perspective
Sue Grand

Vol. 18
OBJECTS OF HOPE
Exploring Possibility and Limit in
Psychoanalysis
Steven H. Cooper

Vol. 19
WHO IS THE DREAMER, WHO
DREAMS THE DREAM?
A Study of Psychic Presences
James S. Grotstein

Vol. 20
RELATIONALITY
From Attachment to Intersubjectivity
Stephen A. Mitchell

Vol. 21
LOOKING FOR GROUND
Countertransference and the
Problem of Value in Psychoanalysis
Peter G. M. Carnochan

Vol. 22
SEXUALITY, INTIMACY, POWER
Muriel Dimen

Vol. 23
SEPTEMBER 11
Trauma and Human Bonds
Susan W. Coates, Jane L. Rosenthal, &
Daniel S. Schechter (eds.)

Vol. 24
MINDING SPIRITUALITY
Randall Lehman Sorenson

Vol. 25
GENDER AS SOFT ASSEMBLY
Adrienne Harris

Vol. 26
IMPOSSIBLE TRAINING
A Relational View of Psychoanalytic Education
Emanuel Berman

Vol. 27
THE DESIGNED SELF
Psychoanalysis and Contemporary Identities
Carlo Strenger

Vol. 28
RELATIONAL PSYCHOANALYSIS, VOL. II
Innovation and Expansion
Lewis Aron & Adrienne Harris (eds.)

Vol. 29
CHILD THERAPY IN THE GREAT OUTDOORS
A Relational View
Sebastiano Santostefano

Vol. 30
THE HEALER'S BENT
Solitude and Dialogue in the Clinical Encounter
James T. McLaughlin

Vol. 31
UNCONSCIOUS FANTASIES AND
THE RELATIONAL WORLD
Danielle Knafo & Kenneth Feiner

Vol. 32
GETTING FROM HERE TO THERE
Analytic Love, Analytic Process
Sheldon Bach

Vol. 33
CREATING BODIES
Eating Disorders as Self-Destructive Survival
Katie Gentile

Vol. 34
RELATIONAL PSYCHOANALYSIS, VOL. III
New Voices
Melanie Suchet, Adrienne Harris, &
Lewis Aron (eds.)

Vol. 35
COMPARATIVE-INTEGRATIVE
PSYCHOANALYSIS
A Relational Perspective for the
Discipline's Second Century
Brent Willock

Vol. 36
BODIES IN TREATMENT
The Unspoken Dimension
Frances Sommer Anderson (ed.)

Vol. 37
ADOLESCENT IDENTITIES
A Collection of Readings
Deborah Browning (ed.)

Vol. 38
REPAIR OF THE SOUL
Metaphors of Transformation
in Jewish Mysticism and Psychoanalysis
Karen E. Starr

Vol. 39
DARE TO BE HUMAN
A Contemporary Psychoanalytic
Journey
Michael Shoshani Rosenbaum

Vol. 40
THE ANALYST IN THE INNER
CITY, SECOND EDITION
Race, Class, and Culture through a
Psychoanalytic Lens
Neil Altman

Vol. 41
THE HERO IN THE MIRROR
From Fear to Fortitude
Sue Grand

Vol. 42
SABERT BASESCU
Selected Papers on Human
Nature and Psychoanalysis
George Goldstein & Helen Golden (eds.)

Vol. 43
INVASIVE OBJECTS
Minds under Siege
Paul Williams

Vol. 44
GOOD ENOUGH ENDINGS
Breaks, Interruptions, and
Terminations from Contemporary
Relational Perspectives
Jill Salberg (ed.)

Vol. 45
FIRST DO NO HARM
The Paradoxical Encounters of Psychoanalysis,
Warmaking, and Resistance
Adrienne Harris & Steven Botticelli (eds.)

Vol. 46
A DISTURBANCE IN THE FIELD
Essays in Transference-Countertransference
Engagement
Steven H. Cooper

Vol. 47
UPROOTED MINDS
Surviving the Politics of Terror in the Americas
Nancy Caro Hollander

Vol. 48
TOWARD MUTUAL RECOGNITION
Relational Psychoanalysis and the Christian
Narrative
Marie T. Hoffman

Vol. 49
UNDERSTANDING AND TREATING
DISSOCIATIVE IDENTITY DISORDER
A Relational Approach
Elizabeth F. Howell

Vol. 50
WITH CULTURE IN MIND
Psychoanalytic Stories
Muriel Dimen (ed.)

Vol. 51
RELATIONAL PSYCHOANALYSIS,
VOL. IV
Expansion of Theory
Lewis Aron & Adrienne Harris (eds.)

Vol. 52
RELATIONAL PSYCHOANALYSIS,
VOL. V
Evolution of Process
Lewis Aron & Adrienne Harris (eds.)

Vol. 53
INDIVIDUALIZING GENDER AND
SEXUALITY
Theory and Practice
Nancy Chodorow

Vol. 54
THE SILENT PAST AND THE INVISIBLE
PRESENT
Memory, Trauma, and
Representation in Psychotherapy
Paul Renn

Vol. 55
A PSYCHOTHERAPY FOR
THE PEOPLE
Toward a Progressive Psychoanalysis
Lewis Aron & Karen Starr

Vol. 56
HOLDING AND PSYCHOANALYSIS
A Relational Perspective
Joyce Slochower

Vol. 57
THE PLAY WITHIN THE PLAY
The Enacted Dimension of Psychoanalytic
Process
Gil Katz

Vol. 58
TRAUMATIC NARCISSISM
Relational Systems of Subjugation
Daniel Shaw

Vol. 59
CLINICAL IMPLICATIONS OF THE
PSYCHOANALYST'S LIFE
EXPERIENCE
When the Personal Becomes Professional
Steven Kuchuck (ed.)

Vol. 60
THE ORIGINS OF ATTACHMENT
Infant Research and Adult Treatment
Beatrice Beebe & Frank M. Lachmann

Vol. 61
THE EMBODIED ANALYST
From Freud and Reich to Relationality
Jon Sletvold

Vol. 62
A RELATIONAL PSYCHOANALYTIC
APPROACH TO COUPLES
PSYCHOTHERAPY
Philip A. Ringstrom

Vol. 63
CYCLICAL PSYCHODYNAMICS AND THE
CONTEXTUAL SELF
The Inner World, the Intimate World, and the
World of Culture and Society
Paul L. Wachtel

Vol. 64
TRAUMATIC RUPTURES
Abandonment and Betrayal in the Analytic
Relationship
Robin A. Deutsch (ed.)

Vol. 65
THE CUT AND THE BUILDING OF
PSYCHOANALYSIS,
VOLUME 1
Sigmund Freud and Emma Eckstein
Carlo Bonomi

Vol. 66
RELATIONAL PSYCHOANALYSIS AND
PSYCHOTHERAPY INTEGRATION
An Evolving Synergy
Jill Bresler & Karen Starr (eds.)

Vol. 67
THE LEGACY OF SANDOR FERENCZI
From Ghost to Ancestor
Adrienne Harris & Steven Kuchuck (eds.)

Vol. 68
SOMATIC EXPERIENCE IN
PSYCHOANALYSIS AND
PSYCHOTHERAPY
In the Expressive Language of the Living
William F. Cornell

Vol. 69
RELATIONAL TREATMENT
OF TRAUMA
Stories of loss and hope
Toni Heineman

Vol. 70
FREUD'S LEGACY IN THE
GLOBAL ERA
Carlo Strenger

RELATIONAL TREATMENT OF TRAUMA

Stories of loss and hope

Toni Heineman

LONDON AND NEW YORK

First published 2016
by Routledge
27 Church Road, Hove, East Sussex, BN3 2FA

and by Routledge
711 Third Avenue, New York, NY 10017

Routledge is an imprint of the Taylor & Francis Group,
an Informa business

© 2016 Toni Heineman

The right of Toni Heineman to be identified as author of this work has been asserted by him/her in accordance with sections 77 and 78 of the Copyright, Designs and Patents Act 1988.

All rights reserved. No part of this book may be reprinted or reproduced or utilised in any form or by any electronic, mechanical, or other means, now known or hereafter invented, including photocopying and recording, or in any information storage or retrieval system, without permission in writing from the publishers.

Trademark notice: Product or corporate names may be trademarks or registered trademarks, and are used only for identification and explanation without intent to infringe.

British Library Cataloguing in Publication Data
A catalogue record for this book is available from the British Library

Library of Congress Cataloging-in-Publication Data
Heineman, Toni Vaughn, author.
   Relational treatment of trauma : stories of loss and hope /
Toni Heineman.
      p. ; cm.
   I. Title.
[DNLM: 1. Stress Disorders, Traumatic—therapy. 2. Child. 3. Family Relations. 4. Foster Home Care—psychology. 5. Professional-Patient Relations. 6. Psychotherapy—methods. WM 172.5]
   RC552.P67
   616.85′21—dc23
   2015004358

ISBN: 978-1-138-81735-7 (hbk)
ISBN: 978-1-138-81736-4 (pbk)
ISBN: 978-1-315-74562-6 (ebk)

Typeset in Times New Roman
by Apex Covantage, LLC

Printed and bound in the United States of America by Publishers Graphics, LLC on sustainably sourced paper.

FOR ALAN
AND
JONAS AND PARKER
WITH THANKS

CONTENTS

Acknowledgements	xiii
Permissions acknowledgements	xv
Introduction	1

SECTION I
Getting started   5

1   **A Home Within: A network to address**
    the emotional needs of foster youth   9

SECTION II
The dynamics of attachment and trauma   15

2   **Relationships beget relationships: The value of**
    attachment theory   17

3   **How can you treat what you cannot speak?**   32

4   **Good guys and bad guys: The temptations of splitting**   45

SECTION III
Systemic impingements   59

5   **In search of the romantic family: Unconscious**
    contributions to problems in foster and adoptive placements   61

6   **Weaving without a loom: Creating a self in foster care**   81

CONTENTS

7 Hunger pangs: Transference and countertransference
in the treatment of foster children   93

SECTION IV
Treatment in the context of scarcity and loss   103

8 Disrupted care and disruptive moods: Pediatric bipolar
disorder in foster care children   105

9 Infant–parent psychotherapy minus one   115

10 Learning to say goodbye: The deaths of three fathers   129

SECTION V
Back to basics   147

11 The essence of Relationship-Based Therapy   149

References   169
Index   177

ACKNOWLEDGEMENTS

Over my years in practice I have been highly privileged to hear important stories from so many people. Some of them have been very sad tales of suffering passed from one generation to another; others have been accounts of triumph in the face of seemingly overwhelming odds. Still others have explored the less dramatic, but nonetheless significant, struggles, pleasures, and uncertainties that are woven into the fabric of all of our lives.

Day after day therapists are reminded that we are innately storytellers because we need to make sense of ourselves and the world around us. Stories help us to create order – they help us learn about ourselves. They allow us to tell others who we are and how we came to be that particular person. When we listen to the stories others tell, we discover who they are and what is important to them.

I want to express my deep appreciation to those who allowed me to learn from the stories they shared with me – the adults who came for therapy, the parents who brought their children for help, and the children who told their stories in play, rather than words. I am also indebted to the students, supervisees, and colleagues who shared stories from their work and lives – giving me the opportunity to learn, as well as teach.

The process of assembling the materials in this volume prompted me to revisit the art of writing with the intent of bringing others' stories to life in a way that would honor their meaning and value. A number of people have been invaluable parts of that process. Particularly when I began writing, I consistently turned to Marian Birch and Daphne de Marneffe for forthright criticism of both ideas and prose.

Writing and editing with Diane Ehrensaft has been an absolute pleasure. We somehow learned very early in working together to turn our frustration with imprecise words and ill-defined concepts into cause for laughter, which consistently helps us to find a way out of the box we have written ourselves into. Wendy von Wiederhold not only makes me laugh at myself and my impatience with the process of writing, she offers a sense of tone that has helped me add important nuances of feeling and meaning to many pieces.

ACKNOWLEDGEMENTS

Most recently, June Madsen Clausen and Saralyn Ruff have helped me to think more clearly about presenting clinical work that is embedded in relationships in a way that makes it more accessible to clinicians whose education and training has been very different from my own. They remind me that there is little point in writing only for those who already understand that relationships hold the key to turning tales of loss into stories of hope.

When I approached Lew Aron about the possibility of gathering some of my writing into a single volume, I had in mind a very simple project. He envisioned something a little different and, fortunately for me, he gently but firmly urged me toward his vision of a book that would give earlier work a fresh voice. Adrienne Harris added new, incisive perspectives on the project as it moved toward completion. I am indebted to the masterful editorial grace of this team and quite honored to have had their guidance.

I have done all of my writing at home – sometimes in the quiet after my two children went to sleep; sometimes while trying simultaneously to meet a deadline and keep the routine bustle of family life from devolving into chaos. As my children matured, so did my writing, in no small part because of them. Jonas and Parker have given me firsthand lessons in the value of relinquishing control – in writing as in life. Their adult independence, ingenuity, and well-placed irreverence reminds me that sometimes you just have to be patient and wait to see how the story unfolds. I thank them for this and the countless ways they enrich my life.

Finally, and most important, my thanks to Alan, my husband and devoted editor, who tirelessly pushes me to think and write more precisely and more clearly. He has learned that the comments he writes in the margins of a work in progress will most likely be greeted with wounded dismay, so he just waits patiently for the initial reaction to pass. When it does, the conversation about how a phrase could be more graceful or a concept more lucid always improves the work. For his patient good humor, dedication to the craft of writing, inspiration, and unfailing confidence in me, I give special thanks.

Toni Vaughn Heineman
San Francisco

PERMISSIONS ACKNOWLEDGEMENTS

Chapter one, A Home Within: a network to address the emotional needs of foster youth, originally appeared as "The Network is Down": Building an Alternative Network to Address the Multiple Disruptions in Clinical Work with Foster Children and Youth, in *Journal of Infant, Child, and Adolescent Psychotherapy, 7: 145–150.* Copyright @ 2008 by Taylor and Francis Group. Adapted with permission.

Chapter two, Relationships beget relationships: the value of attachment theory, originally appeared as Relationships Beget Relationships: Why Attachment Theory is Crucial to Program Design for Homeless Youth, in California Homeless Youth Project: Voices From the Street, 1–13. Copyright @ 2010 by California Research Bureau. Reprinted with permission.

Chapter three, How can you treat what you cannot speak? originally appeared as The Paradox of Language in Treating the Unspeakable, pp. 134–148 in *The Abused Child: Psychodynamic Understanding and Treatment.* Copyright @ 1998 by Guilford Press. Reprinted with permission of The Guilford Press.

Chapter four, Good guys and bad guys, originally appeared as Good Guys and Bad Guys: The Temptations of Splitting, pp. 149–165 in *The Abused Child: Psychodynamic Understanding and Treatment.* Copyright @ 1998 by Guilford Press. Reprinted with permission of The Guilford Press.

Chapter five, In search of the romantic family, originally appeared as In Search of The Romantic Family: Unconscious Contributions to Problems in Foster and Adoptive Placement in *Journal for the Psychoanalysis of Culture and Society, 4: 250–264.* Copyright 1999 by the Ohio State University. Reproduced with permission.

Chapter six, Weaving without a loom, originally appeared in *fort da: Journal of the Northern California Society for Psychoanalytic Psychology, 2: 85–91.* Copyright @ 2007 by Journal of the Northern California Society for Psychoanalytic Psychology. Reprinted with permission.

Chapter seven, Hunger pangs, originally appeared as Hunger Pangs: Transference and Countertransference in the Treatment of Foster Children, 3:5–16. Copyright @ 2001 by Journal of Applied Psychoanalytic Studies. Reprinted with kind permission from Springer Science+Business Media.

Chapter eight, Disrupted care and disruptive moods, originally appeared as Disruptive Care and Disruptive Moods: Pediatric Biploar Disorder in Foster Children, pp. 83–94 in *Bipolar Children: Cutting Edge Controversy, Insights, and Research,* Ed. Sharna Olfman. Copyright @ 2007 by Sharna Olfman. Reproduced with permission of ABC-CLIO, LLC.

Chapter nine, Infant–parent psychotherapy minus one, originally appeared as Infant Parent Psychotherapy Minus One, pp. 225–246 in *Finding Hope in Despair: Clinical Studies in Infant Mental Health,* Ed. Marian Birch. Copyright @ 2008 by ZERO TO THREE. Reprinted with permission.

Chapter ten, Beginning to say goodbye, originally appeared as Beginning to Say Goodbye: A Two-Year-Old Confronts the Death of his Father, *Journal of Infant, Child, and Adolescent Psychotherapy*, 1:1–22. Copyright @ 2000 by Taylor and Francis Group. Reprinted with permission.

Chapter eleven, The essence of Relationship-Based Therapy, originally appeared as Conclusion: Eight Elements of Relationship-Based Therapy in *Treating Trauma: Relationship-Based Psychotherapy with Children, Adolescents, and Young Adults,* T. V. Heineman, J. M. Clausen, & S. C. Ruff, eds. Copyright @ 2013 by Jason Aronson. Reprinted with permission.

INTRODUCTION

Life cannot be lived without loss. We know that, but many of us don't have to think about the implications of that truism on a daily basis until circumstances, either within or beyond our control, compel us to attend to it. If, for example, we are fired or choose new employment – whether with anxiety or excitement – we face the loss of familiar routines and coworkers and must find ways of adjusting to our changed condition.

Some losses seem significant in the moment, and then fade or lose meaning with time. Parents may mourn the loss of one phase of childhood as they prepare for their child's first day of school; there will be only one very first day, but the beginning or end of every subsequent school year means that another phase of childhood is left behind. These, like many losses, will likely shed their noteworthy status and be taken in stride as just one more marker of the passage of time.

Of course, not all losses are so easily absorbed into the continuum of our lives. A divorce means loss for the couple, their children, and the extended family and friends. Familiar activities and surroundings must be given up or altered, along with the dreams of what was supposed to have been. The death of a neighbor or acquaintance may figure largely as a reminder of life's uncertainties, prompting us to vow to "live every day as if it is our last," a promise that usually diminishes relatively quickly in the press of the details of daily life and our reluctance to look death in the eye directly and consistently.

The death of a close friend or family member certainly is different, often plummeting the loved ones left behind to a depth of previously unimaginable despair. This is even more true when the death is premature. The experience of parents who will never again hold their children, the stories about young children who lose their parents completely and forever, attack our sense of what is good and right and fair. Early death is none of these but, like the expectable end of life that comes with old age, it is irrevocable – despite mourners' pleas to higher powers or inevitable temporary escapes into denial. Certainty can be grieved in a way that uncertainty cannot.

We know that even a little certainty can help in times of stress. When we are working with families coping with the disruptions of death or divorce we typically remind parents and other caregivers that children benefit when schedules and

INTRODUCTION

activities are altered as little as possible. Children, as well as adults, find comfort in the familiar – the same foods, toys, pets, routines, and people provide some sense of security when everything important in life seems to be falling apart. In other words, even in the process of reorganization, families can provide stability and emotional safety.

The stories in this volume center on children and adolescents who, because their families could not provide safety or stability, spent time in foster care. The disruptions in the lives of these children involve the loss, whether temporary or permanent, of parents and substitute caregivers along with everything else that is familiar. When children are moved from one foster family to another they leave behind everything that they have come to know and count on in the previous home. Often favorite toys and mementos also disappear, leaving them without reminders of what was lost.

Perhaps the most insidious loss for foster children is the continuity provided by a single person who keeps them in mind – the one person who can provide at least a bit of the certainty in a sea of change. For example, when a family moves to a new community, much of their familiar baggage – furniture, toys, books, pets, recipes – travels with them. This provides comfort as they learn about the culture and mores of the new place and about how they will fit into their new surroundings. Most likely, it will be some time before they feel as if they belong – and nearly everyone desires a sense of belonging and dreads the worry over how to fit in. Yet, this is what we impose on foster children over and over again – we move them to a new place with new people and ask them to adapt – to fit into a place where they don't belong. And we frequently ask them to do that without the benefit of an adult who knows them well enough to help them find their way. Thus, too often, what is most familiar to a foster child is radical unfamiliarity.

Indeed, uncertainty virtually defines life in foster care. It interferes dramatically with mourning, yet paradoxically helps to keep hope alive. Uncertain loss permeates every aspect of foster care, and anyone who comes into contact with a foster child or teen – from caseworkers, attorneys, and teachers to judges, therapists, and community volunteers – will come to know more than they wish to know about uncertainty and unpredictability. Everyone including the adults responsible for their care and the peers who befriend them will be affected – some more and some less – by the instabilities of life in foster care.

Given this, it is remarkable that this system functions at all. Yet it does function – more or less well or poorly. From almost any vantage point it is easy to see its imperfections. Some children are impossible, some adults are incompetent at best, and brutal at worst, some policies and procedures seem designed to do more harm than good. The list of endemic flaws could go on for pages.

But the "system" does also save children whose lives would otherwise be destroyed if they continued to be raised by people who neglected and abused them. Some parents recover and reclaim their children. Some children find "forever families" through adoption. Some young adults leave child welfare well prepared to lead satisfying and productive lives.

INTRODUCTION

All of this keeps hope alive in a system that often seems in danger of collapsing in chaos. Giving in to despair is often easier than holding onto hope. Every day foster care tempts those who live in and around it to surrender, to recognize, finally, that it is broken beyond repair, that there is no longer any point in thinking about how to improve it. But every day, thousands of people, children and adults alike, keep thinking about what is and hoping about what could be.

My personal hope is that in the chapters in this volume you will come to a deeper appreciation of the inexorable connection, despite a tidal wave of failures, between determined, creative thought and the capacity to hope. This volume spans more than ten years of my thinking and writing about loss, anxiety, trauma, and hope. Some of the chapters focus on the therapeutic process – when it works and when it doesn't, including clinical work with children who have suffered emotional, physical, or sexual abuse yet remained with their family of origin. Other chapters reflect on the psychological meanings and constructs that emerge from life that includes trauma, whether from abuse or the chronic loss that marks life in foster care. Some chapters include clinical material that illustrates the protective nature of functional families, in contrast to the personal and systemic consequences of relationships that harm or fail to protect children.

To treat children successfully, clinicians must develop a deep appreciation for the importance of the many structures in which the child is embedded – including the immediate family, the neighborhood, educational and religious organizations, the surrounding community, and the larger world. All of the people in a child's life carry consciously held beliefs and unconscious fantasies that shape their interactions with that child, whether mildly or profoundly. In functional families, parents shape the transmission of extra-familial influences, helping the child to create a coherent narrative from the many, often conflicting messages he encounters. In less functional families or in the midst of the fragmentation of foster care, children are often left without the organizing care that brings cohesion to the disparate information surrounding them.

When working with a child with only one family, even if complicated by divorce, the clinician needs to understand only a single family system, even if fragmented by serious mental illness or substance abuse. When treating a foster child, the clinician may encounter many family systems operating in the context of the child welfare and judicial systems. In these instances therapists can easily feel overwhelmed and utterly alone, having few guidelines for integrating the many conflicting beliefs, values, and fantasies that foster parents, caseworkers, teachers, attorneys, and judges bring to their relationships with foster children. The abuse and/or neglect that propelled the child into foster care has, in almost every case, left the child without a coherent life narrative, a condition perpetuated by the multitude of players and frequent disruptions characteristic of the foster care system.

Yet, it is through foster care that I have come to truly respect the profound connection between the capacity to think and the capacity to hope. Despite enormous pressure, both internally and externally generated, to relinquish both thought and

INTRODUCTION

hope – just to get through the day without giving in to despair, children do cling to hope for a better future and adults do find ways of thinking creatively about how to make that happen. Because it is a system that demands action – when children are in real or perceived danger, something must be *done,* often quickly – it leaves little time for reflection. When we find ourselves wondering about the unthinkable decisions or circumstances we encounter in this vast and complex system, we find that they arise when both the capacity to think and the capacity to hope have been surrendered. Fortunately, both hope and reflection can be recaptured. Creative thinking keeps us psychically alive, allows us to consider even that which initially appears to be unbearable. It is only when we can keep the intolerable in mind that we can consider possibilities for change. I hope that the material in this volume will inspire a sense of excitement and a determination to hope and think creatively even when both seem impossibly hard.

The first chapter in this book tells the story of the beginnings of A Home Within, an organization created to meet the emotional needs of foster youth. The final chapter articulates the basic tenets of Relationship-Based Therapy, an approach that we have articulated with ever-expanding understanding of the unique requirements of therapists working in and around the foster care system. In over 20 years of treating children, teens, and young adults whose lives have been beset with so much loss that they have had no – or only the shakiest – relational foundation on which to build healthy and satisfying relationships we have come to grasp, with increasing clarity, the what and why of successful psychotherapy with those who have endured the trauma of chronic loss. I hope that by elucidating the basic principles of our approach, it will be easily accessible to a wide range of therapists, including the trainees who often find foster youth among their very first clients.

The network of clinicians who offer pro bono therapy through A Home Within because they understand the fundamental importance of relationships continues to grow. Simultaneously, more clinicians who share this view find themselves untrained and ill-prepared to offer treatment that is built on the foundation of the therapeutic relationship. The chapters in this volume offer a variety of perspectives on relationships – those that work and those that don't – both inside and outside of psychotherapy. The final chapter distills the essence of Relationship-Based Therapy into eight elements that can guide the efforts of clinicians who want to make the therapeutic relationship an integral part of their work.

Section I

GETTING STARTED

Imagine that you are beginning your first internship as a graduate student in social work, psychology, or counseling. The first client referred to you is a 13-year-old girl, "Alice," who has had four prior therapists, all of them, like you, interns who moved on when their training year ended. Alice has been told that she "needs to talk to someone" because her behavior in her group home is so disruptive. She angrily announces that there is nothing to talk about, crosses her arms, closes her eyes and falls asleep.

Down the hall, another intern has been asked to work with James, an eight-year-old boy, who has just re-entered foster care when a three-month reunification with his father failed because his father relapsed and entered a residential drug rehab program. The previous foster home where he and his brother had lived for about a year was no longer available; the brothers are now in different homes and attend different schools. James says that everything is fine and wonders if there is anything to eat.

Danielle has been assigned to a third intern. She has been ordered to attend ten therapy sessions as part of the plan for her to address allegations of physical abuse of her children, ages two and four. She tells the therapist that the judge said that the children should come to the sessions, which would count as one of her required two weekly visits, but their foster mother said that she wasn't feeling well enough to take the bus. She then asks, "So how is this going to help me get my kids back?"

Interns finding themselves in these or similar situations could easily feel overwhelmed by a sense of helpless anxiety. This happens every day in clinics across the country when we ask beginning clinicians to attend to the emotional needs of foster children and youth without the necessary education and support for building relationships that can heal the psychological pain that repeated trauma and loss have inflicted on these vulnerable young people. Remarkably, some find the internal resources and external support to forge mutually satisfying relationships with their clients, giving both parties a sense that relationships can and do matter. But theirs is not an easy undertaking.

The experiences of the clinicians who founded "The Children's Psychotherapy Project," as A Home Within was originally known, were not very different from those of the trainees described above. We understood how it felt to sit in a room with an adolescent with far more experience in being a client than we had in being a therapist; we knew the sadness of leaving clients behind at the end of our tenure at a clinic because of regulations over which we had no control; and we had encountered the sense of isolation that too many young therapists discover when they complete training and enter the private practice world.

The clinicians who founded A Home Within did so in order to address some unmet needs: those of foster youth – the need for a stable therapeutic relationship, and those of therapists in private practice – the need for a community of like-minded clinicians who could help them sustain their work with this population (*Building A Home Within: Meeting the Emotional Needs of Children and Youth in Foster Care*). We were a group of 14 therapists with a wide range of experiences including private practice, teaching and supervising, research, and running hospital and community-based mental health programs. We met together every few weeks for about a year over soup and salad at my dining room table. The conversations were lively, as they often are among people with divergent opinions who respect each other. Over the years, three comments from those conversations stand out for me. From my left, "There is so much to do; we need to move faster." And from my right, "We don't actually don't know what we're doing; we need to slow down." This tension continues to inform the way the staff and board of A Home Within think about the organization as we grow and change. It is not easy to maintain that balance, but it is essential to the health of the organization.

The other comment came as we were preparing to invite others to join our nascent enterprise and considering whether we wanted our outreach to be wider or narrower. The deliberations ended when one member of the group noted, "People are going to be doing this work anyway. Let's help more of them to do it better." That premise has stood us in good stead as we continue to invite therapists who are qualified to practice by their state's licensing bodies to join us, not just in providing a service, but thinking and learning together about how to do to it better. The Consultation Groups described below constituted the primary means of education and professional development for members of A Home Within, and continue to do so. As our knowledge about the emotional needs of foster youth grows in breadth and depth we increasingly work to share what we have learned with the wider community through publications and continuing education offerings.

The first chapter of this volume was written about 12 years after we first launched "The Children's Psychotherapy Project" in San Francisco. "A Home Within" now exists in over 40 communities in more than 20 states. It is an organization that builds networks of clinicians in private practice, each of whom agrees to see one current or former foster child in weekly pro bono psychotherapy. The therapists who volunteer their time have a shared and deeply held belief in the vital place of caring relationships in healthy emotional, social, and cognitive development.

The core values that set the original organization in motion continue today. There are three essential elements that describe A Home Within. First, stable, lasting relationships are vital to healthy development, something that therapists can both provide and support. Second, supportive relationships with peers and mentors are necessary to promote the work of the individual therapists. Third, everyone, from the beginning therapist to the most seasoned clinician, has something important to contribute that cannot be measured monetarily but will create psychic space for the emergence of a sense of community and shared purpose.

A Home Within grew out of frustration with "business as usual," which included foster children not only being moved from place to place, but losing one therapist after another when training years came to an end. Our experiences were echoed in the voices of our students and supervisees as they described their frustration and boredom when the foster children they were seeing in their internships just wanted to play board games or fill the hour with meaningless recitations of the week's activities or repetitive, affectless complaints about perceived slights and misunderstandings. We understood that these young clients had deadened themselves to relationships as a means of warding off hope and disappointment.

We also understood, on both an intuitive and intellectual level, that if therapists were to undertake the depth and length of treatment that would ultimately help children who had been traumatized by multiple losses, they would need the ongoing support of mentors and peers. Even if, instead of joining their clients in a world devoid of meaning, they kept themselves open to hearing the pain that relationships had brought these vulnerable young people, they would eventually be tempted to listen to their words without taking in their meaning. Their brains would go numb to protect their hearts.

However, appreciating that when the burden of knowing is shared with trusted and respected colleagues it can be manageable, we elected to create consultation groups, led by senior clinicians, to support the work of the individual therapists. The group helps to maintain the treating therapist's capacity to think – to remain vital and alive in the face of what otherwise would be mind-numbing material. The group also supports the creativity of all of its members as they bring different backgrounds, training, and perspectives to bear. And we have also come to appreciate that the warmth and collegiality of shared experience among group members forms an important part of the therapists' self-care that reaches far beyond the need to revitalize the capacity to think clearly and creatively (Harris & Sinsheimer, 2008; Shapiro & Carlson, 2009). We have been reminded again and again over the years of providing therapy through A Home Within that the whole of the consultation groups is greater than the sum of its parts.

That is also true for the networks of consultation groups that make up each of the Clinical Chapters. Each consultation group is part of the network serving the community in which its members practice, and each Clinical Chapter is part of the regional and national network of Clinical Chapters that make up A Home Within.

The central organizing idea that each member has something valuable to contribute is echoed in the process of replication (Heineman & Ehrensaft, 2005). No two consultation groups are identical nor are any two chapters; each draws on local resources to meet local needs. In one community there may be a great need for therapists to work with youth aging out of the foster care system. In another it may be that there are few resources to meet the needs of children who have been adopted from foster care. The element that binds the individuals, groups, and chapters is a profound belief that relationships are the foundation of mental health and that, by drawing on the wide and varied talents of a diverse group of committed professionals, we can not only change individual lives but also create a system that puts relationships first.

1

A HOME WITHIN

A network to address the
emotional needs of foster youth

Clinical work with children in foster care sometimes feels as difficult as trying to sustain contact through an unreliable Internet network. The network in which the child lives can be disrupted at any time, without warning or explanation. Connections are broken and sometimes reappear with the same unpredictability. In this context it is essential that the therapists have a network of support to contain the anxiety, frustration, and sadness and to share success, for the network can disappear as easily in good times as in bad.

A Home Within is an organization that builds those networks for clinicians. It is a non-profit organization that embodies the belief that we must and can provide lasting, caring relationships for children in the foster care system and that providing supportive relationships for clinicians is the key to their success with the children. It is the only national organization devoted exclusively to improving the emotional well-being of foster youth. By insisting that children must have a single, experienced therapist to work with them "for as long as it takes," we begin to create an atmosphere that provides and protects relationships. We ask that therapists across the country volunteer their professional time to provide a continuous relationship for a foster child, thereby underscoring our appreciation of and commitment to helping provide those relationships to this vulnerable group of children. Even though the therapeutic relationship may be the most stable relationship in a foster child's life, it is not an end in itself – its relational purpose is to help the child build more and better relationships – with adults and other children and eventually with lovers, partners, and their own children.

Leaving the foster care system for a moment, when working with children in relatively stable families the networks to which the family belongs do not always figure prominently in our clinical work, particularly if those networks offer a safe and reliable backdrop that supports the family's activities. These networks, which run the gamut from extended family to relationships with professionals, arc built over time – often over generations – and provide an important means of transmitting the history, values, and culture of family and community.

Whether intentionally or as an unintended consequence of seemingly unrelated decisions, parents build these social networks for their children. The networks vary in physical and relational proximity. Simply because of their propinquity, a family may have frequent contact with the network of neighbors, most of whom are merely acquaintances. In contrast, children in that same family may feel very close to cousins whom they see only infrequently because of great distance between their homes, yet they establish long-term intimacy with those same relatives. Not all networks are equally active or prominent at any given time in the life of a family. The congregants at the family's place of worship may offer a child a consistent network of regular contact, activities, and fellowship throughout her childhood and in adolescence, while the network of families at her preschool or Head Start program may largely disappear over time. A family may intentionally attempt to mobilize one of its networks – for example, by organizing a clothing drive at their child's school. The same family may also inadvertently mobilize a network – as, for example, when neighbors bring food in response to a tragedy or call to complain when the party hosted by the family's teenager continues too long and too loudly.

It is not to be assumed that parents have control over or enjoy participating in the networks surrounding their family. For example, when parents have no escape from a neighborhood controlled by a gang their children will be exposed to the culture that binds the gang members together. Parents of children with a life-threatening or chronic illness may find themselves relying on a network of families in similar situations grateful for their support, but surely not a club in which they wanted membership.

When treating a child, even one whose family is torn by death or divorce, the therapist rarely becomes an active participant in the family's networks – that position belongs to the parents. While the therapist may talk to a teacher or pediatrician or custody evaluator, she typically relies on that person as a source of information or as someone who can help the parents activate a network on the child's behalf. The therapist does not have to become part of the network in order to be helpful to the child.

If we turn to the world of foster children, clinicians working with these children discover a very different experience. They often find themselves unwittingly drawn into the powerful network of foster care in which the child is embedded. Because there is no parental equivalent to direct therapists to the key and appropriate people, therapists may find themselves having to insert themselves to gain access to the network. This "system of care," composed of many, often competing, networks is neither simple, nor easy to navigate. It can bewilder even the most seasoned professional, especially when there is no parental figure who knows how the various networks fit together, understands their roles and functions, can identify the key players, and has the power to mobilize one or more of them on behalf of the child. In other words, therapists can rarely rely on a single person for help in understanding and/or managing the complex world surrounding the foster child.

Unlike the parent, who holds in mind the multiple, interrelated facets of a child's inner and external worlds, the important adults in the world of a foster child often have limited knowledge of and limited responsibility for that child. The foster parent who cares for the child on a day-to-day basis may know little about the child's history and have little influence over the decisions affecting the child's future. The primary responsibility of the social worker overseeing the child's case is ensuring that the parents receive the legally required services in support of reunification, while simultaneously planning for alternatives, should reunification fail.

The judge, who has ultimate authority over the child's future, must rely on information from myriad people, each of whom has a limited perspective on the child, often influences by his/her assigned role. For example, the attorneys representing the mother, father, foster care agency, foster parents, and the child are each legally and ethically bound to advocate for their clients, and each client may have a different idea about what is in the child's best interests. Certainly parents in an intact family also have access to multiple perspectives concerning their child, the difference being that their decisions are made in the context of their intimate relationship with the child. While the judge may care about the child, she does not care for the child; she is not woven into the fabric of the child's daily life and may actually know very little about the child.

The lack of a consistent, reliable, agreed upon "gatekeeper" is one of the crucial factors that separate the childhood experience of foster children from those of children who grow up with their parents. For these children, there is no single person who has the ultimate responsibility for holding the child in mind and for making decisions about the child. For foster children the responsibilities are shared among many, according to skills and assigned roles. Indeed, this process has been institutionalized as "team decision making," which brings together the important people in a foster child's life when there are crucial issues facing those charged with her care. While this collective process recognizes the importance of gathering the differing pieces of knowledge held by the various parties, it can also devolve into child-raising by committee – a process that allows many to contribute ideas and opinions but charges no single person with the responsibility for implementation. This collective process of child rearing in the round is one of the most easily identified ways in which a therapist may be called upon to become an active player in the child's life, as opposed to the person who can stand outside the child's daily life and help her observe and metabolize the feelings, ideas, and actions of those responsible for her care.

When faced with the powerful forces that pull therapists into the role of participant-observer in the foster care networks, therapists working through the model of A Home Within have their own reliable network to provide ballast against the pressures exerted by the foster care system. This is not to argue that a therapist should never participate in a team decision-making meeting, or appear before the judge, or write reports detailing his opinion about what is in the best interest of the child; it is to argue that having access to a network of skilled, like-minded clinicians provides an essential forum for the clinician to consider the meaning of undertaking or refusing any of these activities.

For clinicians in A Home Within, the weekly consultation groups provide the most direct access to the growing network of clinicians. Each week a small group of clinicians meet together to hear about and consult with each other about their work with their A Home Within patients, with a senior clinician serving as their consultation group leader. Because they have collectively come to know the child over many weeks or months of case presentations, the others in the group are in a unique position to offer a forum for helping any one of its members understand the processes that unfold in a clinical session and/or the social, emotional, and systematic context in which the sessions occur. Unlike those brought together for "team decision making," the members of the consultation group have no personal knowledge of the other therapists' young patients – they have only what they know through the treating clinician. Further, unlike most people in the clinician's other personal and professional networks, the members of the consultation group are in the unique position of all sharing a personal experience with the foster care system and the particular challenges and pressures it presents to those working with the children in its care.

Let me illustrate the point by describing the experience of Norman Zukowsky, one of the therapists working through A Home Within who found himself in the painful position of helping his young patient mourn the sudden death of his foster mother, who was murdered by her husband in the family home. Dr. Zukowsky wrote poignantly about how he was sustained by his consultation group's emotional availability, specifically "by my certainty that they were there, even the senior clinicians, if I needed them. In addition, I had the feeling that they knew – somehow – what I was going through. My consultation group was a sanctuary; the weekly meetings were islands of concern, connections, and useful opinion" (Zukowsky, 2006, p. 105).

Each consultation group is embedded in a larger network of A Home Within clinicians working in the same community and meeting in other, similar consultation groups. Periodic professional and social gatherings strengthen this larger network as people come together to share ideas and common interests and return to their work with a renewed sense of purpose and pleasure. As A Home Within grows, we are coming to an ever-deepening appreciation of the power of these multiple interconnected networks. A single therapist working with a single foster child can have a profound effect on that child's emotional well-being and, perhaps, some influence on the way in which other children in the system are viewed or treated. The influence of four or five clinicians working in the same system and meeting regularly in a consultation group will, likewise, extend beyond the work with four or five children. The power of 20 clinicians working in a single foster care system to influence that system is, of course, even greater. If we now connect those 20 clinicians in a single community to networks of five or ten or 20 clinicians working in other communities, the power of the collective voice can truly be transformative, as it becomes the voice that can now be heard throughout the country, carrying the message of all the clinicians who insist and act upon the conviction that stable, caring relationships are essential for all children.

Through A Home Within clinicians find support for offering open-ended therapeutic relationships and, while this may be the ideal, in the current climate this kind of relationship often seems a luxury that is too often out of reach. Finding or creating situations that support relationships without externally imposed constraints can be difficult. Community-based clinics may have little choice except to accept contracts that limit the number of sessions available to a given client. If they cannot bill for missed sessions, therapists may be forced to close a case, even while recognizing that a particular client may be so wary of relationships that she is afraid to show up for an appointment out of a conviction that the therapist may not be there at the agreed upon time.

As I will explore more fully in the concluding chapter, in instances such as these it is best to be explicit about the constraints. For example, the therapist might mention in the first session that they have ten sessions and inquire about the client's thoughts. Or if a client fails to show up for an early session the therapist can explain that the clinic's policy requires her to close a case if there are more than three failed sessions in any two-month period. Comments such as these can open the door to any number of conversations – perhaps feelings about relationships always being limited or a pervasive sense that there is never enough, or relief at being warned about the possible consequences of missing sessions.

When it feels as if our resources are so limited that we can't possibly make a difference, I remember the words of a wise colleague who, after lamenting budget cuts that severely reduced payments for inpatient care, reminded both of us that if we could give a chronic schizophrenic a safe place to sleep, a hot shower, a decent meal, and clean clothes that we might have introduced a tiny ray of hope into an otherwise very bleak view of the world.

Sometimes the most important thing that we have to offer is an honest appraisal of what we can and cannot do. One or two nights of inpatient treatment will not cure the chronic schizophrenic who may or may not remember to take his medication the day after discharge. If the interns we met in the introduction to this section are genuinely interested in the people sitting in the room with them they are likely to have a much greater impact than if they are preoccupied with imposing yet one more therapeutic relationship on clients who might understandably feel that their primary purpose at the clinic is to be the clients on whom interns practice their beginning skills. When we are primarily concerned with being good therapists we are not fully attending to the other person in the room. Genuine and full attention is often notably absent from the lives of foster children and youth. We can't always offer the gift of an ongoing relationship, but we can make ourselves fully present in the time we have.

Section II

THE DYNAMICS OF ATTACHMENT AND TRAUMA

The chapters in this section outline the theoretical foundation for the work that is described in the sections that follow. Most of the people you will meet in these pages are children or adolescents; some are adults. Many of them have spent time in the foster care system and/or suffered the trauma of emotional, physical, or emotional abuse. All of them have important stories to tell about the importance of relationships in the human psyche and interactions.

"Relationships beget relationships" makes clear the importance of early relationships, not only for laying the foundation for later relationships, but for grounding our sense of self in the context of family and community. We want to know where we came from and how we came to be who we are. Parents and other adults carry history for children. Parents remind them of the activities they enjoyed last week or last year. Members of the extended family offer the proverbial "my, how you've grown" with the pinch on the cheek that makes children cringe. And yet, there are those who long for others who "remember them when," people who knew them and their antics well enough to embarrass them by recounting tales from their youth. Those who have grown up in relatively stable families and communities tend to take relationships that stretch back through years of memories for granted. For those whose childhoods have been disrupted by abuse or chronic loss, fond memories of stable, caring relationships may be a longed-for luxury. Perhaps they have no one to hold their memories for them; perhaps the memories are too painful to hold. By examining the lives of homeless youth, nearly one-third of whom have spent time in foster care, this chapter outlines the importance of attachment theory in understanding how relationships develop and are carried over time. It also illustrates the ways in which trauma derails development and interferes with the creation of healthy attachments.

The two chapters that follow demonstrate the ways in which trauma becomes woven into the very fabric of the self, giving the lie to the idea that abuse or the consequences of trauma can be treated as discreet symptoms. "How can you treat what you cannot speak?" examines the conundrum of offering psychotherapy that relies extensively on the spoken word to children who have suffered emotional, physical, and/or sexual abuse. It illustrates the ways in which language can be used both to conceal the traumatic impact of abuse and to bring it into the light so that it can be managed and, if fortune smiles, mastered.

In "Good guys and bad guys" we see how an abusive history becomes re-enacted in the course of therapy. The vignettes in this chapter help us to understand why therapists, teachers, and other would-be helpers are not immune to being drawn into an abused child's drama. It examines the importance of understanding these dynamics so that we do not unwittingly create or participate in situations that, at best, do nothing or little to help, and, at worst, retraumatize the child.

2

RELATIONSHIPS BEGET RELATIONSHIPS

The value of attachment theory

Introduction

Much as we might like to idealize the lives of homeless youth, imagining them, like the characters in *The Boxcar Children* (Chandler Warner, 1989), living happily and cooperatively – independent of parental demands or supervision – the real lives of homeless youth are not exciting, fun, or romantic. Without adults to help, support, and protect them, these young people often live a grim, frightening, and dangerous existence. Why then, don't they, like the children in the *Boxcar* story, come to recognize that they need help from adults? Why do some seem unwilling to accept our offers of food and shelter? Why do some fail to take advantage of the programs we create to help them improve their health, education, and general well-being? If it is because we have not understood or given them what they need, why don't they simply come forward and tell us what we can do to help them? Until we can answer questions such as these, homeless youth will continue to suffer, despite our genuine concerns and well-intended efforts to help them come in from the cold.

Attachment theory, with its descriptions of different relational styles, may offer useful insights into these questions and point us toward answers that will help us develop policies and programs to successfully address the needs of traumatized youth. Because homeless youth have decided to live apart from parents or substitute caregivers, at least temporarily, rather than rely on adults, their stories can heighten our awareness of the consequences of failures in early relationships. At its most basic, attachment theory simply describes the ways in which young children relate to their caregivers – demonstrating that they are either securely or insecurely attached (Slade, 1999). Many researchers, clinicians, and theorists have expanded on the tenets of attachment theory, as first proposed by John Bowlby (Bowlby, 1975a, 1975b). We are now able to draw on a rich body of work to understand the interplay between children's earliest relationships and later behavior (Fonagy 1998; Main & Hesse, 1990; Main, Kaplan, & Cassidy, 1985; Sander, 1975). Because human beings have a protracted period of dependency, extending from infancy through childhood, adolescence, and often into young adulthood, the quality of early relationships profoundly affects all aspects of later life. Initially, attachment theory focused our attention on the importance of young children's relationships with their caregivers; more recently it has helped us understand the impact of early attachments on later relationships.

Attachment theory has also deepened our understanding of the ways in which, for better or worse, we do not easily change the ways in which we view others and our expectations of relationships. For example, we have come to understand that the residue of an abusive relationship makes it impossible for a child to feel protected, secure, and safe from harm immediately upon being moved into an environment in which she is physically and emotionally safe.

These points are crucial to our discussion of the mental health needs of homeless youth. Understanding the importance of early patterns of attachment helps us comprehend their sometimes confusing behavior, and understanding the ways in which later relationships can alter that behavior helps us to create effective programs and policies for meeting their needs. In this chapter I briefly define attachment theory and discuss its implications for homeless youth and programs intended to assist them.

Attachment theory defined

Secure attachments

Infants enter the world with the capacity to form relationships. As utterly dependent creatures, they must rely on caregivers for physical and emotional survival. *Secure attachments* to caregivers provide the foundation for emotional well-being, offering children a solid base from which to explore the world. A sense of security and confidence in relationships develops when parents, or other caregivers, reliably read and respond to their infants' cues. This does not mean that parents must – even if they could – perfectly interpret or immediately react to every signal that a child sends by vocalization or movement. For example, parents may not instantly identify the source of their crying baby's distress or immediately find a way to sooth him or her. Secure relationships are built through "trial and error," with children becoming increasingly skilled at identifying and signaling their moods and needs and caregivers becoming progressively skilled at reading and responding to those signals.

Securely attached children are not overwhelmingly distressed when separated from their parents because they "know," both cognitively and emotionally, that their parents will return. Indeed, as they grow, children can tolerate longer periods of separation because they have internalized the comforting security of the parent. We learn to soothe ourselves by being soothed by another – a young child will seek out the parent in times of distress, while an older child can create a sense of security by thinking about the parent or turning to images or activities that evoke the security of that relationship.

Young adults may carry family traditions forward into their lives as a way of easing the transition from their parents' home to their own. Familiar routines from a secure childhood offer solace well into adulthood because they evoke a sense of reassurance and safety. That is why "comfort food" sustains not just the body, but also the soul. Young parents who have enjoyed secure attachments will intuitively pass along this security to their children because our early relationships are not held just in our minds and hearts but in the very essence of our being. Those whose early relationships have been more troubled will have to work harder to create secure attachments for and with their children.

Secure attachments are relatively straightforward – they are relationships that offer children a solid foundation for later relationships. Not surprisingly, secure attachments, which can be thought of simply as the capacity to love and to work, are associated with positive mental health (Freud, 1930). In contrast, insecure attachments interfere substantially with the capacity for both love and work, often making life exceedingly difficult and unfulfilling.

Insecure attachments

Classification of psychological difficulties is very complex. The causes of mental health and mental illness extend beyond the attachment patterns laid down in early childhood. However, these patterns are crucial in determining subsequent emotional, social, and cognitive development; insecure attachments do not provide a solid developmental foundation (Cicchetti & Cummings, 1993; Cicchetti, Rogosch, & Toth, 2006; Fonagy, 1998; Fraiberg, Adelson, & Shapiro, 1975; Joubert, Webster & Hackett, 2012; Oyen, Landy & Hilburn-Cobb, 2000; Tucker & MacKenzie, 2012). We have a single category for secure attachments because, in essence, they do not show substantial variation. As Leo Tolstoy noted in Anna Karenina, "All happy families are alike. Unhappy families are unhappy in their own ways." And so it is with attachment patterns – we need more than one way to understand and describe them. I will focus on attachment patterns usually referred to as "avoidant," "preoccupied," "ambivalent," or "disorganized" because these are the patterns that we typically see in foster children and youth. In this context, it is worth a cursory note about "Reactive Attachment Disorder," which we do sometimes see in the foster care and homeless populations in the United States, but not to the extent found in children who have spent their earliest months to years in orphanages where they have had only the most minimal and basic contact with adults. (Kay & Green, 2013; Zenah, et al., 2004) Parents who have adopted children from these extreme conditions often feel them to be impervious to caregiving – it is as if the caregivers simply don't exist. It is not so much that they are to be avoided, instead, they aren't recognized. In contrast, the indiscriminate attachments (Albus & Dozier, 1999; Lyons-Ruth et al., 2006; Lyons-Ruth et al., 2009), we do see in foster children underscore their perceived need to take advantage of any available adult in order to survive. Indeed, the structure of the foster care system implicitly rests on the assumption that caregivers are interchangeable and that children can and will adapt to alterations in their environment.

Children and teens with ***avoidant attachment*** patterns often appear to dismiss the attention of caregivers, but they do demonstrate an awareness of others. They behave as if they really don't expect much from adults, so they don't bother to ask for help or soothing when distressed. This type of behavior tends to arise when caregivers are relatively unresponsive to the child's signals of distress or bids for positive attention. As these children move into daycare or school they may pay little attention to the adults charged with their care; they often play by themselves and seem to ignore routines or instructions. Adults may then feel dismissed or irrelevant, as if they have nothing to offer the child. While other children are vying for and obviously pleased by an adult's attention, children who avoid contact are easily ignored or overlooked. Clearly, this pattern easily perpetuates itself – the child asks for little from adults and gets little, which simply reinforces the idea that adults really have very little to offer and that there is little point in asking. Adults may stop offering help, attention, or support when their efforts appear to have little effect on the child's mood, behavior, learning, or sense of well-being.

As the exploration of attachment patterns moved beyond the study of the relationships between toddlers and parents in a controlled laboratory setting, interest developed in the ways in which attachment patterns played out in adolescent and adult relationships (Blatt & Levy, 2003). *Anxious preoccupied attachment* is a pattern we find frequently among foster children and youth. It shows itself as neediness and continual worry about the caregiver or, later, the partner in romantic relationships. Children with this attachment style may literally follow their caregivers from room to room, panicking when they are out of sight. One young woman described the overwhelming anxiety she felt if her boyfriend didn't return her text messages instantly, necessitating her barraging him with more messages and calls. He responded, as people often do to this kind of neediness, by ending the relationship. This did not end her preoccupation with him – it led her to the verge of stalking him. Not surprisingly, people with this attachment style have very low self-esteem and tend to value the caregiver or partner over themselves, leaving them highly vulnerable to being mistreated.

Children who characteristically pull people close and then push them away demonstrate an *ambivalent attachment* pattern. This pattern tends to arise when the caregiver's response to the child is inconsistent – at times responsive and loving and at others dismissive or inattentive. These children need constant reassurance from caregivers. However, even seemingly constant attention does little to calm the child's anxiety or offer comfort. At daycare or in the classroom, children who have ambivalent attachments to caregivers often seem extremely needy and may repeatedly seek the approval or attention of the adult in charge and then discount the attention they get. In addition to being exhausted by the incessant demands for reassurance, adults can easily become frustrated or angry when what they offer does not seem to have any positive effect. (Unlike the avoidant child, who isn't particularly interested in what the adult offers, the ambivalent child often aggressively rejects the offered attention.) Again, it is easy to understand how the pattern becomes self-perpetuating as children demand attention or help and then consistently reject it. Adults often respond in similar ways – sometimes becoming very solicitous of the child's needs and at other times ignoring them or responding angrily.

Children with ***disorganized attachment*** patterns have no reliable, characteristic means of managing emotional distress. They may appear both avoidant and ambivalent in their relationships with caregivers. These children may simply sit – somehow both stiffly immobilized and limp – or they might walk backward toward a caregiver, rather than reaching out for comfort. This type of attachment appears to stem from relationships in which the caregiver is a source of both comfort and fear, leaving the young child confused about whether to seek comfort or "run for cover." In this situation, the child may demonstrate periods of appearing to be emotionally "frozen" or "dazed." In the history of children with disorganized attachments, we often find caregivers whose moods and behavior change rapidly because of mental illness or substance abuse. If we understand attachment theory as a means of categorizing children's typical means of relating to caregivers, it is easy to see how children whose parents are sometimes loving and other times abusive would be so confused that they might either become immobilized or careen wildly through different strategies to cope with distress. Not surprisingly, adults working with these children often feel almost overwhelmed with confusion and helplessness. They may feel at their wits' end or turn away out of a sense of despair.

Fortunately, most children begin life with a secure attachment to their caregivers. This does not mean that they are all equally happy, well adjusted, or well prepared for life. It does mean that most parents, even given enormous variations in beliefs and child-rearing practices, successfully transmit to their children a sense that relationships can, and do, offer at least some stability and continuity. This allows children to move beyond the family with a sense that other people will be relatively welcoming, will respond reasonably to their needs and desires, and will be interested in what they have to offer.

However, many young people who live on the street or in unstable living situations have not had the good fortune to have grown up in homes where they had the opportunity to form stable attachments early on. That is why we can learn so much by looking at the words and actions of homeless youth – as well as our own responses in designing and providing services and interventions – through the lens of attachment theory.

Viewing homeless youth through the lens of attachment

Again, lest we be tempted to view homeless youth through a romanticized lens influenced by pervasive cultural representations of "runaways" – as free spirits eschewing conventionality or teenagers expressing their adolescent rebellion through temporary experimentation with life on the street – we would be wise to listen to what those youth have to say about their lives. A sampling of the interviews from *Voices from the Street: A Survey of Homeless Youth by Their Peers* (Bernstein & Foster, 2008) are used to illustrate some of the issues that are important to youth; they can also be used to inform programs that help youth out of homelessness.

In the course of these interviews youth were asked to explain how they came to be homeless. Their responses give a view of the families they left, or were forced out of, for life on the street.

> I was being bad at home so I wasn't wanted there no more.
>
> (p. 17)

> Because my mom kicked me out and chose a guy over my family.
>
> (p. 17)

> I had a fight with my mother over my gender identity and sexual orientation, and she put me out, and she instructed all family and friends not to help me out financially, so I hitchhiked to San Francisco.
>
> (p. 18)

> Because we have a three-bedroom home and my mom takes care of foster kids so there was no room for me and she gave me a week to find somewhere to live.
>
> (p. 17)

> I grew up in foster care and I was abused in group homes. I've moved around so much. I've been in over ten mental institutes, over 32 group homes and foster houses. I became homeless five years ago.
>
> (p. 20)

> I was getting in so many fights with my mom and I didn't want to be that kind of person. I didn't want to be a burden on my family.
>
> (p. 17)

These are not the words of young people who are living on the street on a lark or who can easily return to the comforts of a loving home. They did not leave home by choice; they left because they felt they had run out of choices.

Nothing in these comments even hints at a home and family in which children are loved, respected, and offered a sense of security. We must keep in mind that families that do build secure attachments for their children are not perfectly happy and calm either, nor without tension and even upheaval at times. Caregivers and children get angry; they sometimes lose their tempers, are preoccupied, impatient, inattentive, overwhelmed, and exhausted. But all of this happens in the context of certainty that caring relationships persist in spite of difficulties, that they can be repaired and restored even when they appear on shaky ground. It is this sense of the robustness of relationships that lays the foundation for mental health – the capacity to manage the inevitable ups and downs of life. (It is also important to note that youth homelessness is not always related to parental detachment, neglect, etc., and the resultant attachment problems that children may experience. There are instances in which parents of homeless youth are searching their hearts and souls, wondering why, despite their many efforts, they were unable to save their children from life on the street.)

We must also remember that an "insecure attachment," in and of itself, does not constitute a mental illness or psychiatric disorder. It simply describes a characteristic way of relating to others, particularly caregivers. However, these relational patterns, which were an adaptive response to the very early relationship with caregivers, can become maladaptive when navigating relationships with others in the world beyond the family. This point is particularly important when considering the attitudes of some homeless teens and young adults toward those who want to help them. While service providers and other adults offering assistance may see themselves as positive "caregivers," homeless youth may not be so sure of their reliability, trustworthiness, or usefulness due to their earlier experiences. They may not eagerly accept offers of help, the options for food and shelter or opportunities that we consider important for improving their health, education, employment, or general sense of well-being. Some may appear *avoidant*, keeping a wary distance and, perhaps, assuming that what is offered may not be real or worth the trouble. Some may be *anxiously preoccupied*, with peer relationships, if not with adults in caregiving roles.

Others may be *ambivalent*, seeming desperately to want help one day and angrily rejecting it the next. Some homeless youth leave service providers and other adults massively confused – not knowing whether they want anything and, if so, what and on what terms – as they struggle to understand the *disorganization* that seems to pervade their interactions with these youth. While the adults wanting to help may have confidence in the value of what they are offering, some homeless youth may be less certain about whether potential helpers really mean what they say, fearing that their offers are meaningless or may disappear without warning if they move to accept them. Therefore, it is crucial that those working with homeless youth bear constantly in mind the ways in which young people's attachment patterns may affect their reactions to offers of support or assistance.

The interviews in *Voices from the Street* make evident how infrequently some homeless youth think of turning to adults for help. Considering the comments these young people made about their parents, presumably their earliest caregivers, in light of attachment theory helps us understand why only 13% of these youth said they would turn to service providers for help. Even when homeless youth said they could rely on parents, they frequently indicated they wouldn't really expect much in the way of contact, let alone help.

> I don't have contact [with my parents]. They told me never to contact them again. That was when I was twelve.
>
> (p. 91)

> My parents are dead . . . because they were both crack heads and by the
> time I was born all of my sisters had been runaways and had children.
>
> (p. 91)

> I visit my dad maybe once a year and call my mom every time I get my
> hands on a free long-distance phone.
>
> (p. 91)

> Probably since me and my mom are a little bit better, I guess if something
> is really wrong or bad I could call her for help.
>
> (p. 88)

> I can call my father. He gives me money, that's number one. Then pretty
> much after that, it's myself and that's it!
>
> (p. 88)

At the age of 18, the young man quoted directly above believes he must rely largely on himself – a sentiment that was echoed by fully one-third of the youth participating in this survey. Their comments about self-reliance have a particularly poignant quality when we understand that this attitude is probably born of necessity and may convey a sense of resignation rather than pride.

> I rely on myself, really. That's the only one who's going to get you
> through it. You're by yourself, really.
>
> (p. 89)

> I usually rely on myself. I've realized that's who I have to rely on. No one
> else is going to change my situation, no one going to change my life but
> myself.
>
> (p. 89)

Unfortunately, this kind of premature self-reliance often stems from the fact that, even as very young children, these young people had to care for themselves. Without adequate parental care, supervision, advice, and help, these youth learned too early to fend for themselves, rather than how to find the help they need. Sadly, we know their sense of self-reliance is often illusory; these youth may not be able to make it out of homelessness on their own.

From compromised attachments to the absence of networks

Adolescents and young adults very often depend heavily on the networks their parents and caregivers have built up over years or even generations. Adults in these networks offer not only their personal wisdom but also links to other adults who can offer advice, connections to jobs, health care, and educational opportunities – in short, those who can open doors into, and guidance through, the world of adulthood. In contrast, the homeless youth interviewed most frequently cited friends as the group they would lean on: 44% would turn to friends rather than parents, caregivers, service providers, or other adults. Friendships provide important companionship, support, and opportunities for shared experiences. However, friendships are different from networks; friendships keep people close while networks connect people to those beyond the circle of their immediate friends and help people reach out into new communities.

This may be one of the most important barriers to homeless youth finding their way off the streets and into the larger community. They don't expect help from adults and if they do want it, they may not know who to ask or how to mobilize networks that could assist them. In the previous chapter we saw the importance of professional networks in sustaining the work of therapists working with traumatized populations. Unfortunately, the primary network available to homeless youth is the homeless population unless and until they can connect with programs that will open doors to different communities and life beyond the streets.

Until that happens homeless youth likely rely on friends because of proximity, ease of access, and the developmental importance of peer relationships. Friends offer a sense of shared experience, belonging, and acceptance they don't easily find in the larger community. Indeed, when asked how they thought people perceived them, the homeless youth surveyed made their sense of being outcasts abundantly clear.

A lot of people ignore me or yell at me.

(p. 43)

Lower than dirt. People look at you with contempt and disgust.

(p. 43)

As the scum of the earth, the lowest of the low.

(p. 43)

People are just mean. It's life.

(p. 43)

While these statements certainly reflect the actual experiences of homeless youth, they likely also reflect the way in which these youth view themselves. Research, clinical practice, and day-to-day experience shows that the world often acts as a mirror for our moods and self-assessment. On our cheerful days we enjoy easy, pleasant interactions with others, while our gloomy moods somehow find their match in the dour expressions of those around us.

Once again, we can look to attachment theory to understand why this would be so. Children learn who they are from their earliest caregivers. Children who hear loving words, experience comforting touch, and see smiling faces in response to their bids for attention come to know themselves as people who are worthy of attention and have the capacity to make others happy – just by being alive. Conversely, children whose bids for attention are met with harsh words, painful touch, and angry, depressed, or simply uninterested faces may eventually come to see themselves as unworthy or useless – a perspective often reinforced for homeless youth by their interactions with adults. Far from having a network of caring adults who offer advice and support, these youth perceive that many of the adults they encounter hold them responsible for their homelessness and therefore find them unworthy of assistance.

None of this is to suggest that those desiring to help are doomed to fail if they don't always respond immediately or perfectly. That is no more possible than it is for parents to be perfectly attuned and responsive to their young children. It is, however, a reminder that if we want to succeed in helping homeless youth, we must be willing to try and try again until we finally get it "right." With homeless youth who have experienced early insecure relationships that undermined their self-knowledge and confidence in relationships, it may take a very long time.

It may also be difficult for homeless youth to send clear messages about what they need and want. If their cues were consistently misread, ignored, or punished as children they may feel uncertain about whether they really know what they need, confused about whether they didn't clearly convey those needs, or convinced that what they think they need is bad or burdensome to the adults they encounter.

With this in mind, we can understand why youth who have started life from an insecure relationship with their caregivers may be wary of relationships with other adults and hesitant to reach out. These young people very often do not tell us how our behavior affects them because they have had very little experience with adults who listen and adjust their own behavior or attitudes, rather than expecting the youth to adapt. Typically, these young people simply turn away without explanation, or at times, they may respond with anger and belligerence.

It is absolutely crucial we understand that, almost without exception, their anger masks profound hurt and self-blame. When parents do not respond appropriately to small children, when they turn a depressed face or deaf ear to a child's gleeful greeting, when they respond to cries with verbal or physical attacks, the children blame themselves. They do not have the luxury of blaming the people on whom they are totally dependent for care; only children in secure relationships have that luxury, because they know – in the very depth of their being – that the relationship will withstand their anger. Most homeless youth, by definition, do not have those secure relationships – at least not with the adults and networks most young people can rely on.

Viewing programs for homeless youth through the lens of attachment

Programs and shelters for homeless youth are a relatively recent phenomenon, arising in the 1980s in response to an economic downturn and a decline in social services that left marginalized youth with few places or people to turn to for help. Good programs recognized that shelters for young runaways needed to meet their developmental needs as well as provide shelter and help them recover from the traumatic lives that most often had sent them into the streets. Even though we have had more than 30 years to learn best practices from pioneering programs, too many programs for homeless youth continue to be modeled on programs for adults suffering from chronic drug and alcohol abuse and mental illness. Those programs often have a punitive attitude toward those who turn to them for help, for example, assuming that, if allowed, they would laze about all day if not forced to leave the shelter to look for work.

Unfortunately, many programs for homeless youth continue to have a punitive stance based on an explicit or implicit assumption that the plight of homeless teens is of their own making. Even if a teen or young adult announces that he enjoys street life and finds family life too confining and impinging on his independence, it does not take much imagination to consider the possibility that behind the bravado lies a very lonely and frightened child who is too afraid to show his vulnerability by asking for help.

Not surprisingly, most of the youth surveyed for *Voices from the Street* did not have the kinds of relationships that allowed them to express feelings without fear of retaliation or the loss of the relationship. We can hear echoes of these fears in their comments about some of their more problematic experiences with programs and services for homeless youth.

> . . . I had a terrible experience. Because I needed them and it was embarrassing that no one wanted to help and they made it such an ugly experience.
>
> (p. 105)

> . . . I'm afraid of getting laughed at.
>
> (p. 104)

> They didn't do nothing. They expected too much, and they didn't see that I went into that program with nothing.
>
> (p. 104)

> . . . sometimes staff have their own little issues and they try to take it out on clients . . . I had some staff say to me, 'If you want we can take this outside.'
>
> (p. 102)

> Any shelter is like prison . . . but I guess it's better than being on the streets. You got food and a place to sleep.
>
> (p. 99)

> The worst experience I've had was when the staff expects you to totally change who you were five minutes ago and act like your life is perfect,

and punish you; they take away your food, they take away your shelter if you don't do what you're told.

(p. 98)

Clearly these young people feel that shelters and other services can exact a very high emotional price and that the responsibility for adaptation falls to them, rather than to service providers. While we can appreciate the attractiveness to service providers of consistent policies and procedures, rules are often perceived by homeless youth as rigid requirements that they must meet in order to have even their most basic needs met. Youth often experience these programs as identical to unresponsive parents who could not or would not adapt to their children or provide for their needs, but instead demanded that their children accommodate their own needs. In other words, as children they had to take care of their caretakers and it often feels to them as if they are once again required to prove themselves worthy before receiving the care they so desperately need. In the context of attachment theory, we can understand why these issues emerged from the survey as particularly problematic for homeless youth.

Curfews, which are often imposed on youth in shelters, appear to have meaning beyond themselves. More than an expected time of arrival, curfews also represent the possibility of being locked out. (Ironically, for teenagers living with their parents, the consequence of breaking curfew is often being "grounded," i.e. not being allowed to leave home.) In addition to standing as a reminder for many youth of the experience of being kicked out of their own homes, curfews can also provoke anxiety because of prior experience being locked in for the night – perhaps in juvenile hall or jail, or perhaps trapped in a house with a physically or sexually abusive family.

The requirement they comply with curfews is but one instance of what many homeless youth perceive as a pervasive tendency of program policies to infantilize them. For better or for worse, many of these youth have tended to their emotional and physical needs for many years before their living situation became unstable. We can safely assume that very few of these young people routinely experienced leaving for school with a belly warm from a lovingly prepared breakfast or regularly settled into a comfortable sleep after bedtime stories or a late-night talk with parents. Then, homeless youth find in programs intended to meet their needs that they are required to surrender the independence and self-sufficiency on which they have come to rely in the absence of the care adults have consistently failed to provide – simply in order to have a meal and a place to sleep.

At times you stay even when you know it's probably better for your psyche to leave. Not better for you physically, but better for your psyche to leave. You are basically harming yourself. You're putting up and making a shell, coating yourself. Shelling yourself. And you are (becoming) more defensive . . . They have certain criteria that you have to follow . . . You have to give up some of your personality in order to be housed.

(p. 100)

Finally, and perhaps most insidiously, some programs require homeless youth to leave during the day, thereby continuing their homeless status as well as replicating the trauma of being kicked out of their families. For most people, leaving home for school or work doesn't mean they are not allowed to return until a specified time; home is always available as a safe haven: the door can be opened when the time is right, not because the clock strikes the magic moment.

Indeed, it is hard to understand how putting a young person on the street for the day could be seen as an antidote to homelessness.

Meeting the attachment needs of homeless youth

In securely attached families, parents and children work together throughout childhood, adolescence, and into adulthood to secure a mutually satisfying relationship – one that can meet the needs of its members through developmental changes and the vagaries imposed by the external world. As we learned from the youth surveyed for *Voices from the Street,* most homeless youth do not come from such families, and many were turned onto the streets by their families when they had barely left childhood.

To repeat, any attempts to address the needs of homeless youth must take their histories into account. As with all of us, their earliest patterns of attachment continue to influence their moods, behavior, attitudes, and relationships. When homeless youth approach (or are approached by) service providers, the encounter is often fraught with the expectation that these relationships will repeat their earlier, unsatisfactory or traumatic relationships with caregivers.

We cannot undo those relationships; we cannot create happy childhoods, but we can generate programs that recognize that relationships cannot be rushed, and that preparation for life as a satisfied, self-sufficient adult occurs in the context of relationships that are built over a long period of time.

Not all homeless youth will need many years of services to begin to heal from the trauma of their early years, but they will certainly require many months of compassionate attention from adults who are willing to listen and to try their best to develop relationships based on mutual respect and understanding. It is essential that those working with homeless youth have, at the very least, a basic understanding of the impact of trauma, particularly the ways in which traumatized young people are vulnerable to overwhelming memories and unmanageable feelings. Experiences that evoke earlier experiences of abuse, neglect, or abandonment are not only disturbing in and of themselves, but are also retraumatizing for these young people.

Programs that recognize that homeless youth bring their traumatic histories with them routinely consider their policies in the light of relationships and the impact of trauma. Good programs understand that traumatized youth have trouble controlling their impulses and act out physically and verbally. When this happens, youth are helped to follow the rules, rather than being turned out. Such programs recognize that cutting a young person off from safe shelter and basic necessities is neither appropriate nor compassionate and that trauma-informed consequences for disruptive or otherwise negative behavior should help to build, rather than undermine trust, and create space for real change.

Trauma-informed programs recognize that change occurs in the context of relationships. Young children learn to follow the rules of the family in order to please their parents; later they behave well to maintain good and positive relationships with teachers, coaches, ministers, and other important people in their communities. Indeed, these adults not only teach them the rules, but help them to follow them, recognizing that it takes time and practice to learn the rules of any game.

Successful programs recognize that insecure attachments and trauma often coexist. Trauma severely interferes with the neuropsychological capacity to regulate feelings and behavior. The capacity for self-regulation, along with the capacity for self-soothing, is developed in the context of a relationship with a regulating and soothing other. When traumatized youth misbehave, they need to be held close – like the teenager who is kept safely at home as a consequence of breaking curfew. They need programs that can keep them safe until they can do that for themselves.

Most homeless youth have had little experience with unconditional love and acceptance. We learned from their interviews in *Voices from the Street* that they have had much more experience with being mistreated and unfairly judged. Programs that recognize this aspect of their histories and the impact it has on their attitudes and behavior are much more likely to devise non-judgmental approaches to supporting homeless youth.

A non-judgmental approach resembles what many parents find effective in raising adolescents. We know that adolescence is a time of experimentation – a phase in one's life that allows for trying on different roles and trying out different behavior. Even though it can be hair-raising at times, many parents of adolescents recognize that the "school of hard knocks" is often more effective than parental advice, but that parental support is essential to help young people navigate this important and often confusing period. This is not to suggest that parents should ignore or give tacit approval to dangerous or self-injurious behavior, or that adults working with homeless youth should behave indifferently when youth act in ways that could cause harm to themselves or others. Indifference is quite distinct from a position of non-judgmental support. These young people need to know that adult support is not contingent on preconceived ideas about how they should behave.

Many of the young adults who contact A Home Within for psychotherapy have experienced periods of homelessness; all of them have experienced difficulties in their earliest relationships. Therapists who participate in A Home Within know how important it is for these young people to have a consistent relationship that doesn't disappear when they do. Unlike publicly funded therapists who must often close cases when their young clients miss too many sessions, the therapists who volunteer their time through A Home Within can keep an opening for as long as they want. Adults need to be available as long as they're needed – "for as long as it takes." It simply makes no sense for relationships to end because a child reaches a certain age or moves from one category of housing to another.

They also know how important it is for youth who have been abandoned to have the opportunity to leave someone else behind – without fear of reprisal or retaliation. The young people who come out of foster care after three, six, or ten different placements often need to miss several sessions or come to sessions erratically before they can be absolutely certain that the therapist will really be there at the agreed-upon time. The experience of keeping someone waiting differs dramatically from knowing that no one is waiting for you – just as the experience of latch-key kids choosing not to go home after school differs sharply from that of children who choose not to go home knowing that a parent is there waiting. Adults working with homeless youth need to remain available even when youth tell them they're not needed. They need to show up when they say they will – even when the youth don't.

As with therapists working through A Home Within, trauma-informed programs recognize that homeless youth are not all alike and that one size does not fit all. Successful programs recognize the importance of meeting the individual needs of homeless youth. The needs of the 14-year-old who has recently run away from home to escape being sexually abused by her mother's new boyfriend are very different from those of the 21-year-old who has been living on the streets for five years and prostituting himself as the only means he believes he has to survive.

Conclusion

When designing programs to serve homeless youth effectively, we need to remember – above all – that relationships beget relationships. By their behavior, homeless youth tell us a great deal about how they have been treated. Initially, many will expect us to treat them in the same ways they were treated in their earliest relationships. Only over time can they learn, from our interactions with them, that they merit care, compassion, and respect. We might follow the sage advice of Jeree Pawl, a leader in the treatment of very young children: "treat others as you would have others treat others" (Pawl, 1995). When we do follow that advice, we will develop and support programs and policies that promote healthy relationships for and with young people. Without those, nothing else really matters.

3

HOW CAN YOU TREAT WHAT YOU CANNOT SPEAK?

The ambiguities and hesitation that show themselves when children attempt to put abuse into language result not simply from linguistic immaturity or confusion, but from the particular meaning language has in the process of experiencing, internalizing, and knowing abuse. Many difficulties attend the task of putting language to abuse – but one that may go unrecognized is that the therapist must sometimes recognize and tolerate the child's contention that utterly no words can name or hold the internal chaos that inevitably emerges in the wake of abuse. The therapist, who typically values the organizing and liberating functions of language, is powerfully tempted to name too quickly what the child finds to be unnamable. Paradoxically, when we put language to an experience that the child either cannot name or has deliberately, whether consciously or unconsciously, endured by separating it from linguistic formulation, we necessarily to some extent falsify the child's experience and run the risk of subverting the treatment. Before language can successfully be brought to treatment, the therapist is obligated to recognize and withstand the wordless, chaotic terror in which abused children live.

Professionals who work with abused children often disagree about whether these young victims can talk about what happened to them. Certainly, some children do actually report abusive events and can do so without prompting by adults. Abused children are neither mute nor incapable of conveying their experiences. However, we must distinguish between children's descriptions of external events and their narrations of internal experiences.

Even young children may be able to give a reasonably clear and accurate account of another's behavior, such as, "He touched my pee-pee"; nevertheless, this information may belie the child's affective and cognitive confusion. A child's verbal report of physical or sexual abuse relies on the ordering function of language in describing experience (Hewitt, 1994). However, a relatively organized narration about behavior may sometimes deflect our attention from the disarray of an internal world. Partly because behavior is observable and feelings are more difficult to discern, the former is easier for a child to describe. Thus, the ordering function of language illustrates a paradox confronting those of us who try to understand the world of abused children. If we too quickly attempt to impose the organizational powers of language or too readily accept the child's ordered and reasonable descriptions of abuse as the whole story, we may collude with the child's defensive use of language to mask the more troubling and less accessible feelings and cognitive confusion. We may very well desire to accept a child's straightforward narrative as evidence that she has internalized and resolved the abusive experiences she describes. Indeed, children are often encouraged to bring order to these experiences so that those who have harmed them can be stopped. However, in a psychodynamic treatment, where the external demands for order are removed, the falseness of this structure often shows itself quite quickly.

The narrative structure evident in clinical work with children who come to treatment from a background absent of abuse frequently stands in striking contrast to the fragmentation and confusion that can and often does permeate the therapeutic sessions of abused children. Because of their different relationship to language, children who have not been abused are far more likely to engage the therapist in a mutually created story (Rachman & Mattick, 2012), whereas abused children often demand a rigidity in the therapeutic relationship and process (Alvarez, 1992; Bromberg, 2000; Heineman, Clausen, & Ruff, 2013; Ippen et al., 2011; McQueen et al., 2008; Smith, 2011). Even in their chaos, abused children must maintain control over the therapy; they allow little to chance and do not easily tolerate the therapist's introduction of modifications or variations in words or play.

Just as we have come to appreciate the importance of narrative structure in the development of a cohesive sense of self, we have come to see psychotherapy as a creative process. This joint endeavor engages both patient and therapist in the development of a unique story (Hewitt, 1993; Ogden, 1997; Raphael-Leff, 2012) that describes and expands the possible outcomes. However, the propensity for action common to children in therapy often adds a dimension that transforms the therapist's office from a quiet sitting room to a stage in which the child's unfolding drama engages patient and therapist. So despite the importance of narrative in psychoanalytic work with adults, it often plays a relatively minor part in successful therapeutic work with children, for whom action is so crucial.

Of course, no one can create a paradigm that can successfully contain all of the possible variations children present in therapy. As a way of conceptualizing the intertwining of behavior and commentary that characterizes psychodynamic work with children, I would like to discuss a continuum of therapeutic communication that ranges from the largely narrative at one pole to almost pure action at the other. Although the concepts of pure narrative without action or simple actions without intended communication are illusory, they offer useful theoretical endpoints on a continuum. Somewhere in the space between narration and action, most of child therapy takes place and might be conceptualized as a therapeutic theater. The child straddles the roles of playwright, director, and actor in his efforts to demonstrate, as well as describe, his compelling internal dramas. This continuum only superficially concerns speaking and doing; more important, it is about the relationship between patient and therapist, the child's desires and capacities to be known, and the therapist's ability and willingness to participate in the unfolding of the child's unconscious processes.

At one end of the continuum, we find those therapies that are largely narrative, where words contain and convey action: patient and therapist talk, listen, and reflect together; impulses and activities are as frequently described as enacted. This occurs exceedingly rarely in therapeutic work with children – and virtually never in the initial work with the child who has been abused. Even if the abused child sits quietly and talks, there is seldom enough trust or comfort for reflection.

The patient who can rely on words alone to convey her thoughts and feelings demonstrates a willingness to entrust her story to the imagination of the listener. The desire to be known by another, not just as presented, but as reflected in the vision of the self created in the mind of the other, requires a rather remarkable capacity for trust. Those who have been deliberately ill treated simply have no access to such faith. Without the reliable and repeated experience of a cohesive self in relation to another, one person cannot simply and straightforwardly tell another about one's self. Thus, the child who has relied on the fragmentation of dissociation to endure repeated beatings or sexual molestation does not have a coherent, cohesive story to tell.[1]

A psychotherapy conducted largely within a narrative structure depends significantly on spoken language with its power to order and organize. For example, rather than arrive late, an adult patient might begin an hour with the comment, "I was so mad at you that I thought about coming late today." In this statement the patient indicates his awareness of his affective state and the possibility of action for expressing that state. However, he made a conscious choice, at least in this instance, to talk about rather than act on his feeling. Perhaps this choice had something to do with the patient's wish to communicate his anger clearly to his therapist rather than allowing any ambiguity. But action (particularly in psychotherapy, which relies so heavily on clarity of motivation and meaning) is often much more ambiguous than words. Suppose our angry patient had elected instead to act on his feelings and come late to his appointment. While waiting, his therapist would have time to reflect on any number of possibilities for his patient's absence, including his being caught in traffic, or staying away in an effort to avoid uncomfortable feelings, or either consciously or unconsciously attempting to invoke certain feelings in the therapist. The actions are ambiguous. Not until he arrives for his appointment can the patient and his therapist begin to talk together, to use language to create a shared understanding of the meaning of and motivations for the actions.

A narrator feels more or less content to tell his story, but the playwright has determined that her tale must be *shown* as well as told. She creates a cast of characters; she scripts their words and choreographs their movements to evoke the changing visual and auditory images that she wants the audience to hear and see. In the context of the narration–action continuum, we should recall that when rehearsals finally begin, the early practices are typically devoted to "blocking," that is, to mapping out the movements that will carry the actors from one scene to the next through the acts that eventually compose the whole. Physical movements can graphically demonstrate relationships and unconscious motives. The attuned therapist pays careful attention to the child's movements as well as to the direct and indirect instructions the child gives her. For example, a child who offers the therapist a toy as a means of bringing her into closer proximity, is relying on non-verbal directions. In other instances, children explicitly engage their therapists as actors in elaboration of their internal dramas with detailed verbal directions.

Joey

As five-year-old Joey settles into a therapy session in front of the dollhouse, he hands me the mother doll; articulating script and stage directions, he informs me how I should play my part.

"She comes home and says, 'This house is a mess!'" instructs Joey.

With the help of the more junior dolls, Joey then gleefully wreaks havoc upon the dollhouse and its contents. On cue, I march the mother doll into the chaos, announcing, "This house is a mess!"

Finding me an inadequate actor in his drama, Joey sighs scornfully, "Not like that."

As he takes over the operation and voice of the mother doll, he relegates me to audience. At least for the moment, he has determined that I am incapable of accurately enacting the drama he has in mind.

Joey's "firing" me bears further consideration. He clearly wants me to know his feelings, but at that instant, for whatever reason, he cannot coach me until my performance meets his expectation. To convey successfully what he envisions, he has essentially two choices – to tell or to show. He does not move toward a narrative description of the scene he imagines with a comment like, "No. She's madder than that," or "You should sound more sad"; instead, he shifts into action in order to demonstrate.

Sometimes, as teachers and parents well know, demonstration works far more efficiently than description, particularly if the language available to the teller or listener cannot sufficiently circumscribe the complexity of the image or action to be conveyed. For example, consider trying to teach a child to tie his shoes without any reliance on demonstration! Even worse, try to imagine having to learn this complex series of twists and turns from narrative description alone.

We make an extremely important assumption that operates when we tell, rather than show, our stories to another – an assumption I believe we take too much for granted. The willingness to trust in the imagination of the other, to allow ourselves and our stories to be created in the mind of another, can, it seems to me, come only out of the conscious or unconscious conviction that the integrity of the self-as-presented will not be destroyed. When we narrate ourselves and our histories, we expect that what develops in the mind's eye of the reader or listener will approximate closely enough the setting, the characters, and the action we wish to convey. Sometimes patients, as Joey did, need to determine whether their trust in the therapist's imagination is justified. Others, perhaps more certain of their skills as raconteurs or with more positive experiences of being benignly held in the mind of another, feel more willing to proceed without feedback, to act on faith, even when that faith is not well placed.

Barbara

Over the course of a lengthy treatment of a young woman named Barbara, I developed a very clear picture of her mother. Since Barbara's relationship with her mother supplied a primary focus of our work together, I had a significant amount of information about the mother, a rather tall, large-boned, blond woman. I had ideas about her friends and knew that she dressed in bold colors and often spoke in a booming voice. Over time, in my mind's eye, I could easily see Barbara's mother moving through the house in which she raised her family and hear the conversations my patient described to me. In essence, I developed a comfortable familiarity with her mother's character and image; I felt that I had come to know her well.

In the context of termination, Barbara described browsing through old photo albums. She commented, "In looking at the pictures of my mother, I was struck again by how much you look like her! And you sound alike, too. You're both so soft-spoken." I was stunned, confused, and annoyed. As I attempted to fit this tall, blond, strong-voiced mother into my self-image as a small, dark-haired, soft-spoken therapist, I felt as if I had just seen a remake of a favorite movie, in which the previously familiar heroine had become almost unrecognizable!

Because Barbara had entrusted her reality to my imagination, her narrative had permitted me the countertransference privacy of creating a fantasy of a larger-than-life mother, quite different from me. Our exploration of the collusion that allowed me to maintain this distorted image of her mother made up an important final piece of our work.

In the context of the narration–action continuum, I want to emphasize that precisely because Barbara did not demand that I describe my visual image of her mother, I was enabled to build from her narration an autonomous fantasy of a mother who could protect us both through her transference storms. Unlike Joey, Barbara did not need to check to see if I was getting it right, nor correct my assumption upon discovering that I hadn't. She could tolerate not needing to know exactly what I was thinking. While my fantasy of her mother did not at all fit external reality, it did accurately reflect Barbara's wish for a strong, sure, and protective mother, one who could tolerate her outbursts without either crumbling or resorting to sadistic retaliation.

I believe that as Barbara shifted between her views of me as either excessively rigid and mean or, alternatively, weak and ineffectual, I must have conveyed in many ways that I had created an image that approximated, closely enough, her wish for a mother who was strong and powerful without being cruel.

In retrospect, a number of factors influenced Barbara's willingness to undertake the process of therapy largely from the position of narrator. She was bright and had a significant command of language. While difficult and not without trauma, her childhood has not included abuse. Perhaps most important, although far from perfect, her relationships had been sufficiently stable and benign for her to develop some faith in the good intentions of others.

Unlike Barbara's therapy, the therapeutic work with abused children begins at the far end of the continuum from narration in the world of action, action often lacking apparent meaning. Listening to these children can prove exceptionally difficult because they are often trying desperately to believe that what they have to say did not happen, is not real, and does not matter at all. The very events that propelled them into treatment often comprise what they most want to deny, negate, or at least minimize. Putting words to these events gives them form and substance – creates meaning and ownership. But that is precisely what abused children are so often mightily trying to avoid. And so they are left without a language to know or share their experiences.

Children who have been physically or emotionally abused exist in the world of action, not merely because the structure of language is developmentally, neurologically, or defensively unavailable, but because narrative structure has been destroyed as a means of psychic survival. If an experience is truly crazy, as abuse is, then it defies the child's attempts to contain it in the orderly, rational world of language. The abused child cannot think or speak or act sensibly precisely because her story makes no sense. This leaves us with a powerful paradigm that may be particular to therapeutic work with abused children: namely the destructive function of language in the treatment of something unspeakable.

We repeatedly encounter the idea that abuse is unspeakable. It is unspeakable because the horrific facts are felt as a shameful secret. It is unspeakable because there are no words to capture events that shatter the child's capacity to integrate experiences. But beyond these and more dreadful than these, it is not speakable because the very fact of putting language to an inherently disruptive experience falsifies that experience.

Paradoxically, this means that to hear what abused children have to say requires being able to listen to their actions without interpreting meaning where none exists. Of course, actions do sometimes have meaning and are used as both conscious and unconscious forms of communication. However, for many abused children, the actions are intended to destroy meaning, to prevent the development of a coherent story.

I do not mean to imply that abused children literally cannot use words; indeed, often they can quite articulately describe abusive events to police officers, attorneys, or therapists. Alternatively, their quick-witted verbal attacks on those who try to help them provide clear evidence that they understand the power of spoken language. Instead, I mean to suggest that, perhaps out of our reluctance to truly know the horrors they wish us to understand, we are often powerfully tempted to focus too much attention on these words as conveyers of meaning and to respond with verbal interpretations. In doing so, we may unwittingly help abused children to create a fundamentally untrue narrative, a façade of cohesiveness and pseudo-meaning that merely masks the underlying chaos. So when the children resist our attempts to talk, to name, or to organize, we might understand their protests not only, for example, as a defense against overwhelming affect or a resistance in the service of protecting the image of an idealized parent, but as a plaintive cry that we are not really listening to the story they need to illuminate. If, instead of talking, we listen, not just to the content or words but to the process of their language – the ways they use speech to connect with us, deflect our attention, inform us, or hide form us we may learn what *they* want us to know.

Louise

Louise was about ten when she was referred by her school because of her lack of friends, difficulties in accepting any kind of criticism, and horribly disruptive outbursts of temper. When her parents first came to meet with me, I was struck with her mother's rage at the school. Her diatribes would permit no questioning or disagreement. She found her daughter virtually perfect in all ways and believed all difficulties were either caused by the school or resulted from their faulty perceptions. Nevertheless, largely because she felt coerced by the school, she elected to have her daughter begin treatment with me.

Louise was a bright, articulate child but far from charming. A pattern emerged very quickly in the therapy hours: Louise routinely gathered several puppets, which she gave unusual and difficult-to-pronounce names. Then, fast and furiously, she would charge through a story in which the character thought to be good was discovered to be bad, or the mother was really the daughter, or the cousin had come disguised as some other character. At first I tried to make sense of the names and to follow the content of the changes, assuming that going from bad to good, for example, might have meaning. The characters exchanged rapid-fire comments, often followed by Louise's eerie cackles. I usually couldn't keep the stories straight, but when I tried to clarify my confusion, my questions were typically characterized as stupid.

During this time, Louise's mother came in for one of our regularly scheduled visits. She began her usual tirade of complaints, but I was astounded to hear that her vicious attacks were now directed at Louise. She described Louise exactly as the school had done, only in far crueler terms. She proclaimed that she could certainly understand why the teachers and students hated this child, who was abhorrent in every way. Everything the school complained about could be attributed to Louise's shortcomings or her incorrect perceptions.

Although I had no reason to believe that Louise or her sisters had been physically harmed, the unrelenting viciousness of her mother's diatribes certainly constituted verbal abuse. Louise and her mother gave me a view into the ways in which a relationship with an emotionally unstable parent leads to disorganized patterns of attachment in other relationships. I now understood the hours with Louise as repetitious illustrations of the unpredictability of her world, both inner and outer. Just as the content of her mother's verbal attacks had to be warded off, Louise used spoken language not to convey the specific meaning of the words, but as props in a confusing, erratic drama. The words, like the names that I could barely understand, let alone remember, were intended to disguise, not reveal. The rapid movement from one character to another, from one affective state to another had its purpose blocking out the words that were too painful and difficult to hear. Louise could not tell me in a straightforward narrative what it felt like to be with her mother. My understanding of the meaning of her play required that I temporarily move away from language, relinquish my effort to analyze the content of her play. Before I could help her put words to her experiences, I had to allow myself to absorb the fear and confusion that permeated her life at home and ripped through the hours with me.

We have all experienced frustrating moments in which we recognize the inadequacies of language. We attempt to describe a dream, a daydream, a tender moment, or our responses to a work of art, and in the very moment of doing so, we feel the experience slip away from our very efforts to capture it in language. Sometimes we respond angrily, feeling that our words have failed us, other times with sadness that we cannot use language to make a connection to those we want to tell about ourselves, or we respond with resignation and defeat, feeling that the story can never be truly told.

Usually we accept and adapt to the limitations inherent in transforming primary process experiences into the linearity of secondary process though. That is, we make meaning as best we can in order to capture and convey the experience. However, the essential difference between these experiences and the experiences of the abused child is that the child has no desire to capture the abusive experiences or little interest in conveying to us the horrors that brought her to our attention. To do so, for her, is to make meaning of something that does not make any sense at all. In my experience these children have a powerful wish to retain the abusive experience as fragmentary, elusive, unnamable, and unnamed in the mistaken belief that doing so will reduce the power of the experience and maintain it in the external world. For better or for worse, once we can name a thing, we own it, and it has a place in our internal world.

A young woman who had repeatedly been abused during her childhood described her reluctance to discuss or know anything about the perpetrator of the abuse.

"I don't want to think for even one half of one second about him, about why he did what he did or even about what he did. That would mean it might make sense. Even thinking about it, having a thought, thoughts come in words, if I can even think it, that he might have had a motive, that he thought about it, then maybe it was something I could understand. Understand? Understand what? How could I understand it? It cannot be understood."

We can comprehend the confusion between understanding and condoning or forgiving. But that is not what this young woman was talking about. Her worries were more basic, they derived from the terror of seeing a coherent picture in the fragmentary confusion of memory and fantasy, with the terror of thinking, lest she give form to something she desperately wanted to relegate to the world of shapeless non-reality.

In the aftermath of abuse, children live in a dark, eerily kaleidoscopic inner world, in which organized images and thoughts can be punctured without warning by fragmented pictures, flashes, sounds, and feelings. An adult patient who had been abused as a child frequently talks of her terror of sleep because of the dreams of abuse. These dreams contain no coherent pictures, no scenes of what was done to her; rather, they are fragmented, disjointed images that fade and flash, one permeated by another, until she wakens in terror and exhaustion. "But," she sighs, "it's no different when I'm awake."

Corrine

Corrine was referred for therapy by her caseworker at the age of 15. She and her younger siblings had been removed from their parents' care when Corrine disclosed to a teacher that her father raped her on a nearly nightly basis and that her complaints to her mother resulted in physical punishment. The children were divided among three foster homes and, as is often the case, both her mother and her younger siblings blamed Corrine for breaking up the family.

Although she had told her caseworker that she wanted "to talk to someone," any kind of conversation seemed almost unbearable for Corrine. Her therapist described the silence in the room as more empty than hostile, as if Corrine simply had nothing to say, no words to say what was inside of her or – maybe – as if she had just tried to empty everything out.

The silences and the frequency of missed sessions made her therapist wonder if the relationship had the possibility of helping Corrine or whether, by calling to remind her of appointments, she was forcing herself on Corrine, as her father had. Gradually, the therapist discovered that when she called to remind her of their next scheduled meeting, Corrine would sometimes engage her in conversation about her day or what had happened at school that week. This "ice- breaker" gave them a place to start talking when Corrine came to her sessions, which she began doing with increasing frequency until she was suddenly moved to the home of relatives in another part of the state.

This provides a good example of the very real difficulties therapists encounter in trying to form an alliance with children who have been abused. Maybe Corrine "wanted to talk to someone." Maybe, more accurately, she wanted to be *able* to talk to someone, but just couldn't. Like the young woman, described above, who didn't want to think about what had happened to her because thoughts come in words, Corrine's silence seemed a powerful statement that the abuse had annihilated her power to put words to her experiences.

Sadly, the therapist will never know whether the treatment was helping Corrine find her voice; perhaps Corrine will retreat even more from finding words because of the sudden loss of someone who was willing to keep listening, even if only to silence. Sudden disruptions of therapy (Deutsch, in press) have a powerful and lasting impact on those left behind, whether patient or therapist and, in this case, both. Often both parties are silenced; in the case of death, permanently, but in other cases, because there seems to be nothing left to say when there is no one there to listen. Therapists who work with foster youth know that they may lose their young patients without words of warning or explanation to help them create a coherent narrative of the experience.

Michelle

The disorganization in which abused children reside was aptly demonstrated in the treatment of a six-year-old girl who was hospitalized following her attempt to jump from a second-story window. This child's physical abuse at her mother's hands was well documented; sexual abuse was merely suspected. Regularly and in myriad ways, Michelle forced her chaotic, enraged neediness upon her therapist. During many sessions she could barely maintain self-control, either virtually or actually hitting, kicking, or lunging for toys to throw or break. Her wails and moaning cries echoed through the hallways. Repetitive, relatively organized play could, at any moment and without apparent provocation turn to primitive, incoherent shouts and invectives. In one session, her therapist's announcement of a two-week vacation prompted 20 minutes of uninterrupted, ear-piercing screaming, which culminated in her vomiting on the office floor. Her therapist left the session in a state of physical and emotional exhaustion born of her having to restrain Michelle while posing to herself the inevitable questions about whether the crying represented an expression of emotional pain or whether she might be suffering from enormous physical pain as well; whether the child would ever stop; whether she should try some other means to stop her; what her colleagues in neighboring offices must be thinking; what she could have done differently; and how she would ever present this hour in supervision. Perhaps Michelle's vomiting was an intentional communication; perhaps it just served to culminate too much crying and too much misery. In any event, it brought the hour to a dramatic close.

Even though Michelle appeared to function at higher levels of ego organization at times, the sudden emergence of primitive states did not appear regressive. Indeed, although the primitive images of neediness, greed, rage, and terror did not always loom at the forefront of Michelle's daily internal life, they always appeared to coexist with states of greater ego organization. It was as if Michelle's psychic "house" contained two adjoining rooms – one organized, the other in disarray. Sometimes she lived in one and sometimes in the other.

This, in fact, appears to be one of the frequent psychological characteristics of victims of child abuse: The movement in and out of primitive states is lateral rather than vertical; that is, the shifts do not involve a regression; Michelle's more primitive behavior did not result from defensive regression, nor did it emerge as a consequence of the safety of the therapeutic environment. It just formed a part of Michelle's story.

Michelle's first session following her discharge from the hospital tells her story well. She began, as she often did, by cooking. This time she made cocoa.

"You're the baby," she said. Looking at an imaginary watch, she continued, "If you're late I'm gonna whup you. You have to take off your shirt, your shoes," pointing to all the pieces of clothing her therapist was supposed to remove. The therapist asked, "You're gonna whup me naked?"

"Unh-huh, in the bath. You're gonna take a bath and then I'm gonna whup you and hold your head in the water until you drown."

Ignoring the therapist's questions about this, Michelle lay on the floor and proclaimed, "You're the doctor. Get your bag. I'm dead."

"What happened?"

"A boy raped me – on Saturday morning – in the park."

"What happened?"

"On my back, with a raper. He hit me."

"What's a raper?"

"Like a glass raper, what they rape grass with," she replied pointing to her back. "He killed me and now I'm a robot and I'm running out of batteries."

"Do you want any battery juice?"

"Yes, now I'm coming back to life, listen to my heart."

"Is it a little girl's heart?"

"No, it's a robot heart. I'm a robot. Bring back the robot girls. Not the boys. The boys are bad. Just girls. I'll protect the girls. Now I'm a baby." She put a toy bottle in her mouth and crawled into the lap of her therapist, who was feeling quite overwhelmed by this flood.

The therapist commented, "Every baby needs a bottle."

"Mama. Mama."

"Yes, you have a mama and a grandmother."

Michelle instantly became a dog and began angrily stuffing the pieces of the tea set, in which she had earlier served cocoa, into her greedy mouth.

I believe it would be a mistake to focus on the content of this hour, to assume that any single story led to another or that the content of the material gave rise to intrusive anxiety leading to what looks like, but is not, a play disruption. There is very little play to disrupt; rather there are a series of images, some of which appear to be more coherent than others. This session occurred very early in the treatment, and the therapist did get caught in attending too much to the content, as, for example, when she assumed that Michelle was trying to tell her in words about being molested.

What matters in this session is that Michelle became disorganized by her experiences of abuse and neglect, and she brought that disorganization to the therapy. I believe Michelle simply acted out the chaos of her internal world, a world in which images do not hold still and words have little meaning. If we assume that Michelle offered these snippets as a deliberate although unconscious means of connection, we would undermine the actual communication emanating from Michelle's actions. Unlike Joey who could use language to describe what was in his mind, Michelle cannot control what pours forth, and when her therapist doesn't quite understand, Michelle's language does little good in redirecting the action. In other words, Michelle, at this point in her therapy, cannot assume the role of either playwright or narrator – she lacks access to the interrelated structures of language and observing ego that would allow her to describe her inner experiences and to shape her therapist's behavior by verbal cues or direction.

Michelle's uncontrollable wailing at the announcement of her therapist's vacation differs in degree, though not in kind, from normative episodes familiar to parents of young children who are just beginning to master language. For example, Johnny has awakened happily from a nap. His mother, anticipating his hungry state, takes him to the kitchen for a snack. When he brushes aside the cookie she offers, she asks what he would like. He answers, "Cookie." His mother briefly offers the original cookie again; then, since Johnny is quickly becoming increasingly agitated, offers, in quick succession, other varieties of cookies and crackers. Johnny pushes them all away, wailing, "Cookie." Finally, stalling for time, his mother pours a cup of milk. Johnny calms and happily downs the milk along with the original cookie.

Though this brief vignette offers many possible avenues of discussion, I use it here to illustrate a normative occurrence of children's inability to turn reliably to language as a means of structuring and describing an affective experience. Michelle's loss of language is frequent, unpredictable, and not easily recovered. In contrast, Johnny's difficulty in finding words emerges in a period of regression, as he struggles to fully awaken. Developmentally, Johnny has not achieved sufficient command of language for us to consider its absence a loss. It is a capacity in the process of developing – sometimes available and sometimes not. What does Johnny mean by "cookie"? Has he condensed "milk and cookie" into one word? Perhaps, although his mother responds as if they have a shared understanding of the word "cookie." His mother's actions, I believe, convey a much more profound understanding of Johnny's repeated, distressed, wailing of "cookie." She offers a number of alternatives, finally shifting to a different category of food. She responds as if Johnny has said, "I'm feeling really miserable right now and what I'm saying isn't working to get what I want, but I don't know what else to say." Ignoring the literal definition, she takes Johnny's word as an affective communication, *including that he has no appropriate words to convey his intended meaning.*

We should also note Michelle's "rape/rake" confusion in this context, because it reminds us how easily children confuse words, meanings, and affects. Was Michelle raped or was she raked? Maybe neither; maybe both. The facts of what happened in the park may well be unknowable to both Michelle and her therapist, but the affect that overwhelms a cohesive story line is almost palpable. Michelle's therapist does want to understand her, does want to listen to the story she has to tell, but like Louise's tale, Michelle's story has embedded itself in a swirl of primitive, disorganized, and overwhelming affects.

As therapists, who appreciate the power of language, we want to help these children create a history out of the fragmented chaos of abuse that repeatedly and unexpectedly threatens to intrude into their minds and relationships. We want them to have stories that they can hold without terror, stories that do not inundate them with overwhelming affect. We can do this effectively only when we can, with them, repeatedly endure the affective disorganization that eludes language. Although we use words, initially, our patient attention and our affective steadiness are far more important than what we say in helping these children settle into a calm, alert state in which their feelings are experienced as signals and we are experienced as benign, even potentially helpful, people.

Only after we tolerate the world of action without meaning can we begin, with the child, to build a vocabulary for actions, feelings, and relationships. If we too quickly name, interpret, or describe a child's experiences, we merely offer children a false narrative – one that distances them and us from the truth of their experiences. When we keep ourselves outside the child's world, our words serve only the purpose of shielding ourselves from the horrors they need us to know.

Note

1 This does not mean that the child will be unable to give a relatively straightforward account of the facts surrounding the abusive events. It sometimes is the case that children either because of developmental immaturity or defensive confusion cannot relay the "facts of the case." However, if the internal experience has been chaotic, confused, and fragmented, then a coherent narrative falsifies, rather than describes that experience.

4

GOOD GUYS AND BAD GUYS
The temptations of splitting

People who abuse little children are bad guys; those who help them are good guys. If the world could be divided so easily and neatly, our clinical work with abused children would be much easier and more straightforward. Out of a conscious wish to spare the child additional pain, we would like to slam the therapist's door in the face of the bad guys. Despicable people; we don't want them in the room with us! The temptation for therapist and child to divide the world into "good guys" and "bad guys" can be quite powerful, especially when we feel pressured by external forces to clearly separate the two – to assign guilt to the perpetrator and thereby, assure the child of her innocence.

In this very delicate arena, it is essential that the therapist remain absolutely clear about the distinctions between moral, legal, and psychological issues. No matter how sexually, emotionally, or physically provocative they have been, children cannot be held responsible for instigating their abuse. It is the moral obligation of the adults in the child's environment to maintain the boundaries between child and grown-up and to exercise control of their impulses. Legal determinants of guilt and innocence are complex and are not the province of psychotherapists. We must focus exclusively on the child's psychological experiences of good and bad, guilt and innocence if we are to be most effective. It is in this arena that the two often come together in ways that makes us uncomfortable.

No matter how much we might condemn an adult who has abused a child, we must assume a neutral stance toward the child's internal representation of the abuser. This does not mean that we assume a morally neutral position. It does mean that we keep ourselves open and equally receptive to all of what a child has to tell us about herself, her experiences, and her representations of her abuser(s).

If we reassure her about her innocence when she feels guilty, she will not believe us and, worse, will surmise that we do not understand her. If we set ourselves the task of educating her about how to protect herself in the future, she will assume that she should have been able to do so in the past – and that she shares in the responsibility for her abuse. If we offer an abused child our patient attention, we will come to know, with sometimes overwhelming intimacy, how it feels to be the "bad guy" and how it feels to be his victim. Given the intense discomfort these primitive feelings stir in us, we should not wonder at finding ourselves often tempted to discover ways around us truly apprehending the mind of the child. No matter how much we would like to keep the "bad guys" out of the therapy, they will inevitably make themselves known through the affective interplay between child and therapist.

Psychotherapy with abused children is not an easy endeavor. These children do not trust easily; they test our patience over and over again. They fear their own impulses and ours, they attempt to provoke our loss of control in manifold ways. They think they're crazy; we begin to feel crazy when we're with them. They feel damaged; we wonder if they are beyond help.

In our initial meetings with the child, we may learn directly, or only through subtle hints, about the dreadfully painful thoughts, feelings, and experiences that will emerge over the course of an extended psychotherapy. This knowledge may, more frequently than we would like to admit, quietly contribute to the recommendation for brief therapy, crisis intervention, or treatment that focuses on symptom reduction rather than introspection. We may support these suggestions by emphasizing factors in the child's psychological status (such as lack of language) or factors in the environment (such as the level of disorganization) that will make it hard to sustain an ongoing, reflective psychotherapy. We may conclude that a psychotherapy that depends on reflection, or learning about intrapsychic processes through the examination of interpersonal exchanges, may be just *too* hard, even impossible.

However, if child and therapist *can* embark on a course of psychodynamic treatment that puts the relationship at the forefront, the complexity of ideas and feelings surrounding the abuse will be woven into their ongoing interchanges. While it may take time for the patterns and nuances unique to this particular therapeutic pair to emerge, there are common paradigms in the work with abused children that may show themselves relatively early in the therapy.

Rescue fantasies can easily be enacted in the treatment of any child, but they may be particularly compelling for those working with children who have been dreadfully mistreated (Cohen, 1988; Esman, 1987; Gillman, 1992; Malawista, 2004). In this paradigm, child and therapist collude in the profound wish that the therapist will quickly and easily deliver the child from the misery that seems to beset him at every corner. The following vignette illustrates how this fantasy can play itself out with people trying to help a desperate child. Their demands that the therapist "*do something*" often intensify when their attempts to save the child have either come to naught or repeatedly have been dashed by the child's seemingly willful misbehavior.

Marcus

People often commented on Marcus's striking features; his unearthly good looks and uncanny charm drew people to him in quite remarkable ways. From preschool through third grade, Marcus had attended a private school that had originated in the era and spirit of the counterculture of the 1960s. While initially an exciting, experimental school, after a few years, it had lost most of its luster and good standing. However, it did continue to draw students from a small cluster of parents who wanted an open and unstructured program for their children. Unfortunately, Marcus's mother, who lived in a state of disorganized psychotic anxiety, was unable to maintain any vigilance over Marcus's home or school activities. So, even after one of the teachers was fired because of inappropriately sexualized behavior toward the children, she continued to use him as a baby-sitter for her son. Marcus began protesting having to spend time with this young man; his mother became convinced that Marcus had been sexually assaulted. Without warning, one afternoon she packed all of their belongings, fled across the country, and enrolled Marcus in the most staid school she could find.

The school quickly discovered that Marcus's skills were far below grade level. Like others before her, the student teacher in his class found Marcus almost irresistibly charming and volunteered to tutor him after school. This lasted a few weeks until one day, when she asked Marcus to try a new assignment he registered his protest by throwing his chair across the room.

This prompted a recommendation for psychotherapy along with her referral to a more experienced tutor. The new tutor, too, was charmed by Marcus. His sad history and the ongoing plight of having to live with his mother's psychosis only endeared him more to her. The new tutor assured the therapist that the student teacher merely had not had enough experience to work with Marcus and, given that he had no obvious learning disabilities, that he could relatively easily be brought up to grade-level work.

Things went smoothly for several weeks. Pleased with her success, the tutor suggested that perhaps others simply had not understood Marcus very well. Indeed, the tutor and Marcus had settled into a seemingly comfortable relationship. One day she presented Marcus with an assignment that was harder than usual. He resisted, but the tutor, confident that Marcus could handle the work, persisted with her expectations. In response, Marcus spat in her face, tore up his book, flung it across the room, and knocked over his desk as he stormed from the room.

This outburst understandably hurt and dismayed Marcus's tutor who, unfortunately, refused to continue with him until his psychological problems were "settled." After a lengthy conversation, the very real hurt behind the tutor's thinly veiled criticism of the therapist became apparent. She had expected her relationship with Marcus to be different, he had initially responded to her care, which only fortified her sense of being the one special person who would get through to this child. She could not fully comprehend the powerfully ambivalent nature of Marcus's attachments. Although initially charming, his inability to withstand any narcissistic injury completely prevented him from allowing true closeness or tolerating even a hint of failure. He made others fail instead.

The tutor was neither the first nor the last of well-intentioned people who tried and failed to rescue Marcus. Many factors prompted these attempts. People responded to his physical attractiveness and superficial charm; they knew the strains his mother's mental state placed on him and felt sorry for him because of his troubled past. They did not realize that Marcus, like many children with similar backgrounds, could not tolerate any closeness in a relationship. Intimacy terrified rather than sustained him. When faced with the possibility of failure, he could not turn to another for comfort or assistance – that would expose an unbearable need for help. And, because Marcus had not had the kind of relationships that allowed him to establish reliable, sustaining internal images, he could not turn inward for comfort. Thus, the moments in which he anticipated failure put him in an untenable psychological position. He responded to the people who were trying to help as if they were enemies, threatening to expose his frailty and vulnerability. In his mind they were bad guys.

With great frequency, we find the important people in the life of an abused child divided into two feuding camps. Often, one group seems to stand for protecting the child, feeling that the other group treats the child too harshly or makes too may demands on a child who has already suffered greatly. The second group often seems to stand for setting reasonable, but firm, expectations, feeling that the child's bids for comfort or leniency are simply attempts to use the hurt she has suffered to manipulate others into meeting her demands.

These divisions among the people around an abused child reflect the split in the child's world of internalized relationships. Because of the actual overwhelmingly bad people in the child's life, his internal world consists of "good guys" and "bad guys." Even when these children can cognitively appreciate that most people are neither all good nor all bad – a concept that is hard for them – affectively, it is even more difficult for them to sustain positive images of people in the face of disappointment, anger, or hurt. In the aftermath of abuse, children have trouble developing and maintaining the capacity to experience negative affects that do not destroy their positive feelings toward those caring for them. Thus, if someone they like or love hurts or angers them, that person becomes "bad." Affectively, this is a very different experience from feeling angry, hurt, or disappointed in someone we like or love; we retain our positive image of that person even in the face of negative feelings. For an abused child, negative feelings, which are often cataclysmic affective experiences, destroy the fragile internal positive images. From this vantage point, we can see why these children often feel so bereft and so utterly alone.

A facet of human relationships that underlies psychodynamic psychotherapy is our proclivity for repeating or revoking aspects of past relationships in current ones. Pushed by powerful forces, we repeatedly create relationships that match those in our world of internalized images. If we expect to be treated well, we will find caring, respectful people and/or tend to evoke those feelings in those around us. If we expect ill treatment, we will find it, provoke it, or see it, even when it isn't present, in the feelings and behavior of others.* Obviously, abused children have every reason to expect ill treatment and, because of the enormity of their own negative feelings, they have the power to provoke intense feelings in others.

Sometimes, children who have been abused successfully and repeatedly provoke those around them into harsh or even abusive behavior. Until the child's world of internal figures contains more benign images, therapists, attorneys, teachers, or social workers can be drawn into an unending, futile battle to protect the child from continued mistreatment. For example, a child who has been physically abused is taken into protective custody. When his first foster parent hits him, he is moved to another home. In the second placement, his behavior so outrages the foster parents that they insist on his quick, unplanned removal. In the group home where he goes next, he so brashly and repeatedly breaks the rules that his counselor's efforts to discipline him begin to verge on the sadistic.

The following vignette illustrates the strong influence an abused child can have on her own environment. Ruby's behavior fueled a battle between school and home that graphically depicts both splitting and the intensity of feeling that a troubled child can evoke in those responsible for her care.

Ruby

Dr. Brown had been seeing seven-year-old Ruby only a short time when he received a call, resonating between pleading and rage, from the principal at her school. The principal insisted that Dr. Brown come in for a conference as soon as possible; Ruby was out of control, her foster mother belligerent, and her social worker unavailable. Dr. Brown agreed that Ruby could be very taxing but wondered if anything in particular had prompted the principal's sense of urgency. The principal, a veteran teacher, relatively new to school administration, described her enormous sympathy for Ruby and the horror that she had endured. Her concern had prompted her repeatedly to intervene with teachers and children on Ruby's behalf. When Ruby became disruptive in the classroom, she had offered her the opportunity to come to the office to "help" the secretaries until she could calm down. Ruby seemed to like this distraction, but if had little effect on her classroom behavior. The principal then decided that, rather than helping Ruby, this program was instead rewarding and reinforcing Ruby's misbehavior. As an alternative, she wanted to consider brief suspensions from school, hoping they might be more effective. However, according to the principal, the foster mother (who was in fact, Ruby's aunt) not only had no interest in coming to the school to remove this unruly child, but had angrily suggested that the principal was just trying to cover up the teacher's incompetence by "dumping" the school's problem on her.

Not unexpectedly, the foster mother, or "Auntie," had a somewhat different view of the situation. She felt that the principal was woefully naïve and far too untried to take on the challenges of this particular school. She experienced the principal's requests for help alternately as "whining" and the result of a white teacher's racial bias, which, to her way of thinking, placed too high a premium on very controlled behavior. She was not the least bit interested in this principal's sending Ruby home in the middle of the day!

Auntie had only reluctantly taken on the responsibilities of foster parent to her niece. The matriarch of a large extended family, she had, in addition to raising her own children, acted as temporary or substitute parent for many children over the years. However, when approached by Ruby's social worker, her genuine fondness for this little girl, along with a deeply held conviction that children belonged with family, had made it impossible for Auntie to refuse the responsibilities of being her foster parent.

From the beginning of her contact with Dr. Brown, Ruby's aunt had spoken openly about feeling "too old and too tired" to manage this very troubled little girl. Despite this characterization of herself, she was a spirited woman who commanded a great deal of respect from family and friends. She knew too much about life in the housing projects to hold an unrealistic optimism about Ruby's chances for recovery and escape.

Ruby had gone to Auntie's following her discharge from the hospital. She had arrived at the hospital in a catatonic state, having been severely beaten and thrown down the stairs of her home, ostensibly as punishment for helping herself to a soft drink belonging to her mother's boyfriend. Because of the mother's long and extensive drug use, the court determined that Ruby should remain in protective custody following her release from the hospital. Ruby's Auntie was well known within Children's Protective Services as an experienced foster parent with a no-nonsense approach to raising children. What she lacked in warmth, she made up for in steadfastness, even in the face of the most aggressive and difficult behavior.

At school, Ruby was a little terror, routinely sent to the principal's office for behavior that petrified her classmates. She moved about the classroom whenever she pleased and aggressively intruded on other children's studies. She frequently threatened to and sometimes actually did throw a chair at children when she didn't like what they said or did. At home, where there was less stimulation, Ruby exhibited more contained behavior. However, even there she suffered enormous anxiety; she anxiously rubbed her head until she created bald spots and was frequently overcome by seemingly unprovoked crying spells. Neighborhood children's understandable fear of her allowed Ruby to win at most games and to commandeer the toys or treats she wanted. Once, shortly after a child refused to give Ruby the candy she wanted, she stole it and bloodied the child's nose in the process.

In contrast to her behavior at school and at home, Ruby approached her therapy with Dr. Brown as a model citizen. She spoke only when spoken to and played with toys only when they were offered to her. Dr. Brown was particularly struck by her carefully controlled one or two-word responses to all of his questions or comments, especially in light of her apparently total lack of impulse control in other settings. She never protested going to therapy; in fact, her foster mother reported that she looked forward to the sessions. Yet she played with excessive control and without joy.

After a few sessions, Dr. Brown voiced his observation that she was particularly quiet whenever she came to therapy. Ruby responded, "You get in trouble at school if you talk out of turn." Silently wishing that Ruby's misbehavior were that minor, Dr. Brown explained that therapy was not like school and that she was free to talk whenever she wanted, adding that he, in fact, would be very interested in anything and everything she had to say. Ruby seemed to take this in, and over the next few weeks, she began to display more openness in both her play and verbal interactions.

In this context, then, Dr. Brown was ordered to appear for a school conference. He and Ruby were just beginning to know each other. Although he had some hunches about what might lie behind Ruby's controlled demeanor in the therapy sessions, his ideas were still untested hypotheses, yet to be explored with his, thus far, exceedingly well-behaved patient. Perhaps Ruby wanted to demonstrate how well she could "follow the rules" in order to win his love or to avoid his anticipated wrath, or both. Perhaps, also, in the quiet of the therapy sessions, Ruby's despair, otherwise hidden behind her aggressive attacks, showed itself. And perhaps she just didn't have any words to say what was in her mind, or else what was in her mind was not in words, so that she was, in fact, showing the pervasive emptiness that emanated when she felt the need to exercise strict control of her thoughts and actions.

If Ruby hoped that Dr. Brown would rescue her, she wasn't saying so directly. However, the principal, having failed in her attempts to save Ruby from herself, was certainly asking to be rescued by somebody.

As a skilled and experienced clinician, Dr. Brown had few illusions that Ruby's behavior could be transformed as quickly or as completely as her teachers, classmates, or principal might wish. Her first seven years had been marred by neglect and abuse; she was a child fighting for her life with no good reason to trust that others would act in her best interests and every reason to anticipate a brutal attack at any time from any corner. Like so many children whose stories of neglect and abuse engender an outpouring of sympathy from those who hear them, Ruby was more appealing when considered from a distance. The day-to-day reality of trying to teach, or discipline, or play with her quickly engendered the expectable responses from adults working with children with ambivalent attachments, turning sympathy and caring to fury, helplessness, and hopelessness.

Not surprisingly, Ruby's world quickly divided itself into "good" and "bad" players. The principal and foster mother found themselves at odds, each seeing herself as doing the best possible job under extremely trying circumstances, while viewing the other as incompetent and difficult. Indeed, the conference confirmed Dr. Brown's suspicion that, through the complex interplay of conscious and unconscious forces that surround an abused child, these two women, with Ruby's help, had actually succeeded in getting each other to behave as badly as they were accused of doing. Dr. Brown saw his task as attempting to bring some ambiguity back into what had become a dangerously polarized world. Without it, the adults responsible for Ruby's care had lost their capacity to appreciate each other's efforts and accept their own inevitable mistakes. If one has placed all of one's unacceptable hatred and loathing into another, one cannot then allow oneself to feel as the other must. The empathic failure that pervaded the relationship between Ruby's home and school seemed to have grown, at least in part, from each woman's reluctance to accept how much she truly loathed this child.

Dr. Brown's clear and unabashed statement that Ruby often made it hard for people to like her temporarily opened the way for a discussion about the problems Ruby created for those trying to help her. Auntie and principal could each grudgingly admit at least to the other's good intentions on Ruby's behalf, but Ruby's show of mean-spirited defiance quickly closed the door on any chance of an ongoing discussion between home and school. Dr. Brown resigned himself to fielding periodic enraged calls from one woman or the other until Ruby could be moved to a new school. There, Ruby again successfully created a split between home and school, but without the racial undertones to fuel the flames, the situation did not become as bitter or decisive.

Although Ruby often treated others quite badly, she had the good fortune to have an "Auntie" who did not mistreat her, even though she often felt like giving her a smack or two. In this case, the split between home and school may have actually protected Ruby from the full wrath of either her aunt or principal; they could direct their anger toward each other rather than at Ruby. At least temporarily, their fight also may have served to keep Ruby's provocative behavior out of the therapeutic relationship.

When a child can successfully, even though unconsciously, split her world into good and bad figures, the therapist may feel strongly compelled to align himself with those who show sympathy toward the child. He may find himself forgiving the child for even the most unconscionable behavior or rationalizing that her ill temper or misbehavior must stem from continued provocation or a lack of care and understanding. When carefully examined, we often discover that these are means to avoid the knowledge that we don't like this child any better than those who complain about the outrageous nature of her behavior. When she successfully provokes people to mistreat her, our harsh criticism of them, though well deserved, may also mask the extent and intensity of the negative feelings she stirs in us.

An abused child's capacity to stir in us the most passionate hatreds (Birch, 1994; Chused, 1991; Ehrensaft, 2007; Hart, 2012; Heineman, Clausen, & Ruff, 2013), not toward the abuser, but toward the child herself, certainly ranks among the most difficult aspects of therapeutic work with abused children. It promotes our participation in splitting, as we look toward external reality for the "bad guys." If we can find them outside of the therapeutic relationship, we can continue the fond, but futile, hope that we will not have to confront them in ourselves. We would like to prevent our entering into the inevitable reenactment of the abusive relationship. However, only by allowing ourselves to accept the various roles the child assigns us will we come to know the fullness of her experiences.

We are relatively familiar with the rage, helplessness, loathing, or impulse to retaliate that abused children can stir in their caregivers and therapists. Equally painful and maddening is a state absent of feeling. However, since many abused children exist in a state of psychic numbness, we would reasonably expect that, if we can tolerate it, they will use the therapeutic relationship as Peggy did, to demonstrate this profound sense of emptiness.

Peggy

Eight-year-old Peggy was referred for treatment following the discovery that she and two other children had been sexually molested by Alex, a 14-year-old boy, at a recreation center they all frequented after school. When the full extent of the abuse came to light, the director of the center expressed doubtful surprise, wondering how the children could have been out of her sight long enough for the events they described to have occurred.

The director had interviewed each of the children, as had the police and an attorney hired by one of the other parents. Believing that participation in the investigation would give Peggy a sense of power, her parents initially supported the interviews. However, when Peggy began to develop increasingly elaborate justification for not telling an adult about the molestation, they became concerned that the questions seemed to focus too much on whether the director could or should have discovered the abuse and on the efforts the children had made to alert adults.

All of this happened within a few days. By the time Peggy reached therapy, she was mightily tired of talking about "this mess." The repeated questioning, particularly about why she had not told anyone, had left her feeling guilty and disappointed in herself. She also felt extremely sad, confused, angry, and anxious. In the first therapy session, she confessed that she knew she should have told "right away." All along she had planned to trap Alex, but now she understood that she should not have tried to take care of things herself because she was "just a little kid and little kids aren't supposed to have to take care of things."

Peggy's plans for an elaborate entrapment had been a means of trying to protect herself from fear and humiliation during the abusive episodes. Inadvertently, the repeated, well-intended, reassurances she received following the discovery of the abuse undermined Peggy's, albeit misplaced, confidence that she could manage on her own. By praising her for talking, the interviewers contributed to Peggy's guilt over *not* talking sooner. The reassurance that she should not have felt responsible for stopping Alex sometimes made her feel that her plans had been "stupid." At other times, she insisted that she just hadn't explained her strategies well enough and that they really would have worked. So, while the cessation of Alex's molestation of these children can only be viewed as positive, the investigative process and the meanings Peggy made of it became an integral part of the abusive experience, retraumatizing the children, and heightening the negative impact.

In the beginning of treatment, Peggy offered a brief description of some of the abuse, though she insisted on leaving out some of the details because they were "too gross" or required using words that she didn't want to say. I commented that she must be pretty tired of talking about all of this, but that I would be happy to listen to what she did have to say about Alex, what had happened at the recreation center, or anything else she might want to talk about.

Peggy's greatest interest lay in telling me about her plans to catch and expose Alex. Tentatively, she began to describe some of the plans she had devised. Since I was genuinely interested in how this little girl had understood Alex's overtures, her compliance with his demands, and her subsequent imagined defiance of his power over her, I listened attentively as she told and retold the plots and subplots. When I expressed sympathy for how hard it could be for a child to think clearly and creatively when feeling very frightened or worried, Peggy declared that I didn't understand how good her plans really had been. She decided to draw pictures of the hideout so she could demonstrate her plans to trick Alex and show the director what he was doing.

My assigned task was to figure out the plans by looking at the drawings. No matter how I tried, there always seemed to be a clue I missed. When I asked about a particular element of the drawing, Peggy frequently chastised me, "I told you that already."

Sometimes she declared that a tiny peephole was hidden in her drawing of the hideout. I had to find it. Peggy assured me that it was "really, really easy to see," unless, of course, you are "really, really stupid." Not surprisingly, I routinely felt and was declared to be "really, really stupid." Sometimes the peepholes were no bigger than a dot left by a pencil tip; sometimes Peggy chided me for being so ridiculous that I couldn't even tell that the holes were "invisible."

Over the course of the hours in which Peggy drew, I made a number of observations about our interactions. Sometimes I noted that as long as I had only really, really tiny clues we could still hope that if I had bigger clues I might be able to learn some of what Peggy wanted me to know. Other times, I spoke about how scary it was for children when adults weren't paying enough attention to keep them out of danger. Sometimes I suggested that, even though it didn't make her feel very good, it might seem better to think that I was stupid about little things than stupid about big and important things. At times Peggy tolerated my direct comments about our interactions, but sometimes she could bear only comments containing more psychological distance. When she could tolerate a connection with me, she might respond by giving more information or allowing me to participate in an elaboration of the drawing. When she too strongly feared my disappointing her, she might simply offer no verbal response or tell me to "shut up."

In the sessions in which the manifest content concerned Peggy's attempts to trap Alex or secretly reveal the molestation to her teachers, Peggy was often quite talkative. Although her narratives were choppy and harder to follow as her anxiety increased, she did try to communicate verbally. A typical description of her plot to trap Alex might go something like, "I put some stuff up there and then over the table, but then it didn't go so we – well, and then on the floor. A tent. A tent with a hole so you could see. You could see in, too. You could, really. The kids were *real* noisy. Teachers don't hear too good when kids are noisy." This chatter might be interspersed with requests for a crayon, a question about whether I had seen her favorite TV show, or a quick, startled query about a noise she heard in the hallway. Peggy imbued these sessions in which she tried to communicate to me about her efforts to act on her own behalf with lively energy.

When Peggy was feeling particularly vulnerable, she frequently came to her sessions armed with one of her many illustrated books of drawing lessons, which followed a sort of line-by-line approach to drawing. Her affect in these sessions was often a pressured, good-natured psuedofriendliness as she carefully demonstrated her ability to follow the directions precisely. Indeed, her figures, which she drew again and again, appeared to be almost identical to those in the books. Any trace of spontaneity, individuality, or genuine affective connectedness effectively disappeared into generic illustrations.

In these sessions, the rules that I had to follow were as exacting as those the books dictated to Peggy. I could comment on how well she followed directions, how hard she worked at the drawings, or how important it was to know that she could make these pictures exactly right. Now and then I might be allowed, without an interruption from Peggy, to say something about how the pictures in the book were very helpful in showing some things and hiding others. Typically, in sessions dominated by the drawing lessons, Peggy simply began talking over me if my comments veered too close to the psychological.

However, my own drawing was permissible. In contrast to other sessions or with other children, at these times with Peggy, I did not proceed with spontaneous drawings; rather, I began with a lesson from her book, but tried to introduce into my drawing some variation, more or less, depending on how frightened she seemed. I assumed that these books, in part, offered a statement about her terror at the possibility of becoming overwhelmed by the emergence of unconscious material. By starting from one of these absolutely predictable drawings and gradually introducing new or different elements, I hoped to indicate that together we might find a way of taking small steps toward discovering what so frightened her.

My suggesting variations on the theme also represented a way of trying to avoid succumbing to the internal dangers of these excruciatingly boring sessions. When I allowed myself to consider the meaning of Peggy's behavior, I couldn't help knowing how successfully these books put a wall between us, as well as any affective connection Peggy might make with her own internal world. The books quite specifically concerned *not knowing* – putting aside one's own ideas or images and following the dictates of another.

Sometimes the pressure to keep still felt almost overpowering. I wanted to break the silence, to share my insights with Peggy, to make a connection with her and relieve my sense of being locked away with my own thoughts. As I made myself wait for those moments when I thought perhaps Peggy could listen to what I had to say, I came to understand the oppressive dread Peggy must have experienced in waiting for just the right moment to trap Alex.

Not knowing when I might find an opening, I waited. Wondering whether my comment would be scornfully cast aside, I waited. Pondering the validity of my wish to speak about my own unease, I waited. Desperate to break the cheerful, unyielding silence, I waited.

I recognized my sense of impending doom in the sessions when Peggy smilingly approached with her drawing books in hand. I dreaded those hours, and I did not like Peggy at all during those sessions. I had come to know how tenuous my emotional survival seemed in these sessions. When I allowed myself to reflect on the process of the hour, I became acutely aware of being trapped with my own thoughts, of feeling utterly alone, unable to find a bridge to Peggy.

Sometimes my mind wandered and I would find myself daydreaming. These trivial diversions allowed no space for Peggy but provided an antidote to my feeling helplessly imprisoned in my own thoughts. Alternatively, when I forced myself to attend, to stay in the room with Peggy, a kind of deadness settled over me. She steadfastly chattered about the drawings, insisting on my admiration, but allowing no space for a genuine response from me.

When I recognized the banality of the daydreams I drifted into at these times, it occurred to me that their appeal for me paralleled the appeal the drawing books held for Peggy. Both were utterly devoid of meaning but seemed to offer a refuge from the life-and-dead struggle Peggy brought to psychotherapy. Peggy used her drawings to eradicate meaning and I, in turn, mirrored her dissociated emptiness in my daydreams. In this way we were joined in a deadly nothingness of not thinking or feeling or knowing.

Like the little girl hiding in the tent trying to communicate through "invisible peepholes," when I could think, I was left alone with my own thoughts. Just as she had felt her knowledge was too dangerous for parents or teachers to hear, I sensed that Peggy felt my thoughts would be too dangerous for her to know. On the other hand, Peggy's quiet insistence on the pretense of a relationship required my emotional deadness as well as hers. We could behave as if our communication had importance of meaning, but, in fact, it just involved drawing the same affectively empty pictures over and over.

In this vignette, we can see how Peggy's behavior effectively communicated her own state of psychic numbing and her sense of the impossibility of a vital understanding between us. Our being together depended on an affective deadness, which, paradoxically, meant that we had no meaningful relationship. However, if we could think together, then we risked having feelings so powerful and awful that they might destroy the relationship. It seemed that Peggy felt she had to settle for an empty relationship, lest her feelings destroy the vitality of a connection that allowed for thoughts, feelings, and genuine interaction.

I hoped that by tolerating that deadness Peggy imposed on me, I would eventually convey my willingness and capacity to bear with her the feelings she felt to be unbearable. When she could not stand my comments about her feelings, I tried to put my interpretations into actions, instead of words. For example, if I could change a drawing just a tiny bit without worry that I had ruined it, then perhaps Peggy could, as well. And if we could begin to look inside for images or idea to introduce into our drawings, then perhaps we could begin to look inward at other thoughts and feelings. Through this process, I could gradually help Peggy put words to the thoughts and feelings that so frightened her and by doing so, help her limit their power over her.

Children who fight, spit, scream, swear, or physically attack their therapists are difficult indeed; our reluctance to walk into a session with them appears rather simple and straightforward. We see ourselves as helpers; they treat us as the enemy.

Even as we try to control our rage and our wishes to fight back, we can take a somewhat empathetic stance toward our responses. We can even expect sympathy from colleagues or consultants.

Although children who have been abused do often overtly behave as if they want to kill us, sometimes their quiet attempts at "soul murder" are even more insidious and successful. When a child hits or shouts or fights, we can, with relative ease, view our wishes to retaliate as a response to the violence they attempt to inflict on us. No matter how difficult it may be, there is an affective connection.

However, when a child hides his terror and rage behind a smiling mask of superficial good humor, he prohibits an affectively vital relationship. In these situations, we run the risk of retraumatizing the child by our attempts to make contact. We are prone to risk rationalizing our attempts to enliven ourselves as being in the best interests of the child – after all, we are simply trying to make affective contact through our comments, or questions, or offers at play. Instead, our task with a child whose physical and emotional life has nearly been snuffed out is often first to endure the profound emptiness – to know with the child how it feels to be among the living dead.

Note

* This is a very rudimentary outline of "transference," which in all interactions, including the therapeutic relationship, is highly complex and nuanced. For example, we evoke feelings in others that we don't expect, as well as those we do; we incorrectly, as well as correctly, interpret the behavior and responses of others; and those with whom we interact contribute their own histories, expectations, and interpretations to the relationship.

Section III

SYSTEMIC IMPINGEMENTS

Every year approximately 750,000 youth are touched by foster care. Some have only a brief stay in the system before returning to their parents or finding a temporary or permanent home with relatives. Others remain in care for months or years while caseworkers, attorneys, therapists, judges, parents, and foster parents struggle to find a plan that will bring continuity, and permanency to lives that have been marked by multiple disruptions and uncertainty.

Perhaps the insidious impingement on the psychological development and emotional well-being of children who spend significant time in the foster care system is the chronic experience of unplanned, unpredictable, and unexplained losses that are a part of their daily lives. While it is certainly the case that some children would have suffered great physical and emotional harm if they had not been taken into the system, it is also the case that they too frequently suffer great harm once they are under the care of the government. It is also true that some children find stability in the foster care system; if they are placed immediately with a family who intends to and eventually does adopt them, the uncertainty about their future may last only a matter of months.

In many circumstances, a few months of uncertainty in the life of a young child would be cause for alarm. However, in the foster care system, while not exactly a cause for celebration, limiting uncertainty to a few months is often viewed as a measure of success. None of us, especially children, manage confusion, uncertainty, and chaos easily. In the face of instability children turn to adults to order their world and calm their fears. But children in foster care may not have a reliable relationship with an adult whose words and actions they can trust. The four-year-old who is found wandering the halls of a residential hotel and taken into foster care for his protection is, at that moment, entirely alone in the world. Although he may be with a kind and caring adult, that person doesn't know him – has no way of keeping his past in mind. If no one knows his story, it doesn't exist, and if his story doesn't exist, how does he?

Every time a foster child loses a foster parent, a caseworker, an attorney, a piece of her history is also lost. The life that is chronicled in a case file is only an outline of a lived life. When a caseworker records notes after a home visit the words capture very little of what is in his memory; if he glances at the notes later, those words have the power to evoke the memories of the visit, including the feel of the air, the smells emanating from the kitchen, the sights and sounds in the neighborhood. However, if that worker moves on, which 30–40% do annually according to the National Resource Center for Family-Centered Practice and Permanency Planning (Sudol, 2009), those memories are lost. The new worker has only the words, no context in which to understand the fullness of their meaning.

Some foster children live in ten or 20 or 30 different "placements" in just a few years. Some placements may be with a family with biological and/or other foster children, others may be in a home with several other foster children. Others may be in a group home that is more like a dormitory than a family home. In many of these situations children not only face the uncertainty of whether they will be moved, but may not know from one day to the next what other children will be in the home.

For example, an adult in her forties who spent some time in foster care described coming home from school to find the foster mother she dearly loved carefully folding her clothes and knowing instantly that she would be leaving. The woman explained that because foster children had come and gone, her own son was becoming fearful that he would someday have to go, too. She felt that she had no choice but to protect her child.

Even though some children are welcomed into a family as if they were an integral member, the periodic visits from the caseworker and the routine court hearings stand as a constant reminder that their status is temporary and can be changed at any moment. Sometimes children are moved because the caseworker or the foster parent believes that the child is becoming "too attached" and will suffer more if he has to be moved later. Sometimes children are moved because they have not made an attachment, which an engaged foster parent may find unbearable, or out of a belief that a change of circumstance will solve the problem.

Despite the barely tolerable circumstances that the foster care system imposes on the children who grow up in it and the adults who work in it, many children can and do manage to keep hope alive. Sometimes it is buried deep within their psyches, where it must be stored in order to protect it. If, with luck, these children come upon a relationship with someone whom they can trust and who understands that such fiercely protected hope can only be brought into the light gradually and with patience, they can begin to heal from too many losses.

The three chapters in this section illustrate the ways in which problematic internal and external forces can and do impinge on development and human interactions. "In search of the romantic family" shows what can happen to people and those trying to help them when a normally occurring developmental phase is not resolved, but continues to influence, distort, and damage relationships. It makes clear that internal forces that interfere with relationships are no less powerful than those emanating from the external world. "Weaving without a loom" considers the question of identity formation in the context of the ever-changing relationships in foster care. It examines the impact of the external environment on the internal worlds of children and those caring for them. The therapeutic relationship is the focus of "Hunger pangs," the final chapter in this section, exploring the contributions and interactions of internal and external forces.

5

IN SEARCH OF THE ROMANTIC FAMILY

Unconscious contributions to problems in foster and adoptive placements

Orphans, foundlings, children in need of substitute parents are an ineluctable piece of human history. The causes and effects of parentless status have captivated the imagination for untold generations. Even a brief consideration of mythology, fairy tales, and literature, especially for and about children, underscores the power of the parentless child to stir both the conscious and unconscious fantasy; attempts to understand the meaning and importance of these fantasies have occupied a pivotal place in psychoanalytic theories.[1] Mythical children are raised by substitute parents for various reasons. Sometimes, as in the case of Oliver Twist or Little Orphan Annie, it is as simple as the death of the biological parents. In stories such as *The Secret Garden*, a child may be emotionally abandoned because he or she is held responsible for the death or disappearance of a beloved parent. At the other end of the spectrum abandonment is an attempt to protect the child's life, as in the case of Moses, who is put into an ark of bulrushes to save him from the Egyptians, or Superman, who is sent away from Krypton before the planet is destroyed (Widzer, 1977). In other cases, the absence of the biological parents is not explained. For example, we don't know why Dorothy lives with Auntie Em and Uncle Henry, or why Joyce's nameless child in the first stories of *Dubliners* lives with his aunt and uncle, or how Huey, Dewey, and Louie come to live with their Uncle Donald.

In these stories the quality of substitute caretakers is as varied as the reasons for children's needing them. Some children are left with kindly, other-worldly creatures as are Romulus and Remus and Kipling's Mowgli, both cared for by wolves, or Sleeping Beauty, alias Blair Rose, who spends the first 16 years of her life in care of fairies disguised as simple peasants. Other children, such as Cinderella, may acquire an unsympathetic or wicked step-parent and fare less well. The fate of children raised by substitute parents varies as well. Some like Oedipus, psychoanalysis's most famous adoptee, inadvertently or unconsciously destroy the parent who abandoned them, while in other cases such as that of Luke Skywalker and Darth Vader, the destruction of the parent is more consciously determined. Others search until they are happily reunited with the lost parent of infancy. And some, like King Arthur, grow to bring honor to themselves and those who cared for them.

The prevalence of these tales and their power to capture the imagination of child and adult alike is fueled by the twin terrors of internal and external dangers. Real-life stories of abandoned, adopted, and kidnapped children become entangled with and absorb unconscious wishes and fears about the mutual harm that parents and their offspring may inflict upon each other. Newspapers, magazines, and television programs repeatedly remind us that parents cannot protect children from all dangers, including behavior emanating from their own unconscious processes, and that some parents actually and deliberately do harm their children. Likewise, these stories become entwined with shared unconscious fears of children's wishes and capacities to destroy parents in order to make a place for themselves in the world. In the world of the "good enough" family, where there is room for benignly derivative and playful expression of these primitive fantasies of parricide and infanticide, parents and children create and hold each other within the powerful confines of a family constellation that accepts the inevitable ambivalence that comes with growth and change.

Before exploring situations in which the idea of "romantic families" hinders rather than enhances development, I would like to examine the place of family romance in normal development. Freud's 1909 essay "Family Romances" provided a brief but powerful contribution to our understanding of the Oedipal resolution and the child's wish to cling to the imagined bliss of the preoedipal relationship. Since then numerous authors have added to our understanding of the developmental and clinical manifestations of this fantasy (Frosch, 1909; Gediman, 1974; Greenacre,1958; Horner & Rosenberg, 1974; Kaplan, 1974). My purpose here is not to explore the many complexities and elaborations of this childhood fantasy, but to focus on the problems that its unconscious persistence into adulthood can introduce into the foster and adoptive processes, particularly in relation to the two themes cited above.

Descriptively, "family romance" is used to refer to a phenomenon most frequently encountered among boys and girls in their early to mid-latency. Young children construct the story that they have somehow been delivered into the hands of the wrong parents and that their true parents, usually people of power, prominence, or nobility, will someday appear and whisk them off to a golden land where they will all live happily ever after.

This fantasy represents the child's attempt to repair the damage wrought by Oedipal desires by the wishes to grow up, to parent, and to assume a position in the world of adults. As the child's cognitive capacities open windows onto the world beyond the family, he must also confront the limited status his parents hold in the greater world. The power of these wishes and knowledge is entwined with the loss of the idealized parent; with whom the child feels once he lived narcissistic bliss. While the perfect parents of the child's imagination never existed, the pre-school child may experience his contemporaneous parents, with their expectations for impulse control, self-regulation, civility, and the beginning reliance on an internalized conscience, as vastly different from those who, in his infancy, offered unconditional love and complete need-satisfaction. However, it is the child who has changed much more than the parents. The development of the child's intellectual capacities and powers of observation has compelled an internal reorganization that admits of expanding knowledge of the world, both internal and external, and the place of the parents within those worlds. Understandably, the child then longs for a return to the earlier state of innocent union. Despite the regressive pull toward the constructed bliss of the parent–child dyad, it is not a developmentally tenable solution, because it would demand a disavowal of what the child has come to know about parents, self, and the relationship between generations.

So, with limited emotional resources and imaginative power, the child constructs, as best she can, new parents, just like the old. She can turn to them when the disappointments in the actual parents of daily life become too much to bear. The anxiety consequent to the wish to leave the actual, if imperfect, parents behind forces the child back to reality, where she gradually comes to accept her parents, with their imperfections, and her limited place in their world.

Freud (1909) notes that these childhood fantasies "preserve, under a slight disguise, the child's original affection for his parents. The faithlessness and ingratitude are only apparent...[T] he child is not getting rid of his father but exalting him. Indeed the whole effort at replacing the real father by a superior one is only an expression of the child's longing for the happy, vanished days when his father seemed to him the noblest of men and his mother the dearest and loveliest of women" (240–241).

Despite her new discoveries of parental shortcomings, the child loves her parents and must rely on them for continued care. She does not entirely replace the corporeal parents, even in her imagination; the two sets of parents, real and imagined, coexist in the child's internal world of object relationships, as do conscious and unconscious fantasies of lost and reclaimed parents (Tabin,1998). The child can turn to parents of the family romance when the disappointments in the actual parents of daily live become too much to bear; at the moments when she lives in harmony with the parents who feed, clothe, comfort, and adore her, she has no need to replace them with more loving or important caregivers. The parents of the family romance provide, temporary solace, but are of minimal use in satisfying the actual, multiple, and complex needs of a young child.

In normative processes, the parents of the family romance serve an adaptive function and gradually fade away when they have outlived their usefulness. While much has been written about the family romance, this process of its decline in the emotional life of the child has received relatively little attention. It seems probable that, like the fantasies themselves, their diminution takes a variety of forms. For some children, the disappointment in the parents may spark a more psychologically distant compensatory fantasy, as in the construction of idealized forebears, rather than of an alternative set of parents. For example, a colleague remembered explaining the fact of having a few blue-eyed relatives with the idea that somewhere in his Jewish heritage there must have been a strain of Viking blood. In this way he added strength and adventure to an "ancestry" he perceived as weak and retiring. Other children may bypass the creation of a personal family romance while becoming enraptured by one or the many heroes or heroines that enliven the family romances of comic books and children's literature. Still others may move from the intensity of a fantasy personally constructed to meet their particular emotional needs and only gradually subsume these stories to the shared myths and narratives of children orphaned, abandoned, or kidnapped and then adopted or reunited with lost parents.

In considering the replacement of a personal family romance with the more sublimated stories of myth and literature, it is important to remember that while the child imagines being reunited with lost, idealized parents, he also does not wish to be separated from his actual parents. The fantasy created to resolve an unconscious conflict creates anxiety stemming from conscious conflict. Suppose the lofty parents of his imagination appeared; would he go with them or stay with the familiar if imperfect parents of everyday life? The anxiety consequent to the wish to leave the actual parents behind forces the child back to an embrace of the parents who exist in his external as well as internal world.

The child initially creates idealized parents in order to manage unbearable disappointment in his own parents and his growing awareness of the limits of his importance in their world. However, with increasing ego strength comes a greater capacity to tolerate disappointment – to manage the inevitable negative affective interchanges between parent and child without the felt need to replace the flawed parents with perfect ones. With this comes the recognition, whether conscious or unconscious, the parents of his family romance are products of his imagination. Thus, through a process of repeatedly moving between fantasy and reality, he strengthens his capacity for reality testing along with his capacity to hold and modulate affect. Through this process he gradually comes to accept his parents, with their imperfections, and their relationship, with its inherent limitations on his place in their affective world. When, through fantasy and playful interpersonal interchanges, expressions of primitive fantasies of parricide and infanticide evolve into a family constellation that can hold and protect inevitable ambivalence that comes with ongoing development, children can gradually relinquish the notion of idealized parents, along with the parallel narcissistically invested sense of self.

When the child can recognize the family romance as a product of her imagination, she can begin to grasp the creative potential of fantasy – whether the personal fantasy of daydreams or the fantasies that are deliberately offered to or accepted from others through conscious transformations into art. The recognition that the romanticized parents are not real but imagined offers the child an extraordinary freedom of playful thought (Bromberg, 1998; Caper, 1996; Dervin, 1983; Hanly, 1909). She is released to create better-than-average forebears to suit her changing needs. In capturing the actual parents in modified but recognizable form, the child preserves a sense of self and family that allows him to move forward. For example, the child who imagined a lost strain of Viking ancestors did not disavow his Jewish heritage; he merely embellished it to create a stronger, more comfortable family for himself.

However, not all families can create sufficient ambivalence to hold and safely express these intergenerational fantasies. In extreme cases either children or parents actually kill or physically harm the other. In other cases the unconscious fears of parricide/infanticide may be only partially contained, leaving family members vulnerable to actualizing these primitive fears in more derivative forms. For example, a retreat into drugs, alcohol, work, or travel may result in extended or frequent separations from the child. In response to this kind of emotional abandonment, children often find refuge in an idealization of the absent parent, which for some children may be captured in the fantasy of the family romance. In situations such as these, the actual family constellation supports the child's fear of abandonment rather than helping her to merge the images of idealized and inadequate parents into ambivalently held object representations.[2] Generally, these partial abandonments are held quietly within the privacy of the family. However, adopted and foster children publicly announce the actualization of primitive fears of destructive familial impulses, the very existence of children whose parents relinquish them to the care of others – whether for good reason or ill, whether eagerly or reluctantly – makes clear that intergenerational dangers are not confined to the world of intrapsychic processes and that not all murderous wishes can be resolved through fantasy, fairy tale, or fiction.

Just as myths and stories help children manage the confounding and contradictory aspects of Oedipal development, they also illuminate the dangers of actions based on an unconscious and persistent belief in an idealized self and family. Consider the boy born James Gatz:

> I suppose he'd had the name ready for along time, even then. His parents were shiftless and unsuccessful farm people – his imagination has never really accepted them as his parents at all. The truth was that Jay Gatsby of West Egg, Long Island, sprang from his Platonic conception of himself. He was a son of God – a phrase which, if it means anything, means just that – and he must be about His father's business, the service of vast, vulgar, and meretricious beauty. So he invented just the sort of Jay Gatsby that a seventeen-year-old boy would be likely to invent, and to this conception he was faithful to the end.
>
> (99)

Fitzgerald (1925) shows us how Gatsby's failure to recognize and incorporate reality – his reliance on imagination alone – results in the construction of a world devoid of meaning – a world that eventually collapses in upon itself. Unfortunately, tragic failings such as this are not confined to the lives of fictional characters – they appear daily in the juvenile justice system.

The stories that come to us in myth, fairy tales, and fiction cannot solve the problems facing adults and children in adoptive or foster placement, but they may offer us significant help in understanding difficulties we routinely encounter in the real-life histories of these children. Two recurring themes in these fictional and mythological tales may have particular importance in our consideration of some of the forces impinging on foster care or adoptive placements. The first is the persistent, though unconscious, belief in the actuality of an ideal parent. Second is the aggrandizement of the transformational power of the child.

Both of these themes are central to the family romance, and I believe that in many cases the tenacity and viciousness of the battle among the concerned adults – whether biological or foster parents, social workers, therapists, attorneys, or judges – stem from an unconscious clinging to the romanticized fantasy of family. The unwillingness to relinquish the notion of the idealized, perfect family represents an unconscious wish to avoid the emotional consequences of fully accepting the oedipal constellation and the acknowledgement of reality it demands.

Manifestations of an unconscious belief in the actuality of an ideal parent

For those adults charged with creating new families for children, the confrontation with an actual orphaned child, in need of substitute parents, may reverberate with their own unresolved acceptance of parental imperfections. Real opportunities for replacing less-than perfect parents with new ones may touch on unconscious childhood longings for the absent, perfect parents and, understandably, stir enormous emotional storms. In many cases, the unconscious fantasies of the children (Glenn, 1974; Wieder, 1977) and those charged with their care merge with mutually reinforcing intensity. Adults who have chosen to work with abandoned children in the unconscious hope of reparation of a seriously flawed or abandoning parental image will be particularly vulnerable to the child's fantasy of being rescued by or returned to idealized parents.

The adversarial nature of legal proceedings also supports and encourages polarization, splitting, and concretization of fantasy. In legal proceedings concerning the choice between parents, even people who have enjoyed relatively healthy childhoods can be drawn into battles over good and bad parents because reality usually demands a choice between two competing families. Unlike the child who moves between two sets of parents – one real and one created – until he can merge them into one, the adults working with foster and adopted children must move between two sets of real people wanting to parent a child. In some cases, the choice closely mirrors the fantasy of the family romance – one set of parents is truly inadequate, perhaps with a long history of drug and alcohol use and physical or sexual abuse of the child, which tends to cast an idealized glow around the parents who would rescue the child from an unhappy fate. In other cases, the two sets of parents are relatively evenly matched in terms of what they could actually offer the child, but the legal and psychological impossibility of a consciously arbitrary choice pushes the competing forces into increasingly extreme positions – idealizing the attributes of one side while diminishing the qualities of the other. Of course, the most powerful impetus to the creation of idealized parents is the wish to keep unconscious the emerging recognition that the impulse to hurt or abandon children lies not only in the parents who have actually done so but also in the adults who are attempting to repair the damaged or abandoned children.

Because foster and adoptive placements specifically concern absent parents, they provide fertile ground for the enactment of the pathological consequences of unrelinquished family romance fantasies. In these instances the fantasy often persists that for the orphaned child an ideal parent exists. Whether held by parents, therapists, attorneys, or judges, these fantasies admit of no ambivalence, relying heavily on externalization as a solution to the dilemmas, contradictions, and disappointments posed by internal object relationships. From this perspective, one would understandably try to help a hurt or abandoned child through a manipulation of the external environment. However, when attempts at foster or adoptive placement repeatedly fail or are beset with difficulties, we reasonably suspect that previously undetected unconscious processes may be at work.

Vera and Barbara

Vera and her 12-year-old daughter Barbara were referred to me for evaluation following years of Vera's persistent verbal and occasional physical abuse of this child. Repeated efforts to guide them into individual and family therapy had come to naught. The social worker wanted to place Barbara with her maternal grandmother but was concerned that the placement, which had been tried before, would fail yet again. The social worker hypothesized that when Barbara was living with her grandmother Vera would tire of caring for the younger children by herself and would entice Barbara back home with promises that any abuse would cease. She felt that it was understandable that Barbara would return out of a wish to believe these promises and to win her mother's love.

Though Vera was far from an ideal mother, she apparently had never been abusive to her other children. Eventually I was able to discern a recurring pattern in which, either following a particularly harsh period or chafing from the cumulative effects of routine verbal abuse, Barbara would run, or be sent by her outraged mother, to her grandmother for care and comfort. This arrangement would seem to suit everyone well. Vera would claim to be pleased to be rid of this hateful child who, unlike her other children, made her appear to be a bad mother. She commiserated with her mother about the very real difficulties that Barbara's provocative behavior presented for anyone trying to care for her. Eventually someone – Barbara, her grandmother, another relative, or a social worker – would suggest that Barbara's tenure at her grandmother's become a formal and more permanent arrangement. This suggestion would typically evoke enraged protests from Vera about how her mother was trying to steal her daughter from her. Barbara would quickly join in and renounce any earlier claims of abuse, happily returning to her mother's care, where they would reside in joyful, though short lived, harmony.

In the course of the evaluation, it became clear that Vera's relationship to her mother represented a disorganized attachment. She was continually in cyclical, though unpredictable, relationship to her mother, sometimes going to her for help with Barbara's incorrigibility, at other times complaining to anyone who would listen that her mother was an evil witch who wanted to steal her most precious child, Barbara, from her. Her one consistent idea was that Barbara was never, ever to have a permanent home with her maternal grandmother.

At one point, I tried to pursue her reasons for this, observing that all parties seemed to agree that grandmother and granddaughter enjoyed quite a nice relationship. Vera began shouting at me that this woman who was trying to steal Barbara was in fact, not her mother at all. She continued her enraged story that she alone of the mother's several children had been stolen from her real parents and adopted by this woman who claimed to be her mother, but was actually keeping her from her true parents to serve her own selfish needs. She went on in increasingly paranoid detail about how her siblings were all jealous of her because they knew her real parents and knew that they were more important than their parents. She saw their support of her mother's wish to care for Barbara as their attempt to assert that she was really "one of them," and to deny her true heritage.

Many aspects of this multi-generational cycle of love and hate lie outside the scope of this chapter. However, I present the story as an illustration of the regressive and pathological persistence of a family romance, grown out of an attempt to manage the loss of an idealized parent and later the loss of an actual object. When I spoke with two of Vera's sisters, I learned that Vera's fantasy of adoption had been known to them since childhood. They remembered that any attempts to assure her that she was their "real" sister would only intensify her fury. With the exception of Vera, who sometimes acknowledged looking forward to the days when she would enjoy the greater wealth and lavish affection of her "true" parents, the children felt well cared for and enjoyed reasonably good relationships with their parents. Her sisters had difficulty understanding the nature of Vera's relationship to their mother who, to the best of their memory, had not treated Vera differently than she had them. The family was comfortable and well respected in the community; I could find no corroboration of Vera's belief in her adoption and the reasons for her very troubled relationship to her mother remained a mystery.

With some hesitation about the absolute certainty of their memories, both sisters independently reported that Vera's contention that she had been adopted usually followed her being disciplined or denied a request by her parents. Thus, it seems possible that as a child Vera would turn to a romanticized family as an attempt to manage the disappointments suffered at the hands of her actual parents. However, because of her incapacity to tolerate ambivalence, she remained fixated on the notion of idealized parents as if they actually existed, rather than being a created externalization of her own wishes.

Over the course of the evaluation it became clear that Barbara could never successfully be placed with her maternal grandmother because of Vera's identification with Barbara as both the bad child who had been abandoned by her true parents and the special child who needed to be rescued by the idealized parent. Obviously, much more could be said about Vera's split identifications between loved and hated child and loved and hated parent, but I believe that her unconscious, paranoid clinging to the notion of a perfect, romanticized family (Watters, 1956; Lehrman, 1927) aptly and concisely captures the problems this family presented to the social service system. The plan that should logically have offered a perfect and simple solution did not take into account the profound disorganization of Vera's attachment to her mother and actually reactivated deep unconscious conflicts that could only doom that solution.

In this context it is important to remember that the family romance is an externalization, a defensive attempt to resolve an internal conflict and relieve distress. As a temporary psychological maneuver, it seems to serve many children well, particularly if they develop the capacity to hold an ambivalently loved object. When this is the case, the evocation of the imagined, idealized parent leads the child to an awareness of his or her demeaning of the actual parent. The anxiety arising from the capacity for ambivalence leads to a cessation of the fantasy in order to quell the anxiety.

However, with little or no capacity for ambivalence, the child need not squelch the fantasy, since it stirs up little anxiety. Ambivalence requires that positive and negative experiences be incorporated into the mix of early human relationships in relatively equal measure. When the parent–child relationship has provided the child with a preponderance of negative experiences, the child cannot balance negative feelings with genuine positive feelings/memories. When reality is not available for comfort, he has nowhere to turn to offset the overwhelming disappointments and hurts emanating from the actual parent–child relationship. In these instances, the fantasy of ideal parents is not diminished by positive interactions with actual parents and can persist far beyond latency.

Nicholas

Mr. Randall was a 27-year-old moderately wealthy playboy when he met and impulsively married Ms. Miller. They had savage arguments from the beginning of their relationship. Ms. Miller became pregnant within weeks of their marriage and, following a few more weeks of vicious verbal exchanges and accusations, Mr. Randall left their apartment one morning and did not return. This precipitated a psychotic episode for Ms. Miller, who had a history of decompensation in response to loss. After a brief hospitalization she was discharged to a halfway house, where she resided for several months.

During this period, through her friendship with another resident, she became intensely involved with a small, devoted religious community. When she left the halfway house, the church became the focus of her life. She worked part-time, performing clerical duties that provided her enough income to move into a small apartment shared with two other parishioners. Prior to the birth of the baby, church members helped her to secure furniture, equipment, and clothes. One family in particular, Mr. and Mrs. Anderson, offered substantial help and support, including accompanying Ms. Miller to the hospital for Nicholas's birth.

Not surprisingly, the unpredictable and incessant demands of a newborn quickly began to take a toll on Ms. Miller's emotional stability. She seemed relieved at the Andersons' frequent offers to baby-sit and began to leave Nicholas with them more often and for longer and longer periods. When another failed love affair again plummeted Ms. Miller into a psychotic episode, she asked that the Andersons care for Nicholas during her hospitalization. They suggested that Ms. Miller live with them for a while following her discharge; this arrangement persisted for several months, until Ms. Miller could no longer tolerate what she felt to be the Andersons' excessive demands for her to be "religious," and the Andersons could no longer tolerate behavior that violated their moral code.

Presumably by mutual agreement, Ms. Miller moved into her own apartment. However, she did not take Nicholas with her. Instead, again by apparently mutual, though unspoken, agreement, Nicholas remained with the Andersons. Ms. Miller visited on a somewhat regular basis. After Ms. Miller, without explanation, had not visited for some time, the Andersons requested and were granted licensure as foster parents for Nicholas. Subsequently, Ms. Miller returned from her unexplained absence and seemed generally satisfied that the Andersons had become Nicholas's official foster parents, though during periods of emotional instability she would rail against their religious rigidity and berate them for their insensitivity to her needs.

The Andersons' request for foster parents status set in motion the mandatory search for Nicholas's close relatives. Several attempts to elicit a response from Mr. Randall failed until he appeared unannounced on the Andersons' doorstep on Nicholas's third birthday. Startled and uncertain about how to respond, the Andersons greeted Mr. Randall, who threw his arms around Nicholas, began helping him open the elaborate gift he had brought for him, and announced that from now on he would be living with his daddy. He appeared oblivious to Nicholas's obvious confusion and severe distress. Eventually, Mr. Anderson, by threatening to call the police, was able to get Mr. Randall to leave their home. He did so in anger and tears, calling over his shoulder to Nicholas, "Daddy'll be back to get you, little boy. Don't worry, I'll get you away from here."

The court ordered an evaluation to determine whether Nicholas should remain with the Andersons or be moved to Mr. Randall's home during the legal proceedings that would determine his future. Convinced that Nicholas knew he was his real father and wanted to live with him, he was furious at having to participate in the evaluation.

Questioned about whether Nicholas might miss the Andersons, who had served as his parents for most of his life, he angrily retorted that he would be relieved to get away from them, since he was so obviously unhappy in their presence. It never occurred to Mr. Randall that the discomfort he correctly observed might be due to *his* presence. Later, perhaps in response to conversations with his attorney, Mr. Randall acknowledged that Nicholas might miss the Andersons. However, he continued to elaborate his expectation that he might be a little sad for a few days and that he would then forget about them.

Here we see Mr. Randall's version of the family romance, in which he enacts the role of idealized parent come to rescue the beleaguered child from the lower-class parents into whose care he has inadvertently fallen. This case too vividly demonstrates the extent to which the family romance relies on externalization and defense against disappointment; Mr. Randall could imagine no shortcomings that he might bring to parenthood. Just like the fantasized perfect parents of childhood, his mere presence would erase all of Nicholas's discomfort. This is not to say that he presented himself as a perfect parent, but that he expected that any difficulties that might arise would be minor and easily corrected by his reading a book or talking with friends. Paradoxically then, he both expected to rescue Nicholas from a horrible situation and did not really expect to have an impact on him. He truly did seem to believe that the problem merely involved getting him into the correct scenario, the one that ended, "and they all lived happily ever after."

Not surprisingly, Mr. Randall had not enjoyed a particularly happy childhood. His father had left when he was very young, and Mr. Randall spent much of his youth and young adulthood searching for him. By the time Mr. Randall located him, his father had squandered most of the family money and was subsisting on earnings from occasional articles he wrote while working on a novel. According to Mr. Randall his father had several offers for the screenplay, even though he had no publisher for the novel. Mr. Randall was undaunted by any of this information, happily presenting his father as a romantic figure, tragically unrecognized by the world. Mr. Randall's identification with the abandoned child, longing for the return of the idealized father, was obvious but far too painful for Mr. Randall to confront.

It appeared that the Andersons were also operating under the cloud of unrelinquished family romances, but that their unconscious fantasies were absorbed and, to some extent, given social sanction, by their religious beliefs, even though their church was not in the mainstream of organized religion. Because Ms. Miller's psychopathology was so obvious and so well documented, they could easily assume a seemingly benign protective stance toward her, and because Mr. Randall's attitudes were so egregiously narcissistic, they were easily accorded the position of wanting to do what was best for Nicholas. However, it became increasingly apparent over the course of the evaluation that they had every intention of rescuing Nicholas from "bad" parents and that their views of Nicholas's biological parents admitted of little ambivalence or compassion. To cast their views in the light of the family romance, they saw themselves as the down-to-earth peasants, who, by virtue of their humble origins, were both obligated and entitled to save Nicholas from the neglectful and decadent life of the rich and powerful. In their minds, they were not merely rescuing him from two actually inadequate parents, but from a lineage of arrogant godlessness.

These two cases demonstrate the extreme failures of reality testing that can emerge in the context of primitively constructed fantasies of idealized/romantic families. Vera's shifting identification between child and parent mirrored her oscillating views of her daughter as perfect or evil and suggest a psychotic organization. Mr. Randall's narcissistic self-aggrandizement made it impossible for any of the characters in his internal drama to be regular people. Because his world necessitated sharp distinctions between good and evil, he could not accept a real-life solution that would have allowed him an active place in Nicholas's life. His need to see himself as the idealized, returning parent actually forced him to remain in the role of the abandoning parent who relinquished all contact with his son. Despite the intensity of feelings among the family members, these dramas were relatively well contained. The social workers and attorneys maintained a professional distance and relatively balanced views of the problems and possible solutions they had before them.

However, as I noted above, the terror of recognizing and accepting the internality of wishes and impulses that result in child abandonment or endangerment can pull professionals into ferocious battles in which boundaries are blurred and reality testing begins to fade. Truly inadequate parents who abandon a child, make efforts at rehabilitation, and subsequently assert their parental claim on the child seem, in particular, to touch on these vulnerabilities. Their unconscious connection to unrelinquished representations of the idealized parents who would someday return for the lost child unleashes enormously powerful emotional forces in the adults charged with the care of the child they have come to claim. A colleague noted that when a missing biological parent is located he – it is often the father who is absent – is sometimes greeted by the social service system as if he's just been dropped from heaven! This situation actualizes the family romance – the longed-for parents really do appear. Paradoxically, to reject them is to recognize that they, in fact, are not ideal – they can return only because they previously walked away, and therefore they must be accepted, even if it means breaking a psychological bond with the imperfect substitute parents of the child's day-to-day life.

Deanna

Deanna was almost three years old at the time of evaluation. She was born addicted to numerous drugs and placed in a special foster care program for drug-addicted babies. Her mother visited sporadically for a few weeks, then disappeared into the streets. Because Deanna was the fourth of the mother's children to be taken into protective care, there seemed little hope of her regaining custody; it appeared that Deanna would eventually be freed for adoption, and she placed with potential adoptive parents.

Meanwhile, unbeknownst to Deanna's social worker, the mother had again entered drug rehabilitation, this time with some success. As the social worker, who was thrilled with the placement she had found for Deanna, was preparing her case to terminate Deanna's mother's parental rights, the mother's attorney was preparing to argue that mother was now entitled to resume her rightful place in Deanna's life. The attorney's premise was that precisely because Deanna was such a delightfully perfect child her mother's incentive to stay drug-free would be guaranteed. The mother's expert witness supported this view, contending that because Deanna's development had proceeded so well, this child (unlike her other children, who appeared to have been more damaged) would provide, virtually by herself, the necessary impetus for her mother to maintain her clean and sober status. Thus, the attorney's argument on her client's behalf rested on the idealization of the child in order to guarantee the creation of a potentially ideal parent.

In order to support this position the expert, an experienced clinician, also seemed to rely on concrete thinking – devaluing the importance of Deanna's psychological relationship with her foster parents while emphasizing the significance of the biological bond. While it would simply be foolish not to acknowledge the importance of biological connections, in this case the clinician seemed to have overlooked another very important factor – namely, that at that point in the child's life, the foster parents were the psychologically true parents, while the biological mother had not yet been fully created as a parent in the child's mind. This idealization of the biological mother was evident in the expert's emphasis on the mother's struggles to overcome her addictions so that she could reclaim her child, with relatively little focus on the fact of her abandoning Deanna.

The pressure from the mother's attorney apparently touched on unresolved issues for Deanna's social worker, who began to express doubts about the foster parents she had previously respected and valued. She began to describe them as difficult and demanding, characterizing their descriptions of Deanna's regression and distress following visits with her biological mother as disruptive and in opposition to the plan for reunification. When they complained on Deanna's behalf, she took this as evidence of their unconscious wish to undermine her plan to convey Deanna into the care of her biological mother.

One of the striking elements in this and similar cases is the insistence upon the language of "reunification," despite the absence of any previous post-natal "union" between parent and child. We might rationalize this linguistic "slip" as evidence of the prevalence and importance of legal considerations, but I feel that such statements reflected, on a more profound level, unconscious beliefs about the inherent goodness of the original/biological parents. When it is simply too terrifying to acknowledge profound and powerful destructive impulses within ourselves, we treat another's enactment of these unconscious forces as a temporary, relatively unimportant lapse. The "true" parent is the one who returns for the child, not the one who drugs an infant or leaves him without physical or emotional care.

In Deanna's case, the child's healthy development was used to support the possibility of transforming a previously inadequate parent into one capable of caring for her child. When abandoned children have not fared so well, when their development has fallen behind or they have been caught in the throes of serious psychopathology, holding them up as ideal or even "good-enough" children, able to create parents of parallel stature, may require significant denial. This wish to give a child a parent who can hold and care for him often causes otherwise well-grounded and thoughtful professionals to embrace the shared parent–child distortions that maintain the romantic view of the parents beyond all plausible possibilities for the actualization of that potential.

Bobby

Bobby was 11 at the time of evaluation. He spent most of his life in protective custody, much of it in a therapeutic group home associated with his treatment program. His father, the most important figure in his life, was exceedingly unreliable, despite his obvious love for Bobby. His father would sometimes visit weekly and maintain almost daily telephone contact; during other periods, the father would disappear, without explanation, for weeks at a time. Bobby often became psychotic with suicidal ideation during his father's absences.

Bobby demanded frequent visits from his social worker and attorney. During the visits he would offer them detailed complaints about the inadequacies of the day treatment program and the group home, including instances of neglectful and abusive behavior. These complaints were always thoroughly investigated, but were never validated. Bobby continued to insist that he wanted to be released to his father, who verbally supported Bobby's plan to live with him, but would then arrive drunk or fail to show up for a weekend visit.

Despite serious organic and emotional impairments and these most distressing disruptions, Bobby continued to improve. The staff maintained their affection for his father, largely because they recognized that he assumed tremendous importance in Bobby's life and that he suffered even greater impairment than did his son.

When Bobby's new social worker first heard Bobby's complaints, he was understandably alarmed and called for the usual investigations. Because he could not locate Bobby's father, he contacted the father's attorney and suggested that he bring suit against the treatment facility. His review of the record left him suspicious that earlier investigations had been biased in favor of the institutions and that Bobby's attorney was not adequately representing his interests. Consequently, against the advice of all mental health personnel, the social worker insisted that Bobby appear on his own behalf at the hearing to determine whether he would be removed from his placement. Bobby was agitated and anxious during the hearing. His reports of neglect and abuse because increasingly incoherent. Since his father could not be located, Bobby's wish to be released to him could not be granted. When the social worker returned Bobby to the group home he was flagrantly psychotic and acutely suicidal. During his subsequent hospitalization, Bobby's father appeared. He was adamant in his talks with the staff about his desire and capacity to care for Bobby, but appeared drunk at a crucial meeting involving representatives from all of the relevant agencies. Bobby's social worker attributed this behavior to the father's understandable anxiety and his reasonable expectation that all of the professionals would be against him.

This case might be used as a demonstration of many of the problems that can arise around a child in the foster care system. However, I present it here as an example of the aberrations that can occur in maintaining the parallel constructions that form an integral component of the family romance. In the family romances of childhood, flawed children belong with flawed parents, while ideal children fit with ideal parents. This unconscious fantasy can persist into adulthood, sometimes requiring extensive and dangerous denial to maintain it. In this case, the social worker, out of a wish to create an adequate parent for Bobby, had to make Bobby into a normal child, capable of a realistic appraisal of his surroundings and sufficiently able to differentiate and represent internal and external processes. This is quite a lot to ask of any 11-year-old, let alone one as seriously impaired as Bobby.

Ironically, I believe this maneuver grew out of a wish to protect Bobby from a recognition of his father's frailties. Just as a young child creates ideal parents because he fears he cannot tolerate knowing the flaws of his actual parents, this social worker attempted, albeit in a potentially very destructive way, to rid Bobby of his defects out of an unconscious expectation that Bobby's father would then demonstrate his capacity to care for Bobby. Indeed, in some cases, the success of biological parents in reclaiming their lives and their children does seem truly miraculous. When their success is reality-based, their children will undoubtedly benefit from renewed contact. However, when the success is illusory, based in wishful fantasy rather than reality, we must be more guarded about the possibilities for solid, growth-promoting parent–child interactions.

Clearly, Bobby's father had not been cured by conventional means; therefore the magic of fantasy provided the only solution – for him to become a "regular" father he must be paired with a "regular" kid, and vice versa.

Manifestations of an unconscious belief in the transformational power of the child

The cases cited above highlight the rigidity of idealization contained in those family romances that do not give way to the capacity to hold an ambivalently loved object. However, Deanna and Bobby's stories, in particular, also point to the second important motive, namely, the transformational power of the child. Family romances of childhood are stories of mutation – ordinary parents become nobility, while the distress arising out of disappointment changes into calm, excited anticipation, or later perhaps to anxiety and guilt. However fleeting or illusory it might be, the child's act of creating new parents demonstrates enormous, if unreal, power. We recognize that in the family romance the child is the creator, and by making her parents into the king and queen, she of course recreates herself as the princess. Idealized parents would most certainly have no less than an ideal child! Concomitantly, if the child is perceived as being ideal, then the parents must be as well. As these families demonstrate, the idealization of parent or child often introduces another source of tension in the already difficult cases presented to dependency court for resolution, not because of the child's fantasy, but because of the collusion with these unconscious ideas by the relevant adults.

While unconscious fantasies about the transformative powers of children and parents may cause problems in the social service and legal systems designed to help families, we must remember that these institutions are built on consciously held notions of the possibilities for change in parent–child relationships. Indeed, that is often why children are referred to therapy or placed in foster care – we expect the therapist or substitute parent to change them from frightened, hurt, or ill-behaved children into stable, calm, or even happy ones.

Family romances also remind us that the hope we place in the transformative powers of substitute parents has counterpart in the child's capacity to change an ordinary caregiver into the most wonderful parent imaginable. Indeed, Little Lord

Fauntleroy, sentenced to life as a foster-child with his grandfather, changes this callous and unfeeling grandfather into a humane and loving nobleman, through his decency and kindness, thereby restoring his mother to her rightful place in his external as well as internal life.

Stories such as these speak to the romanticization of parentless children and our expectation that they possess the magical capacity to create a loving and nurturing parent where none exists. We less frequently acknowledge, because of the idealization of and sympathy for the orphaned or abandoned child, that the child may also have the power to transform a loving adult into a hateful parent. Some children, particularly those who have been abused, seem determined to find the worst in the best of people (Heineman, 1998). These children can and do wreak havoc on the array of foster parents, social workers, attorneys, and therapists gathered to help and protect them.

Sally

Sally came into protective custody at the age of 18 months. Her mother, reportedly saying that she would return in a few hours, had left her with other residents of her hotel, whom she had apparently met a few days previously. Two days later, tired of their child-care responsibilities, this couple returned Sally to her missing mother's room for a nap. At some point Sally left the room and was discovered by the manager wandering aimlessly through the halls. The manager contact Child Protective Services.

Sally spent a few weeks in an emergency foster care home with a professional foster mother who cared for up to six children on a temporary basis. During this period her mother was eventually located in jail in a nearby county. Her arrest record was long. A well-documented history of drug use made it seem likely that her parental rights would be terminated and that Sally would eventually be adopted.

Therefore she was moved to a foster care placement with the Wagners, who had been approved as adoptive parents. They were a professional couple with two older boys, one an adolescent who was soon to leave for college, the other a ten-year-old whose cancer had been in remission for an extended period. Unfortunately, a few weeks after Sally arrived, the younger boy again became acutely ill. During the many trips to the hospital and doctors offices, Sally was frequently left with neighbors, the Greens.

Mr. and Ms. Green were the parents of three children and were regarded by all who knew them as ideal parents. While Mr. Green maintained an active, successful career, he still found time to coach at least one of the children's many sports teams. Ms. Green had left her teaching career to raise her children and was sought after as a room parent, den mother, coach, and companion. Despite her rather firm household rules, the neighbor children tended to congregate in her kitchen. She had always expected that she would return to teaching when her children reached school age. However, she had discovered that she thoroughly enjoyed her children and felt that they continued to need more of her attention than she had expected.

Nevertheless, she had strong convictions about being involved in the community and had been moved by a presentation at her church about the pressing need for foster parents. Her social conscience was stirred by her recognition that very few middle-class families, who are often in a position to offer the emotional stability and additional financial resources so desperately needed by foster children, make themselves available to these children. So when the Wagners, who knew of her growing interest in foster care, turned to her for help with Sally, it seemed like a perfect match.

Gradually Sally spent more and more time with the Greens and less and less with the Wagners. The social worker began to sense that the Wagners commitment to Sally was waning in the face of their son's illness. Since Sally was already familiar with them, she approached the Greens about taking Sally into permanent foster care, which they did willingly but with some concerns. Ms. Green commented to the social worker that Sally often seemed withdrawn, distractible, and somewhat disconnected. Both Ms. Green and the social worker attributed this dysphoria to the many changes Sally had endured and the emotional unavailability of her caregivers.

After Sally moved into their home, Ms. Green became increasingly worried about Sally's misbehavior and her inability to control her. Ms. Green was used to commanding respect from children through reasonable, firm, and loving expectations; even the wildest children managed to behave well in her home in order to be allowed to visit. But Sally, by now three and a half, was different. She seemed oblivious to Ms. Green's requests or demands. Her praise and affection mattered as little to Sally as disappointment and punishment. Within a few weeks of full-time care of Sally, she was at her wits' end and arranged for Sally to begin therapy.

The therapist, immediately impressed by Ms. Green's warmth, sensitivity, and concern, quickly joined the ranks of those who saw her as an almost ideal mother. In fact, as an inexperienced mother herself, she often wished she could set aside her role as a therapist and turn to Ms. Green for advice about raising her own young children. Gradually, over several months of twice-weekly therapy, Sally seemed to become more attached to her therapist, who found herself increasingly devoted to her despite the repetitious, often seemingly contentless nature of the play. Meanwhile, Ms. Green's complaints increased and her hostility toward the therapist became obvious. When Mr. Green attended collateral sessions his sarcastic comments about Sally barely contained the sadistic content of his thoughts.

As Ms. Green's attitude toward Sally grew increasingly mean and hateful, the therapist's admiration of her turned to distrust and dislike. Ms. Green had moved from appearing devoted and determined to despairing and depressed. The therapist began receiving more and more calls between sessions, each detailing Sally's worsening behavior at home and in the neighborhood. Eventually, with desperation seeping through his usual sarcasm, Mr. Green called to inform the therapist that he was taking his wife to Mexico for a two-week vacation. He saw this as his last defense against her increasing depression. He announced that if things with Sally didn't change soon, they would not be able to keep her in their home.

In the sessions, Sally continued to behave as an adorable, though somewhat disconnected child. There were no signs of the horribly aberrant behavior described by the parents. The therapist found herself feeling ever more anxious and helpless. Her contention was that Sally could change only if Ms. Green could allow herself to love Sally and be loved by her; she felt that the responsibility for the change lay with Ms. Green as the adult. Despite this she would occasionally find herself compelled to try to reason with Sally, to try to cajole her into being a "better" child, as if Sally were responsible for making Ms. Green into a better mother.

Shortly after the trip to Mexico, which Sally clearly understood as a much needed vacation from her, she was observed maliciously tormenting a much younger child in the neighborhood. The children who observed her threatening taunts were visibly frightened of Sally and her behavior; they were worried that she might have actually harmed the child had they not called an adult to intervene. The situation had clearly escalated beyond control, necessitating Sally's hospitalization. She was now six years old and the people who had been most devoted to her did not want her back. After a hospitalization of many weeks she was placed with a couple who had been successful foster parents to several developmentally delayed children. Sally's new social worker, who had known her only for a few months, was adamant about his placement despite the very serious reservations expressed by Sally's therapist, the Greens, and the hospital personnel.

This couple, particularly Ms. Eliot, who was to be the primary caretaker, approached Sally's care and potential adoption with an almost religious zeal. Though she agreed that Sally would maintain contact with the Greens and her therapist of three years, it was clear that she was merely giving lip-service to the stated requirement of the placement. Ms. Eliot was insistent on her program for Sally's future and unabashed in her dislike for and distrust of mental health professionals. She arranged for Sally to be placed in a regular classroom, signed her up for sports and scouting activities prior to her discharge from the hospital, and began the process that would enable her to adopt Sally legally as soon as possible. Only Ms. Eliot and Sally's social worker were confident that Sally would be transformed into a "normal" child by virtue of her association with this new family. Ms. Eliot was clearly contemptuous of the Greens and what she saw as their obvious failure to rescue this child.

Though Ms. Eliot would not permit Sally's previous therapist to speak with the family therapist she had found, she did allow Sally two visits with her. Ms. Eliot sat in on both sessions. During this period, Sally and Ms. Eliot had outings of gradually decreasing frequency with the Greens. Ms. Green felt that Sally was increasingly withdrawn and depressed over the course of the visits. Though her behavior with Ms. Eliot was superficially compliant, she felt that Sally was smoldering and barely able to meet the unrealistic demands being placed on her.

Sally remained with the Eliots for about three years. The adoption was never completed. Instead, Ms. Eliot, in a rage, arranged for Sally to be placed in residential treatment following a long history of increasingly dangerous activities. A fire-setting incident finally prompted her to place Sally in residential treatment and, having done so, she never saw her again.

IN SEARCH OF THE ROMANTIC FAMILY

Following a brief period of sexually provocative and potentially dangerous behavior, Sally settled into a comfortable routine in her placement. Her academic performance improved dramatically, her affect brightened, and her peer relationships became increasingly important and pleasurable. After a time she asked if the Greens could visit. When contacted by the center, they expressed enormous relief upon learning that Sally was no longer with Ms. Eliot. Though saddened that she was still without a family, they also worried that her parentless status seemed to leave them uncomfortably obligated to this child who had so nearly destroyed their own family. They did visit Sally and, over time, worked with the center staff on her behalf. As she was more able to accept their positive attention, they were more willing to give it. Gradually their visits to the center increased in both frequency and duration. They found themselves visiting out of pleasure, rather than from obligation, and wanting to invite Sally home with them. Eventually, Sally spent more and more holidays and weekends with the Greens and fewer and fewer at the center. After almost ten years she had finally created a family for herself.

Why did it take so long? When Sally first encountered the Greens she had not had the experience of a reliable "good enough" parent. Consequently, when faced with the loss of a parent, whether through the parent's actual disappearance or emotional withdrawal, Sally could not, through a defensive regression to idealization, attempt to repair the loss; she could not make a romanticized family for herself. Instead, she created what she had lost – a bad mother. Whether it was predominantly her unconscious need to find a mother to match the one she lost or a compulsion to be cast out because of her badness, as a means of explaining and justifying her repeated losses and rejections, in some ways does not matter. What did matter was that the hard-fought, well-intentioned attempts to rescue her were no match for Sally's unconscious need to create a bad object.

Sally's tormented childhood demonstrates the power and persistence of attachment patterns and the sometimes inexorable slowness with which they change. Sally's unconscious determination to find a mother just like the one she had lost resulted in a series of problematic relationships with mother substitutes. It seems likely that Sally's improvement in the residential treatment program was facilitated, in part, by the less intimate relationships with staff. No single person had to bear the brunt of Sally's projections, softening their effects and, in turn making it less likely that staff would feel the need to enact the role Sally unconsciously created for mother substitutes.

Returning to the place of family romance in Sally's emotional life, we can see many threads of this fantasy running through Sally's early history. The Wagners perhaps had a notion of the transformative power of the orphaned child who would restore their family to health, or perhaps replace the child they feared losing. While there was some sound reasoning and sensitivity backing up their beliefs and behavior, I believe that Ms. Green and Sally's therapist also shared an unconscious conviction about the idealized parent who could create an ideal child. When these unconscious notions could not withstand Sally's primitive affects and behavior, both turned to the idea of the inadequate or flawed parent as explanation for the loss of the idealized child, each holding the other responsible for Sally's incapacity or unwillingness to be transformed into the perfect child they expected to create. Ms. Eliot's approach demonstrates the notion of the parallel status of child and parent contained in the family romance. If she was a good parent, Sally was a good kid, not by virtue of any transformative powers on either of their parts, but merely by association and assertion.

Orphans, children whose parents are physically or emotionally unable to care for them, and children who have been abandoned or mistreated are among the saddest children we encounter. The problems they bring to and pose for social institutions, as well as individual parents, teachers, attorneys, social workers, and therapists, are enormous and complex. There are powerful conscious and unconscious pulls to rescue them, to create for them an ideal, or at least good enough family. After all, if any child deserves an ideal family, is it not these who have suffered so much and so early?

I believe that some, though certainly not all, of the seemingly incomprehensible problems arising out of the relationships between these children and their caregivers can be understood, or at least approached, by a consideration of the remnants of unresolved family romances that may be operating in the individual or shared unconscious convictions of the relevant adults. We expect that, like many elements of the oedipal drama, vestiges of this defensive fantasy may persist, unconscious and unnoticed, into adulthood. We have come to understand that normative defensive patterns of childhood are seldom left completely behind. Long after they have outlived their usefulness, they may become conscious or appear as unconscious contributions to behavior; the consequences, in many situations, may be relatively benign. However, in the case of foster or adoptive parents, biological parents who choose or are forced to relinquish their children, and the professionals who work with them, there are real parents, whose competition for the child is not the child's fantasied creation. Any or all of the numerous players may carry with them multiple layers of expectations and fantasies. Unless we carefully consider the participants' unconscious processes, we may not be able to understand or intervene in the destructive, externalized polarizations between inadequate or idealized parents that too frequently bring these cases to our attention.

Notes

1 In this chapter I am considering "family romance" as a phenomenon in the developmental processes of children in intact families with heterosexual parents. The questions of whether and how this fantasy may serve children of homosexual parents, children in interracial families, or foreign-born adopted children, for example, is a compelling and important question that is beyond the scope of this work. There were no mixed race foster placements or adoptions in the vignettes used for illustration in this chapter.
2 The stories constructed by children who did not receive unconditional love and sufficient need satisfaction obviously differ from those created in "good enough" families. A consideration of the place of family romance in the normative developmental thrust toward growth provides a striking contrast to its place in the lives and children and families who become stuck in the world of idealized and denigrated figures.

6

WEAVING WITHOUT A LOOM
Creating a self in foster care

We know from theory, research, and common sense that stability and consistency in relationships promote children's healthy development. Unfortunately, the foster care system often fails to provide reliable, sustaining relationships. The propensity of the system to look to the external world for explanations and solutions to problems too often overlooks the child's internal distress. When we suggest to unhappy or anxious children that their feelings can be relieved by a change in the environment, we insidiously undermine and disavow the fundamental importance of the child's internal world as a source of pleasure, pain, upheaval, and regulation. Moving children from one "placement" to another when problems arise is a primary response of the foster care system. In the following, I will explore the potential impact of this philosophy on identity formation.

We marvel as we watch children grow from tiny, helpless beings to young adults who carry within them a sense of self that is cohesive and reflects the multifaceted nature of personality. We watch and wonder as they move through the days and nights of 18 or 20-odd years of interactions with parents, siblings, aunts and uncles, grandparents, neighbors, teachers, playmates, friends, and enemies, emerging with a sense-of-self-in-relation-to-people-and-community. The question of how and why this happens fascinates us – we look backward through analysis or biography or memoir for events and interactions that explain the fabric of a person's life. We look to longitudinal studies to describe patterns as they unfold. Whether through carefully controlled studies that consider the effects of different variables or by sifting through anecdotal evidence, we try to understand the influence of heredity, the effects of the minutiae of daily life, and the importance of organizing events in shaping character and forming identity (Bosma & Kunen, 2001; Erikson, 1980; Waterman, 1982).

Even as we discover patterns, we know that some of those we see aren't real – that sometimes we impose order on an incoherent surface for our own comfort. We are confused by lives in which people have no apparent connection to each other or in which events happen for no discernable reason. How can we get to know a person who greets us without a coherent history and no cohesive story to explain who she is and how she came to be that person? How does a child weave a history for herself out of random events and unrelated people (Mulkerns & Owen, 2008;

Smith, 2011)? How does she do this without a loom – without the solid structure of home and community? How does she do this without the warp of parents and relatives and teachers in the background to hold the rules, history, and values of family and community with just the right amount of tension? How does a child understand the self that is reflected in the eyes and words and touch of another if the reflecting other changes repeatedly? What does a child do with the threads of her life when there is no home – no loom to hold the warp? How does she contain the colors and textures of experiences and relationships if there is nothing in the background to help hold them together?

Rachael, who lived in four group homes between the ages of 14 and 18, describes the difficulty of finding an identity surrounded by an instability of people and place:

> I had no identity until I was 25. I basically got it through other people. I didn't think for myself. I didn't project any goals for myself. I let some-one else do it for me. And now I find myself at the age of 30 trying to find out what I want. What do I really want to do? What do I really want to learn? Everything seems fresh because I'm still in a learning stage as a group home kid right now.
>
> (Bernstein, 2000, p. 86)

At the age of 30, she still feels like a kid, lost in the parentless, disconnected world of group homes, uncertain about her identity and how she fits into her rela-tionships with others. The patterns that, for most people, emerge over childhood and adolescence eluded her until her early adulthood.

When thinking about the children in good-enough families, rather than about the Rachaels of the world, I imagine children gaily moving to and fro across the time and space of childhood, like the shuttle that carries the woof back and forth, slowly but steadily creating a pattern across the threads of continuity that adults hold for them. For some children a pattern may emerge early and remain relatively unchanged; for others the fabric of their childhood will be made up of many and varied patterns. All of this assumes a relatively firm and reliable warp, perhaps with some broken threads or variations caused from unexpected pulls in one direc-tion or another. We know that children succeed – more or less well – even when the warp doesn't hold as firmly as we might wish. Along with less dire stresses, most children can and do manage to weave a sense-of-self in the face of parental death, divorce, family illness, and poverty.

However, sometimes the stresses are too much for any child, particularly one who feels she has little choice but to care for herself. Christine entered foster care at the age of seven and lived in foster homes, group homes, and juvenile halls for the next 11 years. She was raped and beaten in the first foster home, merely beaten in the second. At the age of 11 she stole a bike and spent six months in juvenile hall because there was no place for her to go. At the age of 12 she was raped by the son of new foster parents, and, at the age of 13, she placed her first child for adoption.

If I had been adopted when my brother was, I would have had a family – a good loving family. I would have got a better education. I would have had parents who loved me, who would try anything they could to help – like a family should be. I would have a family who wasn't corrupt. I would be a much stronger person because today I'm dealing with a lot of stuff, and feel I don't have anybody to help me get through those hard times. I lost a lot of trust in foster care. If I would have had a family it would have been a lot, lot better.

(Bernstein, 2000, p. 31)

We see how powerfully a belief in the sustaining and protective function of family persists, even when a child has endured sexual and physical abuse in the context of a family. Despite what she has suffered, this young woman clings to an idealized view of family as a structure that holds its children dear and fights to help them through their troubles.

What is a child to do if those entrusted with his care repeatedly abuse not only the child's body but the child's trust? What is a child to do if the adults who are supposed to hold the warp against his woof change without warning and without apparent reason – if the pattern is suddenly just left dangling? Frankly, I don't know. The more I think about how foster children emerge from repeated moves and multiple homes with some sense of identity, the more I am awed by the human psyche's capacity to create meaning – to weave a story of self without a loom.

John, part one

Some years ago I consulted regularly with a group of foster care workers. Most of the stories from those days have faded, but one has stayed. A caseworker came to the group for help with John, a 12-year-old boy who was demanding to be moved from his foster home. During every monthly visit, he lodged complaints against his foster parents and threatened to run away if his worker didn't remove him. Her question for the group was whether to shift him to another foster family or wait until he was old enough for placement in a group home.

As we talked more, other pieces of the story emerged. He had been in several placements before this one. He had been threatening to run away for nearly a year and was planning his get-away for his 18th birthday – some six years into the future! At the time, the worker's question about the planned move struck me as quite strange. If a troubled teenager living with his biological parents came to us asserting vehemently and angrily that he was going to run away, I wonder if our first – or second, or nth – thought would be to remove him from his home permanently. I wondered then, and still do, how many orphanages we could fill with adolescents who threaten to run away from home and how many children we would terrify if we took their threats of self-determined emancipation seriously.

Creatures of habitation

There are many important issues in this story – a tale that unfortunately no longer strikes me as odd. We are creatures of habit – as anyone who has unwillingly had to relinquish familiar habits, or has had to adjust to a new, externally imposed, routine, or tried to change a word in a three-year-old's favorite story knows only too well. When we successfully solve a problem we tend to try the solution again, even if the issue before us is actually of a different order. In this case, there had been trouble in John's original family, and the previous response had been to remove him from his home. We don't know what the trouble was or whether this was the best approach, only that it happened. Several more removals and moves followed in the wake of the first removal.

In this way, "removing" and "moving" can too easily become the ubiquitous solution for problems encountered by children, parents, and workers in the foster care system. We learned long ago from Piaget that we are far more inclined to try to assimilate new information into previously developed schemata than to develop new theories or solutions to accommodate data that cannot be assimilated. When we encounter a novel situation or new information, we test it against internal schemata – we want to know how it fits with patterns that we have already created for understanding the world. Unassailable data make our brains itch; it's easier to think about horses with stripes than to create a new category for zebras. In many ways we continue to treat foster children as "horses with stripes" rather than having to accommodate our systems to their needs. They are not simply children in need of substitute families. The experiences that brought them to foster care leave lasting scars; the loss of a family is almost unthinkably overwhelming to a young child, even if that family was neglectful or abusive. When children lose family after family for reasons they don't comprehend, they are understandably often bereft and unable to find comfort easily.

The number of "placements" encountered by foster children and adolescents arouses great interest and concern in the literature about these children. However, I want to emphasize that every "placement" involves a "replacement" and every "move" requires a "removal." Every time a child says "Hello" to one family, he says "Goodbye" to another. The warp is severed and the pattern of his life is left dangling until he can reattach it. How many times can a child do this and remain even relatively intact?

It may or may not surprise you – depending on how much time you spend working with or thinking about foster children – to learn that the idea that multiple placements may actually cause emotional breakdown has emerged relatively recently in the world of child welfare. The prevailing notion has been that emotionally disturbed children cannot easily be contained in families, that it is mainly their psychological problems that cause "failed placements." Even though, as we reviewed in Chapter one, attachment theory has provided us with decades of insight into the ways in which our characteristic understanding of and approach to relationships, we move children from one home to another assuming that somehow they will be different or better in the next placement. Indeed, if there are changes, it is usually that their behavior is worse, rather than better.

Some of us take for granted that a three- or six- or nine-year-old child may not have the ability to adapt repeatedly to the new sights and sounds and smells and tastes that characterize every family. We assume that young children may not have the emotional and cognitive capacity to read and respond effectively to the complex nuances of continually changing family dynamics. However, the mental health of foster children may not be on the agendas of the agencies responsible for feeding and clothing and housing foster children. This is not to suggest that the people in charge of foster children are a uniformly malicious, callous, or ill-informed lot – it is a complex system with multiply determined agendas, confusing rules, and inadequate resources. Sometimes it seems staggering that any child leaves the system unscathed. Remarkably many do; they manage to grab hold of whichever adults come their way, to make use of whatever they have to offer, and to keep weaving even when the tapestry is hanging by a thread.

"Taking for granted"

Over the last several years I've spent a great deal of time reading and thinking about what it must feel like to be a foster child – each of whom, like Blanche du Bois, is utterly dependent on the kindness of strangers. The contrast between that experience and the experience of children who simply, with good reason, presume that their parents will know and care for them is ineluctable. For example, I mentioned earlier the difficulty in changing a single word in a child's favorite story. As I was writing that phrase, I became acutely aware of the many assumptions it contains. It posits a calm and quiet time for reading, a child who has enough experience with stories to have a favorite, an adult who knows the preferred story, and a mutual pleasure in sharing time together. Perhaps the adult has read the story enough times to be tired of it or perhaps has enough curiosity about the child's memory to see if a changed word will be noticed.

Happily, many children take these kinds of interchanges for granted – they feel entitled to bedtime stories. Children of reasonably attentive parents simply assume, from experience, that their parents know them and will continue to know their preferences in food and clothes and activities. This sense of entitlement, along with the child's presumption of the parent's knowledge of his needs and desires, of course, inevitably leads to the occasional disappointment. For example, as his mother is heading for the grocery store a young child asks for a new, much advertised cereal. But when Mother gets to the grocery, cocoa puffs, cocoa flakes, cocoa pops, and cocoa "Os" all blur. She grabs one and hopes for the best, only to be greeted with a disappointed, "That's not the one I asked for!" Though the child might argue differently, we can see that the wrong cereal is the symptom rather than the problem. The problem for this child is his disappointment, with its implicit recognition that his mother does not always adequately attend to his needs. It represents a small narcissistic injury – one of the inevitable tears in the fabric of relationships, probably relatively easily repaired with an apology, a hug, a plan to exchange the cereal on a subsequent trip, or a decision to try the cereal that did appear.

I use this as an example of the minutiae of everyday life that contribute to the patterns of childhood and that we too frequently forget about when considering foster children. Too often their lives are punctuated by events so vast and horrific that we fail to attend to what they lose when they are removed from one family and placed with another. Each time the warp is severed, they must attach themselves again – perhaps to another with a different texture and tension or with threads larger or smaller than the one before. Maybe a child was just learning to like the macaroni and cheese in the most recent foster home but doesn't yet have the language to tell a new foster parent about her preferences. She doesn't know how to say, "I am a girl who likes mac and cheese. That's part of who I am." That is just one tiny piece of her identity that can be lost in changes from one caregiver to another.

As we know, continuity is incredibly important to these conservative little beings. Do it once, it's an event – twice, it's a family tradition. They are comforted by well-known stories and love the predictability inherent in watching the same video over and over again. Children are not inclined to express boredom with familiar foods or to suggest that a new and exotic family menu might be in order. They take comfort in repetition and predictability – parts of the warp created by family and community through which they can weave an identity and to which they can return when they feel lost or hurt or confused.

Although the impact of terrifying events – such as natural disasters, mass murders, or preventable accidents that kill and maim many – effecting families, communities, or nations inevitably fade in our collective memory, those memories make us acutely aware of the need for a regressive retreat that overtakes us when forced to confront our individual and shared vulnerability. In the face of terrorizing unpredictability, people go home and stay there; newspapers and magazines fill with stories of neighbors helping each other and offer recipes for "comfort food": nothing new or exotic in a time of emotional crisis. Of course, again, the food itself is not entirely the issue – its primary value is to help restore the connection to the people and times when we felt soothed and cared for. The familiar smells and tastes and textures helped us relocate ourselves in a world that at one time offered at least the illusion of predictability, safety, and security.

What if you spent your childhood in five or six or nine different homes? What if you didn't stay in any place long enough to feel comfortable? What if the sounds and smells and tastes changed so often that they always seemed new and unfamiliar – things to which you had to adjust, rather than made you feel at home? What if the differences were too great to allow for assimilation and repeatedly demanded accommodation? An unexplainable assault on a community is almost too much to bear; how many emotional assaults can a child bear – particularly one who is all alone in the world?

The comfort of home

Lauren was a 15-year-old runaway who lived in 22 foster and group homes in three years. She has something to tell us about trying to meet unreasonable demands for adaptation:

> I left foster care at 13 because I went to go stay with mom. That's a very significant event because she left without me after four months. It was the second time she left me. That's when I just kind of knew that you're all by yourself. I always feel like I'm all by myself. It's probably because of her leaving me, and then never trusting I'm going to stay anywhere too long. I always think I'm gonna go back someplace and it's not gonna be there anymore, and no one will have told me, and I won't be able to stay there.
> (Bernstein, 2000, p. 55)

An adolescent without memories of comforting places and people to turn to in times of emotional distress, Lauren feels utterly alone in a world that could quite literally disappear when she isn't looking. This is one of the insidious and lasting consequences of having to weave without a loom – in times of emotional crisis, the child's sense of comfort must too often be largely self-generated and self-contained, rather than offer a solid connection to a soothing other.

When a parent helps a child calm herself, or tolerate the frustration of waiting, or return to sleep in the middle of the night, the child is eventually able to soothe herself by evoking the image of the protective, soothing parent – perhaps murmuring the same words or using the same tone of voice. Through practice and repeated help from parents and caring adults, she gradually becomes able to rely on her own internal resources for comfort. Thus, for a child who has enjoyed the presence of a comforting other, self-soothing, paradoxically, is an other-related, intrapsychically contained, interpersonal activity. Just as the tastes of "comfort food" contain the memories of the nurturing mother – whether or not consciously evoked – the comforting other, is embedded in the process of self-soothing.

However, when a child grows up without a predictable comforting presence, he must learn, as best he can, to soothe himself. Perhaps he rocks in his crib, sucks on his fingers, or stares into space. Whether he autistically uses his own body for consolation or escapes painful feelings through dissociation, he learns to turn away from others to find comfort. Through practice and repeated dependence on his own resources, he gradually builds internal resources that evoke memories not of a comforting other but of loneliness, solitude, and self-reliance.

John, part two

In this context, let's return to John, our would-be runaway, and try to understand what he is saying, what his social worker is hearing, and how they communicate through a language of loss. We can understand John's comments and behavior as emanating from an ambivalent attachment style: he says he wants to leave, but he stays. There are various possible paraphrases and interpretations of John's ongoing commentary on his foster home, including:

"You'd better get me out of here before I decide to leave. No rush."

"Things are okay for now, but I know I can't stay forever."

"In case I get kicked out, just know I was planning to leave anyway."

"Don't think you can just dump me and forget about me – things aren't perfect, you know."

"I know I have to leave when I'm eighteen – don't think I'm planning to stay where I'm not wanted."

When the social worker presented this case for consultation, it initially appeared that she had heard only John's complaints and his requests to be removed from his foster home. Her explicit question was not whether to move him, but where and when. However, her actions suggested an implicit recognition of the complexity of feelings driving John's complaints. Over the year of his placement in this particular home, she had not acquiesced in his demands for a change in living arrangements. Apparently she recognized that John was not in danger, that this was not a situation that demanded immediate or even swift action. However, she did not perceive the inherent contradiction between her past actions and her future plans. Neither was she consciously aware that she was talking to John as if she heard only the complaining part of his message and acting as if she heard only the satisfied part of his message. When pressed about the reasons for planning to move John, she explained that he had run away before and she was worried that he would again.

Viewing the interaction between John and his caseworker through the lens of attachment theory, we can see that John has an ambivalent attachment to his foster family. He complains about them, but he stays, apparently keeping his positive feelings toward them out of conscious awareness. The caseworker responds in kind; she seems aware only of John's negative feelings, but her actions belie her stated concerns. Had the caseworker recognized this as an ambivalent attachment, she might still have chosen not to point out John's positive feelings, but her anxiety about whether leaving him in that home might have been eased.

Here was a child perfectly capable of voting with his feet who chose instead to vote with his seat! We can reasonably easily understand John's difficulty in articulating the complexity of his feelings. In the first place, he was 12 – still a child; we can appreciate how hard it is for children to put words to highly charged, ambivalent feelings, particularly when talking to strangers about parents or caregivers. In the second place, he was 12 – almost an adolescent; we know that this can be a time of heightened vulnerability hidden behind a defensive nonchalant or tough facade. We also know that John had gone through multiple placements and we might reasonably wonder if he was one of those children who learned too early to care for himself rather than turning to adults for comfort. Perhaps in this new family, which he apparently judges adequate to meet his needs for the next six years or so, he may find comfort from others.

Finding comfort from others is a terrifying possibility for children whose self-soothing rests on solitude and self-reliance. They expect, with good reason, that people who appear will disappear, often without warning and without reason. The pattern of identity they have woven over the constantly changing warp of relationships with adults typically boldly announces, "I do not trust you or anyone. Do not take me for a fool." Perhaps this is an important aspect of the underlying message in John's complaints to his social worker. "Just because I'm staying, don't think I'm foolish enough to trust these people. I know how to take care of myself." Like too many foster children, John's idea of self-care is to know that there is a way out of any situation. Or, as Bryan Samuels, former Commissioner of the Administration on Children, Youth, and Families reminds us, "Foster care teaches kids how to start over. It doesn't teach them how to stick around."

In her acceptance of John's request for a change in his living arrangements, the social worker tacitly agreed with his assessment that change is the most expedient solution – even when you haven't fully identified the problem. Obviously, we don't have complete information, but we do know that John insisted and his social worker agreed that John's complaints stemmed from external sources and could be answered by environmental changes. This is perhaps the most powerful legacy of removing children from inadequate or abusive care: because the original, real, external danger in the child's life demanded a change in the environment, some foster care workers have almost overwhelming propensity to assimilate all subsequent problems – both external and internal – into the earlier schemata. New problems can then be treated as old, without a demand for accommodation to changed information that might require a different solution. This appears to be the unfortunate legacy that the social worker brought to her efforts to help John – when there's a problem, change the environment.

Of course, there are a number of possible explanations for her assumption that external change was the preferred course of action. On a purely practical level, she might have had legitimate concerns about having ignored John's requests if he did make good on his threats to run – she would have to answer to herself and her supervisors. Perhaps her plans to remove him to a different setting grew from exhaustion or exasperation with him, the numbers of other children for whom she had responsibility, the system with all of its inadequacies, or feeling overwhelmed by having to face all of this day after day. We hear over and over again from those living in and around foster care that they often feel little hope of making things better, that doing something seems better than doing nothing, and that frequently the only available solution is to move the child. Unfortunately, this perpetuates the idea that problems are generally external and that relationships are more easily replaced than improved.

The possibility that John's complaints might have referred to an internal state of discomfort – anxiety, confusion, discontent, or sadness – did not seem to reach her conscious awareness. She apparently could not let herself know that the internal distress could not easily be left behind. She seemed unable to hear that he planned to stay despite his difficulty in doing so. His situation wasn't perfect – there were some problems. John didn't seem to know how to ask how to make staying better – how to improve relationships. Unfortunately, when there seems so little hope of improving the failed relationships that bring children to foster care, we often have trouble remembering that all human relationships suffer rips from time to time, that they sometimes fray at the edges, and that, in the short term, repairing them may seem to take more effort than replacing them. However, children who have had to weave an identity without a loom, who have had to attach the patterns of their lives over and over and over again to adults who might care for them know too well the utter exhaustion of adapting and accommodating and still feeling utterly alone.

Jessica, who spent her adolescence in foster care somehow learned that, despite feeling alone, life cannot be lived without relationships:

> ... it's not as clear cut as just "Pick yourself up by the bootstraps and move on" when you don't have the supports to do that. People don't understand that because they think everybody has a family. In reality, for a lot of people who have been in foster care, it's sink or swim. If you want to do it, you have to somehow get the confidence. I think I just reached out. Seeing that other people were doing it, I took a chance that I might be able to do it. But a lot of people do sink rather than swim, and that's what scares me. I don't like the idea of having to pick yourself up by yourself. That's not the way it works. Anyone who's made it has had friends or some kind of support to make it through. You don't make it through any stage of life alone.
>
> (Bernstein, 2000, p. 78)

This is what we cannot bear to know – that you don't make it through any stage of life alone, that relationships are not easily replaced. If we truly and firmly held the knowledge that children do not move effortlessly from one set of parents to another, do not easily adapt to new faces, smells, tastes, and sounds, we would not tolerate a system of care that allows children to be removed and moved two or six or ten or 20 times in as many years. We know it and we forget it – we forget that children need the steady and consistent warp of caring adults to hold a history for them until they can hold it for themselves. Forgetting means that we can turn away from the internal world of these children. In the words of one foster care worker, "I can't think about whether moving them is painful; otherwise I wouldn't be able to do my job." Remembering demands that we know and help hold the pain that these changes impose upon children. Every time their relationship with family alters, they lose a bit of the story that helps to shape their identities and eventually allows them to know themselves in the context of friends and community.

The relationship between a sense of a coherent personal history and a solid sense of identity is most powerfully conveyed by people who have spent part of their childhood, even just a bit of it, in foster care. As I was preparing to write this chapter, I discovered a website designed to help former foster children locate their lost foster parents. At the time I last downloaded information, there were well over five hundred postings from people who were hoping to contact former foster parents. Here are a few that are fairly representative, in both content and tone, in terms of being lost and of the hope of being found:

From Renee, who was in foster care for several months:

Over the years I have thought of you often and wanted to thank you for caring for me when I was an infant. All that I was told is that you cared for me for several months before I was placed with my adoptive family. My husband and I are now foster parents ourselves and are intimately aware of the love, time, and selflessness it requires to care for foster children. If by chance you read this please contact me as I would love to hear from you and thank you again.

From Christopher, who was in foster care for about a year:

Was placed in foster care, prior to being adopted. Would love to meet foster parents, and perhaps learn something about myself when I was an infant. Thanks for taking care of me.

From Randolf, who was in foster care for seven years:

I would like to find the Kirklands who were the best and last foster home I lived in. The brothers were in high school or college at the time (1972, I think). My stay with them was by far the best memory I have in the foster homes I stayed in (9 in all). Just wanted to say Thank You! And see how life is treating you.

From Bobbie, who was in foster care for five years:

Shortly after my grandmothers death in 1974, I was made a ward of Los Angeles county. Mother was nowhere to be found, father was already estranged for years, and relatives couldn't or wouldn't take me in.

For the first year I lived with the Gambles in Long Beach near where I'd grown up with relatives. They moved to the San Francisco area and I had to stay behind in LA county. I was put in several temporary homes while waiting for a permanent placement. This did nothing but make my life unstable – all that shifting around. After a few more homes, I started to run away. At least I knew where I'd be staying from one day to the next. I became a hunted runaway and it felt like I was a criminal.

After being picked up by the LAPD, I'd end up in MacLaren Hall for 6 mos. until my worker could find another suitable placement. I was in at least 17 homes in LA county form 74–81 when I wasn't on the run.

I spent 3 to 6 month increments in lockup facilities and fenced placements. In between these places, I'd roam like a gypsy from Santa Barbara to Palm Springs, using whatever means I had to, to survive. I wore out many welcomes, borrowed and stole. I panhandled on and slept under the Hermosa pier some nights. Usually I had a "running buddy" with me, and we'd hitchhike all around the LA area. I met many people I'll never see again.

What prompted me to write this entry today is my need to say thanks to those who helped me along the way. Your faces are blurry and your names forgotten, but your kindness is remembered. My story seems sad, but it was those hard times that makes me the person I am today. Sometimes the most unlikely cases are the ones that turn out the best.

For those who remember having me, know that I landed butter side up.

Conclusion

We have no way of knowing whether any of the people from Bobbie's past found the message, whether they learned that this former foster child "landed butter side up." Curious to see if there were new postings, I returned to the website. I sat in stunned silence, recalling Lauren's worry, "I always think I'm gonna go back someplace and it's not gonna be there anymore, and no one will have told me, and I won't be able to stay there," as the glow from the computer screen announced that the website no longer existed.

It was somewhat accidental that I had downloaded the pages. What if I hadn't? What if I had only my memories of the words and stories that these unknown people had posted in the hope of renewing lost connections? What if I had no external source against which to check and correct my memories? Too often, this is the life of children in foster care – people disappear and with them go some broken threads of the story. The children or young adults have nowhere to turn to discover whether and how those collections of broken threads were ever connected. They are left alone to try to make sense – to find and define the patterns of the relationships of their lives. When they come to us for help it is often with a collection of broken and disconnected threads that have been discolored and frayed from years of neglect or misuse. We must remember that when they come us it may be with the hope of finding someone who understands the importance of the loom of family and community – someone who can hold the warp while they weave these threads into the comfort of a coherent pattern. They come to us, not for help in making sense of a story, but for help in making a story.

Children and the clinicians who treat them bring their stories to the therapy. Whether or not consciously held or explicitly articulated, they inform the relationship and, over time, each therapeutic pair creates its own unique story. The stories created between therapists and adult clients are largely told in words. However, therapeutic work with children also demands action and, often, concrete representations of our care. Sometimes our words are simply not enough to satisfy the emptiness of their emotional lives; they need the actual comfort of real food.

7

HUNGER PANGS

Transference and countertransference in the treatment of foster children

Clinicians who treat children inevitably come into contact with food – not just thoughts of food or feelings about food or the meanings of food – but food itself. Toddlers often enter the office with their bottles of milk or juice in hand (or mouth), while preschoolers frequently travel with little bags of ever-ready snacks. Older children and adolescents, whose stomachs and brains demand caloric comfort and fortification after a day at school, may arrive with the remains of their lunch or a bag of food from the neighborhood market.

Some children, more or less insistently, offer to share their treats, sometimes prompting the need for lightning-quick analyses of complex psychological questions such as how to manage a lovingly offered, sticky, half-eaten chocolate bar. Other children find our words too ephemeral: they demand that we offer something tangible – real food that they can feel in their bellies until they can hold us in their hearts and minds.

Just as food can easily become a battleground for parents and children, it can and does absorb multiple meanings and issues for children and their therapists. Unlike their parents or caregivers we can simply avoid direct confrontation with these issues by electing not to feed the children who come to our offices. However, when children have suffered physical and emotional deprivation, real food frequently becomes a part of the treatment. These are hungry kids and they want to be fed!

Sometimes, as for example when snacks are provided to children being seen in a clinic, or the halls that lead from the hospital waiting room to the outpatient offices are lined with vending machines, child and therapist are thrust into the complex issues surrounding food without the opportunity for prior reflection. While the negotiations over how much food is offered, how it is limited, or who controls its availability become an inherent part of the therapist/child relationship, there is in these situations, always the hierarchical "other," often the unseen but powerful "administration" or "staff" who has final authority in the inevitable psychological and political questions about distribution and care of shared resources (Altman, 1995). For example, if one therapist allows her patient unlimited access to a candy drawer, what impact does that have on other children and their therapists: should one child be allowed to save a block construction if that means there are fewer blocks for the other children who come to the clinic?

93

Some of these issues are more easily addressed in the world of private practice where the therapist usually has greater control over practical issues – for example, not having to share an office or move from room to room in a clinic, makes keeping track of toys and projects easier. However, there is no "other" hovering over the therapist/child relationship when difficult decisions present themselves.

In private practice the decision about whether to make food available to children (or a given child) falls to the therapist alone. Some clinicians argue that food is not the proper currency of psychotherapy and that allowing or introducing it into an analytic treatment actually interferes with the work of experiencing, naming, and understanding thoughts and feelings. In many ways this is the easiest position because "no" sets clear boundaries. There is nothing vague about "none."

"As much as you want," seems to be the most problematic stance, both practically and psychologically. In a residential treatment setting where all children have equal access to unlimited supplies of foods, the meanings of choices, self-imposed limits, or over-indulgence can be addressed within the individual sessions and the milieu. In contrast, children leaving our offices typically enter the milieu of a family and the morass of feelings and conflicts that surround an abundance or shortage of food. In addition, offering unlimited supplies seems almost too threatening, perhaps because it stirs not only our fears of being engulfed by the child's needs but our own greedy desires to "save some for ourselves."

The decision to offer children food usually introduces all of the ambiguities of "some" and the inevitable negotiations and struggles that arise as therapist and child try to determine "how much is enough" what is "good" and what is "good enough."

David

David came to therapy from a background of extreme poverty and neglect. The stability of his foster family, in particular the firm and loving stance of his foster mother, had done much to help David gain some control over his impulsive rages. Nevertheless, he remained a sad, angry, hurt, and incredibly needy little boy.

David hated being a foster child and felt embarrassed and humiliated when his "foster" status was mentioned at school or in the neighborhood. Although she couldn't always be certain, his foster mother strongly suspected that he stole things from his playmates with some regularity.

From the beginning of his weekly psychotherapy with Dr. R., David demanded food and gifts. When she told David that he could pick a snack from the selection she kept in her office, he angrily demanded more. He berated her for withholding from him, pointing out that since she obviously had plenty of food in her drawer there was no particular reason that she couldn't give him more.

The package David typically chose offered not only food, but the chance to obtain a "free" prize in exchange for a (large) number of "coupons" printed on the side of the packages. As David became increasingly excited by the idea of using the coupons to obtain a special prize, Dr. R became increasingly worried about the disappointment that this gift would likely bring. While working together to cut and save the coupons for this special gift, Dr. R and David could think and talk together about needs and desires – disappointments and gratifications. However, the added chance of gratification also brought an additional opportunity for disappointment into the relationship.

Now, by limiting the food David could take, Dr. R was also making David wait for this much-desired prize. If he could have two treats a week the prize would come twice as fast – three treats a week, even faster, and if he could have the whole drawer of treats he could have his prize immediately! Dr. R fluctuated between wishing that she had never offered David food and wishing that she had never placed limits on what he could have. Either position seemed preferable to the weekly struggles and her vision of the likely disappointment David would face when this long saved-for toy finally arrived.

After many weeks David had accumulated the required number of coupons. As he and Dr. R prepared to send them off, the treasure that he would soon find at his therapist's office increasingly excited David. When the prize failed to arrive at the expected time, David implored Dr. R to call to discover the reason for the delay. She did as he asked, often calling during his sessions. During this process, which took several weeks, Dr. R's anxiety intensified as she imagined that this prize would never arrive or would be disappointingly shabby. However, David's expectation that it would arrive seemed not to falter. His view of her as someone who could and would negotiate on his behalf was evident in his reminders to call between sessions and checking to see if she had. Finally, the toy arrived. David was delighted!

The process of acquiring the prize seemed more important than the object itself, since David explained to Dr. R that you could buy these toys at the store near his house. Indeed, as soon as he had his toy David began accumulating coupons again. This time he began saving for an even bigger prize – a safe in which to keep his valuables!

During this time David began asking Dr. R to bring him food from home. He didn't want cookies from the store, he wanted a cookie that she had baked for him. While Dr. R recognized David's wish to have tangible evidence of his being special to her, she found herself quite resistant to granting this seemingly simple request. She felt that David's unconscious question was whether she would take him home with her, and that he would greet the home-baked cookie as a promise that one day he would have not only something *from* her home, but would be welcomed *into* her home. At the same time the process of working together, as they had toward the accumulation of coupons, and Dr. R's willingness to *do* something for David seemed terribly important to David. Eventually Dr. R discovered cookies that came with separate packages of icing, with which she could make a special treat for and with David without blurring the boundaries between home and office, between therapist and parent.

The approach of Christmas provided yet another opportunity for Dr. R and David to explore the complex feelings about giving and getting. A colleague noted that foster children are like "store bought" cookies sitting on a shelf – one among many that might be chosen and might be returned. David had asked Dr. R for trading cards for Christmas; as their last session before the holiday neared, he asked what she was giving him for Christmas. She replied that she planned on giving him the cards that he had asked for. David responded with his usual angry tirade: she should give him more than he asked for because she had so much and could give him so much more than she did. Dr. R gently reminded David that when she gave him something it felt good at first, but then it felt bad because anything he got seemed so little in comparison to what he needed.

When David did get the requested gift, two 60-card packages of trading cards, predictably his initial pleasure faded into an angry feeling of deprivation. However, for the first time David was able to allow Dr. R's words to help him with these overpowering feelings. Before he left for the holiday, he told her not to worry, that he wasn't mad anymore.

David's explanation that he had thought that there were only 17 cards in the packages made Dr. R acutely aware of the power of David's feeling of emptiness and the pervasive and insidious consequences of early deprivation. Her gift not only left him longing for more, but rendered him unable to think. He knew that she had given him "what he had asked for," but the actual gift diminished before his very eyes. The gift served as a reminder that Dr. R could not give him the family he really wanted. As the pack of cards shrank from 60 to 17, the fantasy of having her for a mother collapsed along with it.

In this context I think we can understand David's anger as stemming not only from an intense and complicated sense of deprivation, but also from a fear of accepting Dr. R's affective attunement (Stolorow, 1999). To accept her treats and gifts without protest might allow her to assume that they were enough – that his needs could easily be satisfied. He insists that she recognize the vast difference between them – she is someone who has so much that she can give freely, while he is someone with so little that he cannot freely take.

David's demands that Dr. R know him in all of his emptiness and greediness kept the issue of his foster status in the forefront of their work. He talked about how terribly much he wanted a family. It was impossible for them to believe or behave as if he were a "regular" kid.

Internal vs. external

Perhaps Mary Douglas is correct in her statement that clinicians "are institutionally incapable of remembering that humans are social beings. As soon as they know it, they forget it" (1986, p. 81). Our interest in and adeptness with the world of intrapsychic processes and interpersonal relationships often offers us a haven from our confrontations with lost souls and battered bodies. Sometimes, as with Bromberg's (1998) musings on his daily encounter with the homeless man who unwittingly, but annoyingly, intrudes on his morning coffee, these retreats from external realities to internal dynamics help us in our working or thinking. However, like these musings they also allow us to turn away from the social and the political and to put aside questions of how our greediness may allow us to participate in, passively accept, or even promote programs and policies that both economically and emotionally insure that the rich will get richer while the poor get poorer (Singer, 1993).

When working with foster children I think that we would very much like to forget that they are social beings. We would like to luxuriate in the opportunity to explore only their intrapsychic processes and the dynamics of our interpersonal relationships. We don't like being reminded of the desperate living conditions in which these children began their lives or the dehumanizing effects of poverty on families (Sidel, 1999). On a regular basis these children remind us that the daily existence of the inner city poor is so marginal, so fragile, that families easily crumble under the multiple stresses of poverty, inadequate education, deplorable housing, low wages, and so forth (Newman, 1999).

Once children have tumbled into the morass of the foster care system it may be virtually impossible for their parents to retrieve them. Clearly, many of these children should, under no circumstances, be returned to the people who brought them into the world. However, achieving the conditions for having a child returned may simply be impossible for some poor families. For example, the family income may not be sufficient to allow parents to move into housing that meets the regulations of the foster care agency. Regulations change, as do social workers, attorneys, and foster parents.

The sense of helplessness and lack of professional or personal agency are among the ongoing, maddening challenges of working with foster children. Unlike those whose daily lives are intruded upon and organized by social service agencies, therapists in private practice are used to working with a fair degree of autonomy. All of this changes when treating a foster child. Important decisions about the child's psychotherapy may be made without consultation with the therapist: the child may be moved to a new foster home without warning: a new social worker may, for better or for worse, completely disregard the previous social worker's plan.

Change and instability are too often the hallmarks of the early lives of foster children, leaving them confused, uncertain, unable to trust easily or think clearly. This can, and often does, instill a sense of helpless desperation in both child and therapist as they struggle to manage the enormity of the child's cravings for a family, while they try together to build, in one or possibly two hours a week, the sense of continuity and strength that families provide for children.

Jimmy

Sometimes we come to know the emotional hunger these children must bear by first knowing their physical hunger. Dr. M described the almost unbearable hunger he felt when he met Jimmy in the waiting room. Typically, Jimmy was just finishing the french fries he had brought from a fast food restaurant. Since this was not a food he would regularly eat, he was curious about how much he really wanted some of those french fries. Of course, his response in part was physiological – he saw Jimmy in the late afternoon when he was beginning to fade and was somewhat hungry himself. However, having a snack before the session had little effect – he still wanted some of those fries.

Eventually, in supervision we understood that what he craved was the feeling of satiation and pleasure that this simple treat seemed to offer this young boy. When Dr. M greeted Jimmy he was usually just finishing his food. Jimmy frequently held out the empty container to indicate that there was none left for Dr. M. Every week Dr. M was confronted with the promise of something he couldn't have. It seemed almost overwhelming.

Jimmy was a foster child. Each week on the way from his foster home to his therapy appointment, his transportation worker treated him to a hamburger and french fries. It was one of the highlights of this child's week. Jimmy's pleasure was great – too great for such a small treat.

The therapist's pain stemmed in large part from his confrontation with the paradox that Jimmy seemed satisfied with so little when he needed so much. His weekly snack satisfied a need – it not only calmed his physical hunger but also offered him a connection to someone special and a ritual that defined the relationship.

What the transportation worker had to offer seemed so direct and immediate and satisfying compared to what Dr. M felt he could offer this little boy. (He later learned that the transportation worker had instigated the restaurant stops as a means of keeping Jimmy quiet during the drive to the office and bribed him with candy on the return trip.) Dr. M's craving for the french fries represented an identification with Jimmy's yearnings and concretized their mutual wish for a magical, simple resolution for Jimmy's difficulties.

Like so many other children in his situation, Jimmy was an empty and terrified child who hid his fears and hurt behind an angry, belligerent stance. The quiet satisfaction offered by the french fries rarely lasted more than a few minutes into the therapy session. With his therapist, as with others who tried to reach him, Jimmy was difficult and demanding. His pattern of avoidant attachments made it hard for adults to warm to him. He found Dr. M and his toys and games wanting and consistently demeaned any attempts to put words to his feelings or behavior. In response, Dr. M, as others working with children with avoidant attachment patterns, felt himself wanting to withdraw rather than face the continual complaints and rejections Jimmy handed out so freely.

However, week after week he returned. Despite his expressed dissatisfaction with Dr. M and what he had to offer, he was always reluctant to leave the sessions, typically complaining that he never got to do what he really wanted. Sustaining his commitment to Jimmy and the therapy was extremely difficult for Dr. M in the face of Jimmy's relentless demands and complaints. He understood that in simply returning, Jimmy was telling him how much he cared about therapy and Dr. M. He also understood the truth of Jimmy's complaint that he never got to do what he really wanted.

Jimmy clearly needed psychotherapy, but he needed a family even more. Both Dr. M and Jimmy clearly understood this, but for a long time, it was painfully unspeakable. Like so many young therapists in this situation, Dr. M felt under enormous pressure to "cure" his young patient so that he might, at the very least, avoid a move to yet another foster home and, at best, be adopted into a stable, loving family. However, Dr. M continually struggled with his feelings that psychotherapy was a paltry substitute for the family that Jimmy really needed – it was like the french fries that tantalized rather than satisfied. Dr. M felt as if he owed Jimmy "a home cooked meal" – he felt that since he could adopt him, he should adopt him. He sensed that this was Jimmy's primary, unspoken message to him.

This complementary transference/countertransference entanglement is not unfamiliar. We can be swayed, even if temporarily, by our patients' convictions that psychotherapy or analysis is a poor substitute for a "real" relationship, or that our insistence on the importance of thoughtful consideration merely delays necessary action or that what we have to offer isn't enough or is actually counterproductive. Of course, sometimes these assertions are correct and, with luck, we have the opportunity to explore with our patients the shortcomings and inevitable disappointments of a therapeutic relationship and/or to help them find resources that will better meet their needs.

However, I believe that this paradigm has particular significance when we couple a foster child with a young and inexperienced therapist. Since this pairing is a frequent occurrence both in clinics and the private sector, we must give careful attention to the central place of the particular transference/countertransference feelings engendered by the child's deep and primitive longing for a family. I believe these therapeutic couples frequently have an unspoken, often unconscious conversation that goes something like: "If you really cared about me you would take me home." "If I really cared about you I would take you home." The power of this paradigm arises from the convergence of a number of factors that often typify these particular therapeutic relationships.

First is the actual availability of the parentless child and the likelihood that the therapist, both chronologically and developmentally, is of an age to be beginning a family. The parental vacuum can be particularly overpowering for a therapist who doesn't yet feel professionally tethered by either experience or skill (Jackson & Strickler, 1989). While she may feel herself ignorant in the professional world of psychodynamics, interpretations, and enactments in the world of families she, of course, has many years of experience. The tendency to romanticize the child in need of a parent intensifies the pull on the therapist to rescue the child through the creation of a family for him (Heineman, 1999; Esman, 1987; Frankiel, 1985).

Therapist and child can easily collude in a shared unconscious fantasy that a family not only will cure the child but that *only* a family will cure the child. This shared unconscious fantasy also joins them in demeaning and devaluing the curative power of language, symbolic thought, and relationships that are caring, even though caretaking. More insidiously, it joins them in an unspoken belief that the child can be helped only by concrete ministrations – that he is somehow not capable of making use of what the therapist actually has to offer.

The therapist may find direct or indirect support or even feel pressured toward concrete solutions from the agency or individuals responsible for the child. Those in legal charge of a foster child, usually a social worker and/or an attorney appointed to protect the child's interests and rights, are understandably eager for simple and swift resolutions to the child's difficulties. In addition to their wish to see the child's suffering alleviated or ended, the emotional problems of foster children typically make the lives of their social workers harder. It is easier to find or maintain a family for a happy and well-behaved child than one who is depressed, overly anxious, or unable to control her impulses. In some instances the therapist may experience intense pressure, internally and externally generated, both to "cure" the child and to stand in for the child's family.

The fantasy of providing a home, whether temporary or permanent, pertains almost exclusively to therapeutic work with foster children. Certainly the reality that these children are in need of a stable family offers a backdrop to support these fantasies. However, in this, as in other situations, reality provides an insufficient explanation for the power and persistence of the fantasies. As I mentioned earlier, young and inexperienced therapists may be particularly vulnerable to these fantasies of rescue, which are often described as insistent and compelling. The subjective experience is of a need to act to save the child *because there is no alternative,* i.e. the therapist's experience is often not of being better than the alternatives, but as being the only alternative (Birch, 2000).

The emotional economics of foster care

I believe we might benefit from considering this psychological phenomenon in light of Dalton Conley's (1999) *Being Black, Living in the Red: Race, Wealth, and Social Policy in America.* Conley argues compellingly that the disparity in financial assets or accumulated wealth, as opposed to income alone, plays a prominent role in the persistent social and educational inequalities between white and black Americans. He vividly illustrates how even limited assets can protect families in times of financial crisis – when income is compromised or fails. Psychologically, the status of foster children parallels that of the family with no or very limited assets: neither has money in the bank. In the same way that having equity in a home or money in a savings account can keep a family together during hard times, having a family can keep a child together during hard times.

In good times, families build up emotional reserves. The normal give-and-take of family life, the daily routines, the shared experiences, the mutual love and caring, and the normal breaks and reparations of relationships all strengthen the family bonds. If these bonds are strong enough they will sustain the family and its members during times of psychological crisis. During an emotional crisis precipitated, for example, by a death in the family, an extended physical or emotional illness, a move, the loss of a job, or increased work pressures on one or both parents, families draw on these emotional reserves. It's the money in their emotional bank.

Foster children come into the system because their family's limited emotional reserves were depleted. Whatever the precipitating event – abuse, abandonment, imprisonment of a parent, neglect, etc. – children lose their family when the family no longer has the emotional resources to sustain them.

Without a family the child has no emotional assets, nothing to renew and replenish the psychological resources that are necessary for just getting through a day. Having a foster family is *not* like having your own family – it's analogous to an income stream – not money in the bank. Like sources of monetary income, some are better and more reliable than others, and like those sources of income, they can dry up. Foster parents can and do ask to have children removed: social workers come and go and decide that children should be moved into different "placements"; the rules that governed a child's placement with a family may change into a regulation that demands his removal.

When he turns 18 the income, both financial and emotional, reaches an even more intensely uncertain pitch. He must now generate his own income and/or rely on the meager reserves he may have been able to accumulate during a childhood that rarely provided enough to bank.

With no parents and no extended family able or willing to care for him, a child simultaneously has no place to go and can go anywhere. The chances often seem overwhelmingly great that he, like the family with few financial assets, will "fall between the cracks" and just disappear. In part, it is the recognition of this emptiness, the bareness of the foster child's emotional cupboard that generates the sense of an imperative – not a request or a desire – but a demand that the therapist move from professional to parent.

The fantasies of creating a family for a foster child also gain power from our recognition that they know something most of us who work with them do not know, and never will, and never want to know. They know what it feels like to be without a family, and no matter how quickly or successfully we replace the family they have lost, they will always know how it feels to be a child utterly alone in the world.

In *The Poisonwood Bible*, Barbara Kingsolver writes: "Hunger of the body is altogether different from the shallow, daily hunger of the belly. Those who have known this kind of hunger cannot entirely love, ever again, those who have not" (1999, p. 345). Perhaps the fantasies of rescue, of providing the enveloping, everpresent love of a family for these children also grow from the dim awareness that because of their experience of loss and their awareness of a depth of despair and hunger that most of us have never known, that they cannot ever entirely love us.

Conclusion

If we now return to Dr. M and Jimmy, perhaps we can better understand the tension between them. No matter how strong the hunger pangs Dr. M experienced in response to the tantalizing aroma of Jimmy's food, they were "of the belly" and bearable. Jimmy's hunger for a family lingered in the depth of his being: it was "of the body." Jimmy's teasing Dr. M with disappearing food parallels his sense of being teased with relationships that disappear as quickly as they materialize.

Dr. R understood that David's request for a home-baked cookie came from a "hunger of the body" that she could never satisfy. But she also realized that she could help him know and bear these feelings by her recognition and tolerance of their shared knowledge that possibly he could not fully love or trust her because she had never known a hunger that plumbs the depth of the soul.

Section IV

TREATMENT IN THE CONTEXT OF SCARCITY AND LOSS

Therapists treating children and adolescents understand the importance of developing a working alliance with their clients' parents. But what if there are no parents available? What if there is no single person to whom the therapist can go to learn about the child's history? What if that history only exists in fragments, held in the minds of multiple people? Finding the "right" person to talk to about a foster child can be a daunting task, especially if, as is often the case, the adults surrounding the child have wildly divergent ideas about what plan is in the child's best interests and equally different interpretations of the legal mandates governing his or her care.

When treating foster children, it doesn't take long to learn how hard it is to replace a parent and what happens to children when the people in their lives are there to fulfill discreet and well or less well-defined functions. Take for example, the process of bringing a foster child and therapist together. Suppose the foster mother feels that the child could benefit from therapy. She does not have the authority to authorize treatment. That is the job of the caseworker, and if the worker agrees, the process may be a straightforward administrative process. However, it may require a "needs assessment" by a mental health specialist or team, either within the department or in an agency contracted to offer these services. More often than not, there will be a waiting period before the evaluation can be undertaken and/or completed. If the evaluator agrees that the child would benefit from therapy, the task of finding an appropriate setting or therapist usually falls to the caseworker, who may have to make multiple phone calls just to get the child on a waiting list. If, as happens, one or the other of the child's biological parents is working toward reunification and, through counsel, protests the need for treatment, the question might have to be resolved by court order, necessitating the involvement of a judicial officer.

With court order in place and an opening at a clinic a reasonable distance from the foster parent's home, it would seem that treatment could begin. However, it may be that the foster mother has multiple foster children and cannot realistically provide transportation to and from the sessions. This may require that the caseworker contact the unit responsible for transportation, which may well include one or more people who do the scheduling and others who actually do the driving. If the child is assigned someone to drive her to her therapy appointment, it is possible that she will be picked up and transported by a stranger to meet another stranger in a place that she has never been before. And the therapist will be greeting someone who has known the child only as long as it has taken to drive from home to office.

Of course, this addresses just the logistics, not the meaning of having so many people participating in a process that under other circumstances might be as simple as a parent making a phone call to get the names of possible therapists, calling a clinician to schedule an appointment, meeting with that person to describe the child and the particular concerns, and then taking the child to the appointment and introducing her to someone the parent has already met.

To state the obvious, parents have multiple roles and serve many functions, but their central place in their children's lives is in the steady, ongoing caring relationship they provide. This is different for foster children, who have multiple people in their lives, each of whom is there for a particular reason and to serve distinct functions. Unfortunately, if people are seen as "functionaries," then it is relatively easy to draw the conclusion that they can be exchanged or replaced as long as the duties for which they are responsible are fulfilled. This is evident in "Infant–parent psychotherapy minus one," a painful examination of the treatment of a young child in foster care. "Disrupted moods and disrupted care" illuminates the dangerous consequences for foster children who do not have an adult who knows their history and can advocate for them. The last chapter in this section explores in depth the experience of a child whose grief is helped by family and friends, after briefly examining that of a child who ended up in foster care following his father's death. "Beginning to say goodbye: the deaths of three fathers," reminds us of the protection that families offer children, especially in the most difficult of times.

8

DISRUPTED CARE AND DISRUPTIVE MOODS

Pediatric bipolar disorder in foster care children

There is broad consensus within the mental health community that bipolar disorder (BD) is a serious, genetically influenced mental illness with well-defined diagnostic criteria for older adolescents and adults.

When left untreated, adult-onset bipolar disorder can devastate the lives of afflicted individuals and their families. The depressive episodes that are characteristic of BD carry a high risk of suicide, and the grandiosity and loss of reality testing that accompanies full-blown manic states can lead to dangerous behavior that threatens lives and livelihoods.

By contrast, confusion and disagreements abound among mental health professionals, pediatricians, and parents about when or even whether to diagnose troubled or troubling children with bipolar disorder. Until recently, childhood-onset bipolar disorder was considered rare. Also the diagnostic criteria currently in use for pediatric BD differ so significantly from those used for adult BD that it is not at all clear that the majority of children so labeled are suffering from the same illness as their adult counterparts. Although adults diagnosed with BD typically experience distinct episodes of depression and mania of at least mania of at least one week in duration, the emotional shifts that have become identified with pediatric BD can include moods that shift within the span of minutes rather than weeks. Some researchers and practitioners would argue that rapid-cycling BD in children is consistent with children's generally greater susceptibility to fluctuations in mood. However, broad diagnostic criteria run the risk of labeling with BD those children who are healthy but emotionally intense, as well as those whose emotional development has been derailed through chronic neglect or abuse.

Emotional development and quality of care

Emotions are not simple instincts that emerge full blown at birth. Children do not enter the world with a mature capacity to experience, express, recognize, and regulate their feelings. Rather, emotional development unfolds over time and depends on the quality and stability of relationships with parents and other caregivers. Therefore, even mentally healthy children are more reactive to their bodily states, thoughts, and experiences than adults; and they are less able to understand what causes them to feel the way they do or, at times, to even recognize and name the emotions that they're experiencing. For example, an adult can understand that working long hours for several days to meet an important deadline is the cause of her simultaneous feelings of exhaustion, euphoria, relief, and hyperarousal, whereas a 10 or 12-year-old who has worked intensively to complete a school project may not easily recognize that her unsettled, distractible, excited, and tired feelings are to be expected under the circumstances.

When assessing a child's emotional well-being, it is of critical importance to be knowledgeable about what is expectable and acceptable at a particular stage of development. Parents' appropriate and predictable responses to their children's moods, behavior, and body language build and strengthen the neurological foundation for self-regulation and emotional maturity.

For example, most parents learn to recognize and respond swiftly to the cry that signals their baby's hunger. Intuitively a parent may also name the unsettling feeling and its solution: "Oh, you are so hungry. There, there. Let's get the bottle to fill up your hungry tummy." Over time, the child learns to identify this physical sensation – a particular uncomfortable feeling in the belly – as hunger and to know that the discomfort can be relieved with food. If we fast-forward 15 years into the future, we can imagine this child, now a teenager, striding into the kitchen and announcing to his mother, "I'm starving. How long until dinner? What's to eat – right now?"

But what if his mother was depressed and too self-absorbed to learn to discriminate among his different cries so that she sometimes responded to a hunger cry with a bottle, at other times with a diaper change, and at other times not at all. Perhaps her words and tone of voice mislabeled both the problem and its solution: "You are so demanding. You just need to cry it out and learn to leave me alone."

Over time, her child will become increasingly oblivious to or confused by his feelings. Without the attention of an attuned caregiver, children continue to have the global physiological responses of early infancy rather than the nuanced states that gradually develop over the course of childhood and adolescence. Under these circumstances children do not actually experience more discrete feeling states, let alone learn how to name them. Without the experience of a range of feeling states, a child has no reliable way of signaling his needs and has even less sense of the kinds of responses that might diminish his distress and increase his pleasure. Under these circumstances we can imagine him as an adolescent who barges into the kitchen, unhappy and uncomfortable, but unaware that he is hungry. He might reject an offer of food with, "It's not that easy. Leave me alone. I'll take care of myself."

Relationships beget relationships, and children who have been mistreated are prone to mistreating others. A child or teenager who has been subjected to years of neglect or abuse is likely to have a limited capacity for empathy because she has not learned to differentiate, identify, or name her own or other people's feelings. If she has developed an avoidant attachment style, she may also disregard or vigorously reject offers of help or support when she feels unhappy or uncomfortable. From the perspective of a child whose early needs were routinely ignored, misinterpreted, or discounted, it makes no sense to take later offers of help seriously. Gestures of care can also threaten her sense of emotional safety. A child who has had to learn self-reliance at a tender age does not easily risk making herself vulnerable by placing her trust in yet another person, who might once again break her heart. Instead she may appear needy and dependent one moment and then reject an offer of comfort with an attitude of fierce independence the next. This kind of seeming emotional lability in children with a history of trauma is likely to reflect both a developmental deficit arising from impoverished experience, a defensive strategy to cope with that deficit and a pattern of attachment characterized by ambivalence.

Assessing emotionally disturbed children

As illustrated above, bipolar disorder is only one of many potential causes for emotional turbulence in childhood and adolescence, one that locates the difficulty in the child's genetic makeup. As debate about when to diagnose pediatric bipolar disorder and how to treat it continues, mental health professionals would be hard-pressed to disagree with the following bedrock guidelines:

1   Accurate diagnosis requires a detailed assessment that takes into account the factors and to determine whether there is any familial genetic loading for mood disorders.
2   After a diagnosis is rendered, treatment must be carefully planned and individually tailored, and the child must be closely monitored and have access to continuity of care.

With few exceptions however, research and clinical reports on children diagnosed with bipolar disorder do not take environmental influences such as quality and stability of parenting into account. For children in the foster care system (Biederman et. al., 2013; Keenan-Miller & Miklowitz, 2011; Pavuluri et al., 2006; Rucklidge, 2006; Schenkel et al., 2008), information that might lead to a different diagnosis – reactive attachment disorder or complex post-traumatic stress disorder, for example – is simply not available.

Vulnerable children, such as those who live in poverty, have been subjected to familial or community violence, or have endured multiple losses in the foster care system, are at even greater risk for receiving a psychiatric label, unfortunately often after a cursory assessment and a hastily conceived plan of treatment with little opportunity for continuity of care.

The rise of pediatric bipolar disorder among children in foster care

I have worked with children in the foster care system for nearly 30 years. At the beginning of my career, medicating children with the few psychoactive drugs available was done with great caution. In the intervening years, the armamentarium of medications available to increase attention, stabilize moods, quiet hallucinations, induce sleep, ease depression, and calm anxiety has swelled almost beyond belief. Coincidentally, during the same time period the rolls of the foster care system also swelled and are just now beginning to drop as the children who came into care as a result of the crack epidemic are reaching adulthood and leaving the system. For foster children the diagnosis of bipolar disorder is particularly problematic – for many it connotes "craziness" in a way that anxiety or depression do not. Foster youth can more easily relate to the idea that they are depressed because they have lost their family or friends or community, or are anxious because they don't know where they might live next week.

"Anxious" and "depressed" are used in the general population to describe a wide range of moods. However, "bipolar disorder" is purely a psychiatric diagnosis that locates the problem in the child, rather than taking into account the possibility that periods of intense anxiety juxtaposed with periods of intense depression might also be a response to an unpredictable and bleak environment. The young adults now leaving the foster care system are more likely to suffer psychiatric disturbance, including mood disorders, than their peers. Perhaps they entered the system with a genetic loading from parents who are unavailable to provide a history. They have also been exposed to more trauma than their peers. In those instances when we have at least cursory information about a traumatic history and no information about family history, we must not favor a genetic basis of behavior over environmental influences when most likely a complex set of interactions between nature and nurture is at work.

Children enter foster care from a position of vulnerability. Many of them are born to low-income mothers who have had little or no prenatal care. Many have been exposed to significant amounts of alcohol and illicit drugs in utero. Some go directly from the hospital's newborn nursery to a foster home. Others live for several weeks, months, or years with parents and extended family members who, because of poverty, mental illness, addiction, incarceration, or a background of abuse and neglect, are ill prepared to raise children, particularly those who enter the world with a compromised neurological system.

Children who enter foster care when they are older have frequently suffered from neglect. Some have been physically or sexually abused, many have witnessed domestic violence, and many more have been exposed to community violence. Simply put, stability and predictability in the form of loving and reliable care has been notably lacking in the lives of children entering foster care whether they enter as infants, toddlers, children, or adolescents.

As a result it is frequently the case that their emotional development has been stunted and they have a limited ability to recognize or regulate their emotions. Instead they remain reliant on others to recognize that hunger requires food, that agitation requires calming, that sadness requires soothing, or that fear requires confident protection. Indeed they often have difficulty distinguishing between their internal and external worlds. With limited capacity for self-soothing, they are neurologically primed for heightened responsiveness.

When we place a child who is emotionally unstable and unpredictable into a system that is itself unstable and unpredictable, it is hardly surprising that it is

DISRUPTED CARE AND DISRUPTIVE MOODS

difficult to know, from one minute to the next, how the child may feel or behave. And so it is not unusual for foster children to display both more intense moods and more frequent and rapid shifts in mood and behavior than we would expect from children of similar ages and developmental stages. In a climate in which bipolar disorder is readily diagnosed we can see how easily foster children might be suspected of having this disorder, and how important it is to first rule out other ways of understanding their chaotic emotions.

Angie: A case study

"Angie," a young teenager in foster care, was diagnosed with bipolar disorder. Her brush with the mental health system illustrates how difficult it is for children in foster care to receive an assessment and follow-up care that meet even the minimal standards described earlier. Angie's story may invoke intense feelings – sadness and despair along with annoyance and rage – feelings that we associate with pediatric bipolar disorder and also with a sense of overwhelming helplessness in the face of unbearable circumstances.

Angie, a 15-year-old living in a group home, was taken to a hospital emergency room because she had been crying uncontrollably for ten days. She had been spending most of each day in bed and showed little interest in activities, school, or meals. At times she was unresponsive, seeming not to see or hear when people tried to communicate with her. During the intake interview at the hospital, Angie rocked in her chair with her arms wrapped tightly over her chest. Occasionally her sobs and swaying were interrupted with quiet moans as her hands pulled at her hair. She could barely answer the interviewer's questions and seemed not to understand or be able to explain her unhappiness. After a cursory interview the emergency room psychiatrist gave her a diagnosis of major depression, prescribed an antidepressant, and recommended that Angie return to the outpatient psychiatry clinic for follow-up care. This diagnosis was now part of Angie's medical and social service record.

The piece of the story that did not make it into the hospital record was the fact that Angie's boyfriend, also a foster child, had been suddenly moved to a group home out of the area when his foster mother had become ill and unable to care for him. He and Angie were too young to drive, and there was no reliable public transportation to connect their two communities. This unexpected loss was predictably heart wrenching for Angie, who was fully in the sway of her first love. They had not even had a chance to say good-bye to each other.

Angie had been in her current group home for a very short time when this abrupt separation occurred, and to make matters worse the only staff member whom she had felt close to had recently left.

Angie was bereft; the only two people in the world to whom she felt connected were gone. There was no one to comfort her, to help her think creatively about how she might reconnect with her boyfriend or to advocate for her being able to see him. Angie could only hold and rock herself like the infant she felt herself to be.

She became inarticulate, unable to express her overwhelming grief in words; and no one was available to hear her words, even if she could have found them. In her regressed state, her only forms of communication were moans and sobs. She had no reliable caregiver to help her name her feelings and connect them with the events that had devastated and depleted her emotional resources. Angie desperately needed someone who could not only offer physical comfort in the moment, but also help her to interpret and cope with her feelings so they would not overwhelm her. She needed someone who could hold out hope of a brighter future for her – someone who could know that her emotions, overwhelming as they were, would gradually dissipate and become manageable so that she could reclaim the emotional resources she needed to function.

Lacking the care she desperately needed at this crucial time, the stage was set for an emotional breakdown. Angie began to emerge from her depression after about two weeks, and she did so with a vengeance. She angrily refused her boyfriend's phone calls, insisting that she hadn't really cared about him and didn't miss him at all. In like fashion, Angie rebuffed the efforts of staff in the group home to re-engage her in activities she had previously seemed to enjoy. Instead she filled her time by frantically and compulsively text-messaging everyone on her contact list. Her school performance declined as a result of frequent absences that, more often than not, involved sexual encounters with boys older and rougher than she had formerly associated with. When she did attend school, her teachers noted that she was disheveled and seemed to be particularly distracted and disorganized.

The staff at the group home became increasingly irritated with Angie, and she with them. It seemed that whenever there was a verbal or physical altercation in the home, Angie was at its center. After two weeks the owner of the home, who had a reputation for "running a very tight ship," initiated Angie's removal. Angie's behavior in the next group home continued to escalate, and after two weeks she was placed in a short-term residential treatment facility. Based on the earlier diagnosis of a major depressive episode and on her recent behavior, Angie's admitting diagnosis was early-onset bipolar disorder.

Experts agree that a diagnosis of bipolar disorder cannot be made definitively without a thorough assessment. But conducting an adequate assessment hinges on a series of unarticulated assumptions that (1) the child will be consistently available to participate; (2) qualified mental health specialists will conduct the assessment; (3) the evaluator will have access to adults who know the child; and (4) there will be sufficient funds available to pay for the assessment. These assumptions ignore the reality that, more often than not, hospitals, clinics, and individuals working with foster youth face insurmountable challenges in finding the time, money, and information necessary for a careful and thorough assessment. Although government funding may be available, the rate of reimbursement is typically so low that clinicians in private practice often refuse to see foster children or strictly limit the number of hours they make available to them. As a result, the pool of experienced child psychiatrists and psychologists available to this population in the private sector is very small. Foster youth referred to a hospital or clinic for evaluation and treatment sometimes have access to more resources. However, as we will see, other factors frequently interfere.

Angie's placement in a residential treatment setting took her to a community more than one hundred miles from the city of her birth and childhood. Because of her changed status, she was assigned a new caseworker. The transfer of her most recent file from her former caseworker to her new one took nearly a week. The transfer of those records to the residential treatment center took another week; and retrieving two other folders, which contained the remainder of her records from storage, consumed an additional two weeks. By the time those records arrived, Angie had been discharged. The staff had diagnosed and treated her without having any significant information about her history. Angie was able to give them some information, but her willingness to engage with the staff varied significantly, as did her moods. She was sometimes depressed and tearful and sometimes angry, sullen, or stubbornly silent. The information she did offer was sketchy and sometimes confused, but reality based.

When the file finally arrived at the treatment center, it confirmed Angie's report that she had been in foster care since the age of five. Prior to that, she had lived for some period – possibly a year or two – with maternal relatives. She had apparently moved from household to household, depending on which relative had the space, time, and energy to care for a small child.

The recorded information about her early life was limited. Her parents had grown up in the same neighborhood. Shortly after Angle's birth her father was killed in a gang-related drive-by shooting, although it is not clear whether he was the shooter's target or an uninvolved bystander. Angie presumably had little or no contact with her paternal relatives.

Her mother was 16 when Angie was born, and was in and out of Angie's life for the first few years. By the time Angie entered foster care, her relatives did not even know how to reach the mother. They believed she supported herself largely through prostitution, and reported that she would show up periodically, wanting to see Angie and demanding money. Angie's maternal grandmother suspected that Angie had witnessed her mother engaging in sex on many occasions.

Angie began her tenure in the foster care system as a sad, quiet little girl. During her first six months, she was in two different emergency placements followed by three years in a long-term foster placement with an elderly woman who typically cared for four or five foster children at any time. When her foster mother died, Angie became even more quiet and withdrawn. Members of the extended family of her foster care mother expressed interest in adopting Angie, and at the very least wished to stay in touch with her. For reasons not made clear in the file, the adoption didn't materialize. With the move to a new foster home she lost her friends in her old neighborhood. Her grades in her new school declined, and she was described as a child who was distant, kept to herself, and didn't make friends easily.

Over the next four years Angie was in three more foster homes. One foster mother moved to another state in order to be with her children. Another asked that Angie and her other charges be sent to respite care for two weeks during her vacation, but if the woman did return from her travels, she didn't notify anyone. The respite-care family did not want to become long-term foster parents, necessitating Angie's move to yet another home. While she was in that home, another foster child accused the foster parents' biological son of molesting her, and all of the children were removed. Angie, who was then 12, was moved to the first of two group homes and from there to residential treatment.

Angie was discharged from the residential treatment center before an evaluation was completed because she was not considered a danger to herself or others and she exhibited no psychotic ideation. Her caseworker felt that her treatment could be adequately continued at an outpatient clinic in her own community. Angie returned "home" but went into a different group home placement. The diagnosis that had begun as major depression, based on her visit to the emergency room, and then transformed into bipolar disorder on the basis of descriptions of her behavior by staff members who barely knew her, was now "official," not as the result of a careful and thorough assessment, but because, very simply, it just got passed along. Unfortunately, Angie's story is all too familiar in the foster care system. There are simply not enough people with enough time, information, or funding to adequately assess and properly treat these vulnerable young people.

Based on the limited information about her mother's lifestyle, it is possible that she exposed Angie to street drugs in utero, potentially compromising her neurological development and making her vulnerable to psychiatric disturbance. Angie's primary responses to losses in her early life were depression and withdrawal, and her depressed, angry reactions to her boyfriend's departure were intense. Perhaps her response was indicative of a genetic loading for mood disorders, but without access to her family history, this supposition remains speculative. However, we do know that the chaotic and disrupted care that Angie received throughout her childhood posed significant risks to her emotional development, so that Angie's responses to her circumstances may have been simply those of a child who has lost too many loved ones without the support to manage the attendant feelings.

Young love is particularly intense – whether the love of a baby or toddler for her parent, or the first romantic love of early adolescence. The sudden and unexpected loss of her first boyfriend may have triggered in Angie memories and repressed feelings of grief and loss from her earliest years. If Angie had had a loving parent or caregiver to support her and to know, when she couldn't, that the pain of her loss would diminish, she might gradually have been able to cope with the rush of confusing emotions she was experiencing. If someone – anyone – had understood how important this relationship was and had helped Angie find and contact her lost love, things might have been different for her.

If the emergency room psychiatrist had known about Angie's loss, would the diagnosis have been different? Psychiatrists receive much more training in the diagnosis and management of biochemically based mental illnesses than in understanding suffering that stems from the losses, disappointments, setbacks, and disillusionments of life. Compounding the tendency to diagnose what can be medically treated is the reality that funding for treatment hinges on a medical diagnosis.

Paradoxically, clinicians sometimes give foster children a diagnosis that may not be entirely accurate – such as depression, obsessive-compulsive disorder, or bipolar disorder – in the belief that the diagnosis will ensure treatment. Although this may be true, the treatment that follows an incorrect diagnosis often does more harm than good.

Foster children commonly report that they were either given medication when they just wanted to talk to someone, or were denied mental health services because their problems weren't "bad enough." Of course, some of these children do benefit from a medical intervention and their descriptions of their encounters with mental health professionals are subject to distortion, but these negative reports occur with such frequency that we cannot reasonably ignore them.

If we now revisit the minimal criteria for accurately diagnosis and treating early-onset bipolar disorder – a careful and extensive evaluation that establishes a genetic predisposition and a clear and well-coordinated treatment plan – we see that Angie's experience falls significantly short. Although the staff at the residential treatment center had consistent contact with Angie for two weeks prior to her diagnosis, they had no history – no baseline against which to view her moods and behavior. The information in her file, when it finally arrived, provided a patchwork history because it had been compiled by a series of caseworkers based on very limited personal contact with Angie, her biological relatives, and a series of foster parents.

A typical emergency room visit does not allow any clinician, regardless of training or experience, sufficient time to make a definitive psychiatric diagnosis. This is particularly true for a diagnosis of bipolar disorder, which requires a knowledge of family history. Arriving at an accurate diagnosis is all the more challenging when the person in distress is a young, virtually speechless adolescent like Angie. The reports of group home staff members provided the basis for the next stage of the diagnostic process – depression was transformed into manic depression. When Angie moved from residential treatment to yet another group home, there was no treatment plan, only a supply of medication.

And so we see the inordinate difficulties in trying to construct, coordinate, and monitor a treatment plan for children in the foster care system. It is entirely unclear who in this cast of characters should have had responsibility for formulating a plan for Angie's treatment, which adults would be involved in its execution, and who would monitor its effectiveness. Although there were many adults in Angie's life, none of them knew her – who she was or where she came from. There was no one to keep Angie in mind – to hold for her a past and a future so that she could live in the present. The loss of a coherent narrative – a cohesive picture of one's life – is perhaps the most enormous and insidious loss for foster children.

Bipolar disorder is an illness that causes great suffering; we trivialize the experiences of those who struggle to overcome its terrible power by carelessly confusing it with other disorders. As we move forward in our efforts to describe, define, and accurately diagnose early-onset BD, it is imperative that we strive to conduct a thorough assessment for each child with a detailed personal history and description of current conditions, in addition to gathering information about genetic and behavioral history.

Alumni of the foster care system are diagnosed with a wide range of mental illnesses including bipolar disorder at a significantly higher rate than their peers. And so we must pay particular attention to this vulnerable group of children, adolescents, and young adults and must develop better resources for early detection and accurate diagnosis. At the same time, we must carefully consider the possibility that in many instances, it is the system, rather than the child, that is the carrier of the disorder. Foster children often grow up with no sense of their own history in a system that frequently fails to provide them consistent access to responsible caregivers. Children simply cannot develop the capacity for emotional stability in an unstable system. We must not further traumatize children who grow up in foster care by callously ignoring the impact of the external world on their internal lives.

Angie shows us how a child can get caught in a system of care with more disruptions than continuities. In the next chapter I introduce you to Christina to illustrate the ways in which a child and her therapist can become enmeshed in that system and that it is not always possible to "keep your head when all about you are losing theirs." This chapter grew from a request by a colleague to "write about the case that broke your heart." Christina did that and at times our work together also made me lose my mind.

9

INFANT–PARENT PSYCHOTHERAPY MINUS ONE

Infant–parent psychotherapy is based on the assumption that young children in emotional distress come to us in the company of a parent. Often we undertake the process of intervening in the infant–parent relationship when the parent either cannot hold the child in mind or holds a distorted picture of the child that, in large or small measure, threatens to interfere with the child's development of a cohesive sense of self. It is difficult for a mother suffering from depression to make space in her mind for her child; her own preoccupations consume all of her available psychic energy. The distortions of reality arising from psychosis or character disorders make it virtually impossible for a parent to create a reasonably accurate picture based on the cues the baby sends rather than the expectations and assumptions arising from the parent's own internal processes. Despite the enormous difficulties these situations pose for a clinician wanting to realign and strengthen the parent–child relationship through infant–parent psychotherapy, the clinician can come to know the mind of the parent, the mind of the child, and the ways in which they influence and alter each other. This is very often not the case for the clinician undertaking psychotherapy with a very young child in foster care. That child has been separated from one or both parents, possibly at birth. He may have gone directly into the care of a single foster parent or he may have had a series of substitute caregivers who may have very limited information about his background or his experiences in previous foster homes. The status of the child's future may be as murky as the details about his past. The agency responsible for his care is legally bound to work simultaneously toward his reunification with one or both parents, and arrange suitable, permanent, and substitute care should reunification fail. The tasks of providing services to support reunification typically fall to the child's caseworker or a series of caseworkers, depending on the administrative structure of the foster care agency. The biological parents may be required to participate in a drug treatment program, psychotherapy, parenting classes, and other activities designed to ensure that they can provide a safe environment for their child. While the parents are working to regain custody of their child, they are usually required to have somewhat regular visits with their child, which may be supervised by a professional supervisor, a relative, or the child's foster parent. Alternatively, the visits may be part of the parent's treatment program or, particularly if reunification is progressing well, may not be supervised at all. During this period, the caseworker(s) must also look for people who might be willing and able to raise the child, in the event that the parents voluntarily relinquish their parental rights or those rights are terminated by court order. This process involves the legally mandated search for relatives, ascertaining their interest, willingness, and suitability. Typically, relatives, even if they are not available to step forward as potential adoptive parents or guardians, want to visit with the child. Sometimes this visit takes place in the child's foster home; often it takes place in a neutral setting – a park or a playroom at the foster care agency. Very often, particularly in highly contested or unusually complex cases, each of the parties will have legal representation – the governmental agency responsible for the care of the child, the child, and the parent. If there are siblings in foster care, they may all have different attorneys, and the same attorney typically does not represent both parents. If, as happens not infrequently, two or more relatives want to become guardians or adoptive parents, they will each have legal representation.

Finally, a pivotal player in the life of a young foster child is often the court appointed special advocate (CASA). This person is a trained volunteer from the community who is charged with developing a relationship with the child, gathering information, presenting it to the court, and advocating for the child's best interest with the court. It is not surprising that in the foster care system the job of identifying the "parent" is rarely simple or straightforward. Sometimes there simply is no one who can give information about the child. At other times multiple people, with overlapping, ill-defined, or conflicting roles, rightly feel that they have some claim to the role of "primary caregiver." When adults are at odds over the "ownership" of a child, it is nearly impossible for them to create a unified and cohesive narrative about the child – each must construct a version of the child that supports his or her claim to primacy in the child's life. This makes identifying the infant an even more difficult psychological task. The actual child, too young to create or hold his own story, may appear in the therapist's office accompanied by an adult who is a virtual stranger to him. That person is often merely delivering the physical being and has nothing in mind about the child except the appointment time and place or the contents of the case file. The file does not contain information about the way in which the child was held in mind during pregnancy, what kind of greeting the world offered at birth, or the nature of his relationships.

The joys of infant–parent psychotherapy

This relational void is quite different from our contacts with children in a reasonably well-functioning parent–child relationship, in which the parent mediates all of the young child's relationships. The parent knows the important people in the child's life – relatives, neighbors, family friends, babysitters or day care providers, and playmates. The parent knows what each of these people brings to the child and what each expects in return. It is the job of the parent to hold all of these people in mind and to help the child gradually come to know each of them – which grandparent expects good manners, which is generous with cookies, which neighbor sounds frighteningly gruff but will answer endless numbers of questions, or which playmate is likely accidentally to break a fragile toy but will happily share every plaything he owns. In these cases, the clinician can reasonably assume that the parent can and will give a clear and coherent picture of the child, her likes and dislikes, and the nature of her relationship with these important people. In the event that the therapist had reason to meet any of these people, it is unlikely that they would be markedly different from the expectations created in the clinician's mind by the parent. In this way, the clinician's experience mirrors the child's experience. The "good-enough" parent gives the child information that is reasonably accurate, complete, and developmentally appropriate about the important people in the child's life, along with the information that the parent conveys to the child about herself, including that she is loved. Through this process, she learns about relationships and the ways in which people value and care for each other. Clearly, communicating important information about relationships is not simply a recitation of facts. Parents convey their excitement about visiting some people and their hesitancy about seeing others. They may be angry about the intrusiveness or emotional distance of a relative, disappointed when the director of the day care center retires, or excited when an old friend moves into the neighborhood. If a clinician is called upon to intercede in this kind of a parent–infant relationship, it is most likely because of an event or situation that has stressed the relationship beyond its usual functional capacity. Patricia and Nicholas illustrate this kind of situation. Patricia sought consultation following her brother's diagnosis of a terminal illness that threatened to claim his life in a matter of weeks. She worried enormously about the impact this would have on her young son, Nicholas, whom she expected to be inconsolable and to suffer lasting harm from the loss of his favorite uncle. Patricia was fond of her brother, but not very close to him, describing him as somewhat emotionally distant. She could not imagine how she would explain death to a toddler and could not figure out how to have the necessary phone calls with relatives and medical personnel without having Nicholas overhear them. The daily decisions about whether to leave him playing alone so that he would not see her crying on the phone or to keep her close to him, even if it might be upsetting to him, seemed impossible. Patricia's sense of enjoying a close relationship with Nicholas was echoed by her husband who was confused by her sudden loss of confidence in herself as a parent. He did not entirely understand her absolute conviction that she would be unable to soothe her son. As the consultation progressed, Patricia talked more about her unhappiness at the approach of Nicholas's third birthday and her guilt over not feeling excited about this milestone in his life. She felt that he had been more distant than usual and worried that her grief was driving him away. Nicholas's outbursts of temper and enormous sadness in the face of disappointment or frustration seemed to her to be more frequent and intense. She worried that he would become uncontrollable. Gradually it became clear that, for Patricia, the anticipation of her brother's death coincided too closely with Nicholas's developmentally appropriate bids for autonomy. Previously, she had been able to help Nicholas manage the intense feelings that are an integral part of the life of a toddler (Lieberman, 1993). However, with the unexpected news of her brother's impending death, Patricia felt overwhelmed and undone by her own grief and the sadness she felt for her mother as she faced the loss of her child. Understandably, she could not be as emotionally available or reliable for Nicholas as he had come to expect. Equally understandably, he became more unpredictable – sometimes withdrawing from his mother's sadness and sometimes becoming more demanding of her attention. Just as he was learning to manage the intensity of his own feelings, he was confronted with the unexpected force of his mother's grief. The relationship that had been a predictable source of pleasure and mutual regulation was becoming derailed by an unexpected, tragic external event. Fortunately, Patricia recognized very quickly that her distress was threatening to overwhelm her and her relationship to Nicholas.

In this case, the parent–infant therapist did not actually see Patricia and Nicholas together. He felt that could know the relationship and Nicholas through Patricia, and that the most important step was to help re-establish Patricia's confidence in her capacity to parent successfully, even under difficult circumstances. Nicholas did not need the help of a professional to resume his positive developmental trajectory. He needed to regain his mother and her sense of parental authority in order to learn that they and their relationship would not only survive the intensity of their feelings but could also draw strength and grow from their shared experience of grief and loss.

This is the kind of case that our dreams are made of – a psychologically minded parent, a child who is securely attached and developmentally on track, a single non-life-threatening event, and adequate social and financial resources. Patricia's confrontation with the premature death of her brother was relatively uncomplicated. Because it did not raise the ghosts of past traumatic losses, she had the luxury of dealing with it for what it was – a loss that made no sense and came too soon. With the therapist's help, she recognized relatively quickly that her identification with her mother was causing her to merge and confuse her own expectable and normal feelings of loss in the face of Nicholas's developmentally appropriate separation with her mother's anticipatory mourning for a child she was about to lose forever. With this awareness, she could reclaim her dual roles: first, as the parent of a little boy who needed her help in the emotional process of separating from and returning to her, and second, as the daughter of a mother who needed her help in the process of separating from a child who would not ever return to her.

Grief is an underappreciated luxury. People who have the opportunity to mourn the loss of a loved one without the intrusions triggered by previous unresolved traumas often do so simply with the help of family and friends. When they do ask for professional help, like Patricia, they often make quick and good use of what we have to offer. Although their lives may have not been without turmoil or trouble, typically they have enjoyed enough satisfying relationships based on mutual value and respect to expect more of the same. These cases make it easy for us to be helpful and to give the best of what we have to offer.

The pains of infant–parent psychotherapy

However, the cases that make up the reality of our day-to-day working lives infrequently offer simple satisfaction, gratification, or opportunity to enjoy a sense of professional competence and confidence. More often, the children and parents who come to us for help are beset with multiple current and past stressors that continually threaten the stability and coherence of their internal and external worlds (Birch & Zorrah, 2012; Cicchetti, Rogosch, & Toth, 2006; Clausen, Aguilar, & Ludwig, 2012; Lemma & Fonagy, 2013; Papoušek, 2011; Siegel, 2011; Tuters, Doulis, & Yabsley, 2011). The difficulties they bring to us endanger our sense of clinical identity and well-being. Because they have rarely enjoyed a preponderance of satisfying relationships, based on mutual value and respect, they do not look for or expect to find them. When they do – and relationships form the foundation of what we have to offer – they either do not know what to do with them or feel an almost overwhelming need to destroy them in order to preserve reality as they have come to know it. One of the gravest difficulties facing therapists working in foster care is that it is a system that, despite the rhetoric, fundamentally does not value relationships. Because relationships stand at the core of our beliefs and our insistence that they are essential for children's healthy development, we will at some point find ourselves at odds with the system charged with the child's care. In some cases, this conflict will destroy the treatment; in other cases, the disagreement may be barely noticed. The toll on the therapist is particularly onerous when "the system," which often feels like a disembodied, uncontainable force with power far greater than the sum of the players in it, purports to support relationships while steadfastly interfering with the child's opportunities to build important, consistent connections to nurturing adults. In these situations, I have often had the feeling that even if I devoted every waking minute to my therapeutic charge, I could never possibly protect her from the misery that will be inflicted upon her by a system whose supposed task is to rescue her. This certainly characterized my work with Christina. Indeed, the CASA who volunteered with Christina and her older brother and I both frequently wondered whether, even together, we could sustain the energy and resources needed to keep the lives of these young children from spinning completely out of control, let alone help them overcome the effects of the tragic events that had brought them into the foster care system. Christina and her brother, Jack, entered foster care when she was 2 years old and he was 4. They were delivered to the foster care office by an elderly great aunt who had tried to care for them following the death of their mother some months earlier from a drug overdose. At the time of their mother's death, the children were living in a single room of a residential hotel with their parents. Following her death, their father's drug use continued unabated. Their great aunt took them to her home when she found them unkempt and the room without food. The aunt was frail and in poor health. She explained to the intake worker that she could not manage two young children whose behavior was totally uncontrollable and unpredictable. In addition, their father, Harry, frequently came to her home angrily insisting that if she did not let him see his children, he would report her for kidnapping. He also raged at her, demanding money and food before he would leave. The aunt had been a foster parent as a younger woman, and was extremely reluctant to have these children placed in foster care. She had tried to prevail on her own daughter to take the children, but she refused to do anything that might bring her own family into contact with Harry, who had stolen money from her in the past. As a working parent with a marginal income, she felt that she and her husband could barely take care of her own children. She worried that she might lose her job any time she had to take time off work to attend a doctor's appointment or meet with the school counselor. Christina and Jack simply had too many problems, and she had too few resources.

When they entered the foster care system, both children suffered from chronic diarrhea. Jack had severe tooth decay; Christina had a bilateral ear infection. Neither child slept well – they had trouble falling asleep and woke frequently with nightmares. Christina wailed almost incessantly – everything seemed to frighten her and nothing seemed to soothe her; she seemed immobilized by fear. In contrast, Jack could not hold still. He ran, he jumped, he screamed, he fought. Both children had seemingly insatiable appetites. Their foster mother felt as if they would eat "until they exploded." She worried that Jack would make himself sick by eating the food he tried to forage from the garbage or hurt himself while climbing to reach food on the kitchen shelves. Christina and Jack, who spoke only English, spent their first month in an emergency foster home with a very caring, experienced Spanish-speaking foster mother because there were no other homes available. However, they did begin to calm down, and their physical health began to improve in that foster mother's care. In the next foster home, where they were to spend the next three years while the legal system moved with inexorable slowness toward what was supposed to be a permanent plan, they again had the good fortune of having a patient and experienced foster mother. Maria had two adult children and a grandchild who visited frequently. Her daughter helped her with the day care center she ran in her home. Most days there were six preschool children in the home during the day who were joined by Maria's grandson between the end of school and the dinner hour. At the time of this move, the children's case was transferred to another social worker as a matter of routine practice. Their social worker was concerned that Maria might not be able to keep the children in her home because of Jack's behavior. She referred him for therapy about six months after he entered the foster care system because he was so out of control that Maria feared for both his safety and that of the other children in her care. He recklessly climbed to high places, and frequently lashed out at other children when his wishes or will were thwarted. Jack also grabbed anxiously at his crotch throughout the day, gyrated in a sexualized way when he was being dressed or bathed, and liked to sneak into the bathroom to watch other children on the toilet. Maria was also worried about Christina's continual inconsolable sadness, but the social worker felt that she was too young for psychotherapy. When they had been in foster care for about nine months, Maria discovered Jack in Christina's crib. Her diaper was off, and Christina was in tears and appeared to be frightened. At that point the social worker asked for a psychological evaluation of Christina, fearing that Jack had molested her. She also began to worry that Jack might have been sexually abused while in the care of his parents.

At the time of these events, Jack was approaching 5 and Christina was 3 months shy of her third birthday. The evaluation to establish sexual abuse was inconclusive in regard to Jack. However, the therapist who saw him in individual therapy felt that his play strongly suggested that he had either been engaged in or witnessed explicit sexual behavior. The evaluator found no evidence in Christina's play or behavior to warrant concern about sexual abuse or exposure. However, she did refer Christina for therapy because of her extreme sadness, rote and repetitive play, and propensity to make indiscriminate attachments. She noted that during the course of an evaluation that stretched over several weeks, Christina had made overtures to every adult in the clinic – therapists, secretaries, and adults sitting in the waiting room. She showed little interest in the other children at the clinic. Christina was referred to me for therapy. Her social worker scheduled and brought her to her first therapy appointment because the foster mother was unable to leave the other children at her day care center and did not drive. Maria felt very strongly that Christina should have therapy because of "the things that had happened to her." However, she was adamant that she did not have the time to take Christina to appointments, could not take time away from the children in her day care center to take part in home visits, and did not feel that she had any reason to participate in Christina's therapy. She explained to the social worker that she would be happy to speak with the therapist by phone at anytime and would gladly pass along important information about events in Christina's life and any changes in her behavior. She felt that her relationship with the little girl in her care was good, that Christina's troubles had started long before they met, and that Christina had only improved since coming to live with her. Of course, all of that was true, but it also aptly demonstrated the limits of Maria's attachment to Christina. She truly cared very much about this little girl – perhaps even loved her; Christina often said that Mama Maria loved her. However, she saw herself as a substitute and temporary caregiver. In the three years I worked with Christina, I never met her foster mother. During this time, the court ordered two additional evaluations of this child, and neither of the other psychologists met her foster mother – the adult who had primary responsibility for her day-to-day care. When I was asked to see Christina, I was told that this would most likely be a brief intervention to help her with an expected move into a permanent placement with relatives in another part of the state. The social worker explained that she had tried desperately to find a therapist who saw young children on the list of approved therapists; there were very few and they had no time. The clinics had waiting lists and generally were not taking new patients because it was at the end of the training year. My schedule was very full at that time, and it was with more than a little reluctance that I agreed to see this little girl, but I expected that I could make time during the summer months and that she would be settled in her new home and with a long-term therapist when

I returned from vacation. Like Maria, I saw myself as a substitute and temporary caregiver. Writing this triggered my original confusion, horror, outrage, embarrassment, and exhaustion at the reminder that I treated a young child for three years without ever having met her primary caregiver. When we started, it didn't seem to matter so much – this was to be a short-term relationship. Maria and I both saw ourselves as transitional folks in Christina's life, charged with helping her move on with as little disruption as possible. Then we just continued as we had begun. Perhaps we did not meet because of force of habit, inertia, or denial of the reality of our relationship to Christina or some form of acting out our resentment of being expected to deliver far more than we had promised, or all of the above and more. The fact that both evaluators also neglected to meet with Maria suggests another possibility that is a frequent aspect of the transference/countertransference paradigm in our work with foster children – we "forget" about the other adults in the child's life. The immediacy of the child's emotional needs in combination with tenuous attachments to caregivers who can be replaced without warning can make it easy for us to set them aside or to overlook their importance. The neglect of this important person also, of course, reflects Christina's reality – there was no parent available for infant–parent psychotherapy. We spoke by phone with some frequency. Maria readily called me when there was information that she thought would be helpful to me. She never asked for advice or for suggestions about how she might help Christina. Periodically, I would plan to call to see if I could arrange to visit on a weekend, when she would be free from her childcare duties. These good intentions briefly assuaged my guilt and temporarily covered the swells of outrage, resentment, and sorrow that frequently overwhelmed me as I helplessly watched and participated in a system, in this instance, so consumed with meeting the letter of the law that the spirit of the law intended to protect the best interests of the children was continually overrun.

When I returned from vacation, Christina was still with Maria. The relatives who were supposed to materialize had withdrawn their offer to care for the children. There were no alternatives on the immediate horizon. Their father was in a drug rehab program, and was demanding reunification services and visits. His program was expressly designed for drug abusing parents with the intent of bringing families back together. His continuing in the program – which contributed to their funding – required that he have increasingly greater time with them, and that the children would eventually live with him at the center during the latter phases of his treatment. So Christina and I continued to see each other on a somewhat regular basis. We talked and played. She especially liked the dollhouse, from which the dolls came and went in an unpredictable and haphazard way. I was never sure who would bring Christina to her appointments. Sometimes it was her social worker; sometimes it was one of several drivers. Christina and I had our two favorites of this group – they brought her on time, picked her up on time, chatted with me, and had running jokes and stories with her. Things could seem almost normal – it could seem as if a parent was looking after her and that I was delivering her back into the hands of someone who knew and cared about her. During one stretch of several weeks, for reasons that I could never understand, the transportation became wildly erratic. Christina probably had seven or eight different people driving her to and from therapy sessions. Sometimes she arrived just as her appointment was scheduled to end. Sometimes I had to reschedule the appointment of the patient who followed her because the driver was so late.[1]

During these times I often found myself drawn toward anxiously joining Christina in her vigil at the window. One day, as our wait was approaching an hour, I was stunned by the fear on Christina's face. I then recognized the anger in my voice as I was leaving a message for her social worker. When the driver had not arrived, I had called Maria, only to discover that she had rushed to a doctor's appointment because of an urgent medical problem. Her daughter could not fetch Christina because she had to mind the children in the day care center. I had called the social worker, who was not in. I had then tried the transportation office, only to receive a recorded message instructing me to call the emergency number. At the emergency number, another recorded message greeted me, explaining that the machine was full and that I should call back at a later time. That prompted my helplessly enraged message to the social worker, which was interrupted only by the look on Christina's face and her panicked response to my unthinking intrusion of my mood into the therapeutic space (Aron, 1991). I tried to remind myself that we needed a least one person in the room to act like an adult. I seemed only a slightly more likely candidate than Christina. Perhaps the truism that children need parents most when they are least available extends to therapists. Christina and I had been left stranded, helpless, and, for that moment, alone in the world together.

This wait, that lasted a little more than an hour, provided me an intense, affective glimpse into Christina's world. Even though I knew better, when I could pull my rational self together, I felt as if we had been totally and completely abandoned – forever. My calls for help went unanswered. No one cared. No one even knew I needed help. It was past lunchtime. I had not brought my lunch that day. Should I take Christina and go for food? What if the driver came while we were gone? Would she wait for our return? What if someone called while we were out? What if no one ever called? What if the driver had actually forgotten about us? We were hungry, scared, and confused, and our resources were diminishing rapidly. Maybe that is what if feels like to be stranded on a desert island. Maybe that is what it feels like to be a foster child. There was no one to call. Indeed, during much of the time that I worked with Christina I alternated between feeling that there was no one to call and that I had to call everyone all the time or all would be lost.

Fortunately, as a volunteer member of A Home Within, I had the wise and supportive counsel of the clinicians in my consultation group. At the time I began seeing Christina, I was leading a consultation group; when her funding ran out, I continued with her on a volunteer basis and brought her story to the group. It is difficult for me to imagine how I would have been able to manage all of the feelings – particularly the sense of despair – without the group's help. Our talking together made it possible for me to maintain some capacity to think when the facts of this child's life made a state of blissful ignorance seductive. The three months that I expected to see Christina stretched to three years. Over the course of this time, I developed a deep affection for this little girl and a profound feeling of sadness about the limitations – both internally and externally imposed – on my capacity to help her. Christina had a beautiful, engaging smile and a delightful sense of humor. She flourished in the care of Maria, and became one of those children who seemed always to get the best that people have to offer – within limits. Maria did not want to raise another family; she had agreed to take Jack and Christina on a short-term basis, not to consider adoption or legal guardianship.

After protracted legal battles and additional evaluations and reviews of evaluations, Christina and Jack went to live with the relatives who had initially come forward and then withdrawn. Unfortunately, after about a year that "placement failed," and these children were returned to the county that held jurisdiction, but not to the mother with whom Christina had spent more of her life than any other. Christina been "sent back," but she had not returned home. Maria was out of the foster care and day care business. Christina was distraught – her overwhelming sadness and confusion showed in angry temper tantrums and massive regression. When she left her relatives, she had expected to return to the one adult she felt loved her and whose love she could count on.

Beyond infant–parent psychotherapy

When I again saw Christina she was 7 years old. She entered my office hesitantly and stopped to inspect the dollhouse. In a quiet voice she offered, "It's been a long time since I've seen you." I agreed and said that I was glad to see her. She responded, "No one in that place liked me." Fighting back tears, I told her that I was so sorry and that I had heard that it had been very, very difficult. She began to explore the office tentatively, commenting on what was new and what she remembered from our previous life together. What made me want to cry? Everything about this child's life and our therapeutic life together. I had to take care of her and I could not take care of her. I had battled the system for three years and had been defeated; I did not want to resume that fight, but I had no choice. My relationship with her was not only just about psychotherapy; it was also a battle about emotional life and death and one that I stood a very good chance of losing. I knew the players in this drama, and I had enough experience with the tragedy of foster care to predict that we were moving Christina inexorably toward life in long-term foster care. Christina was a beautiful child whose sweetness and charm masked an emptiness that could make an hour with her feel like an eternity. It was often tempting just to go through the motions of psychotherapy because fighting to stay psychically alive and connected to her was so difficult. It was equally tempting to go through the motions of psychotherapy in relation to the foster care system because fighting for Christina to have a chance to stay psychically alive and connected was just so difficult. I wanted to cry because when Christina walked through my door, I instantly knew that there was no turning back, and that I had just put my sanity on the line. Despite my split-second recognition that I had already implicitly agreed to resume psychotherapy with Christina, I behaved as if the question was still open and a matter of rationally weighing the pros and cons of an argument. Christina's return came at a particularly busy time in my professional life. Because of other commitments, I knew that I would have a very difficult time maintaining a regular schedule for this child for whom any disruption was overwhelming. I knew that my schedule would not allow me to attend all of the meetings that would determine Christina's future and that it was essential that her therapist be present. Christina's distress was threatening her placement; she really needed to have therapy two or three times a week, at least until her overpowering feelings could be contained. I did not have that kind of time. Every bit of logic argued for my transferring Christina to a new therapist.

However, this was not about logic. In one sense, this phase of my work was the most clearly defined in any of the time I have known Christina, yet it also caused me the greatest ambivalence about my relationship to her. The recurring message from all of the many players in Christina's life at the time she returned was that I had to "stabilize the placement." Christina was in very grave danger of being moved to yet another home, which would have been absolutely disastrous for her. Because her disruptive behavior clearly had psychological origins, everyone was expecting therapy to accomplish this task and, fundamentally, really did not care whether that job fell to me or someone else. I felt that on the most basic human level, I had no choice about resuming my therapeutic relationship with Christina. I had to see her. However, I also knew that my schedule would not allow me to give her the time and attention that she needed and deserved. What if I failed, and she lost both her current foster family and me as a result? I wondered if it would be better if I referred her to someone who could be more available while I stepped into a role more like a special friend. So often this is the dilemma facing the therapist working with young children in foster care – which is the least bad of the available choices. Christina was not my child. Christina was not Maria's child. When their children are in overwhelming distress, as Christina was, parents drop everything. They rearrange their schedules; they put their busy lives on hold. No one in Christina's life had that connection to her. With the help of my consultation group, I struggled with the limited options facing me. Fortunately, in the process of sorting through them time and time again, I had the opportunity to talk with Jeree Pawl about this case. With her usual wisdom, Jeree redefined my task. She counseled that my job was to "want" Christina. This cogent advice eased the anxious burden of "stabilizing the placement" that had been defined by the foster care agency. I had to reconnect with Christina. I did want her, but I did not want full responsibility for her emotional well-being. If I could want her, others could want her as well. My wanting her would allow her to become a "want-able," loveable child.

I continued to see Christina on a regular basis. Her new foster mother was loving and experienced, and she or a member of her family brought Christina to her appointments. The legal process that would ultimately decide her future resumed. The judge ordered a new evaluation that included a review of the evaluation that was done when Christina was living with her relatives, along with the two evaluations that took place when she lived with Maria. During that time when Christina came to my office, we would talk and play in old and new ways. She liked to go through the office and remember what is old and discover what is new. In a session a few months after our reunion her eyes lit up when she found a toy that I had bought at a craft fair. She exclaimed, "I made this for you and it's still here. Do you remember when I made this for you?" I really did not know what to say. Much of the time in my work with Christina, I really did not know what to say because I did not really know what my job was. Obviously, she had passed through the age of infant–parent psychotherapy, but in a very profound way we were still at the point where we started – without any clear idea of who the parent is in this parent–child relationship. When Christina first moved into her current foster home, I included her foster mother in some of the sessions in order to help her understand and manage Christina's anger, confusion, and grief about not being with Mama Maria as she had so fervently wished and reasonably expected. After a while, Christina protested having to share her time. Her relationships at home and school were beginning to offer her pleasure, and her foster mother was increasingly confident about her ability to understand and respond to the full range of Christina's behavior and feelings. When the family moved a distance from my office that made her continuing impractical the foster mother and I agreed that Christina did not need to be transferred to a new therapist.

It is not unusual for therapists working with young children in foster care to feel that the full weight of the child's life is on their shoulders. In a system that is geared toward action as the solution to most problems, this overwhelming feeling is often concretized into plans for action. Particularly for young and inexperienced therapists, it frequently manifests itself as a wish to adopt the child (Birch, 2000; Heineman, 2001). In other instances – perhaps with older, more experienced therapists or with clinicians working with adolescents or older children who do not as easily pull on our heartstrings as potential adoptees – it may take the form of a wish or attempt to take charge of the myriad players in the child's life (Weston, 2006). In either case, I believe that these concrete solutions can best be understood as a profoundly experienced need to create a parental mind to watch over a child. We know that there are no babies without mothers. When we are confronted with the vacuum of maternal care that engulfs children in foster care it surely stirs a primitive panic in us. We know that a child simply must exist in someone's mind – always and completely. When faced with the absence of a parental mind, we imagine filling the void permanently with adoption or, at least completely, by gathering and ordering the fragments of information and responsibility that are held by the many people in a foster child's life.

However, when we, as therapists, step into the void – because a child must be held in mind – we may inadvertently preclude another from filling that psychic space. When we feel or act as if we are the child's parent, we may not leave room for a real parent to begin to hold the child in mind. We frequently see this played out in relation to foster parents, who are given sole responsibility for a child's care, but often not allowed to voice an opinion about how best to meet a child's needs. We ask them to assume parental responsibility without conveying parental authority. I believe that my contribution to the crisis that we narrowly averted when Christina returned from the relatives who did not want her was my sense that I had to step into the parental void – not by adoption or becoming her foster parent – but by pulling all of the pieces and players together and holding them in mind for and with her. It was a job I had no hope of doing successfully and in the face of this formidable task, I felt hopeless and anxiously overwhelmed. Having psychically put myself into the center of the melee, everyone understandably looked to me to solve the problem. They themselves became anxious when they recognized that the limitations on my time, energy, and psychic space would make me fall short. When I found the freedom to step back and simply "want" Christina, her life began to shift subtly, but remarkably quickly. With more space to assume the parenting role, her foster mother introduced more structure. With my help, she began to act more independently and to solve problems at home without continually asking for advice from the caseworker, which only made both of them worried that she could not handle Christina. As Christina calmed down, the caseworker turned to other, more demanding situations, which, in turn, created more space for her foster mother to parent. Psychotherapeutic work in any system or culture imposes particular pressures and expectations that create unique psychological dangers. In some instances, the culture creates a pressure to politicize the therapy; in others, it creates an enchantment with the life of the mind that can undermine the work of true introspection.

In the foster care system, the pressure to *act* often and profoundly endangers the therapist's capacity to think. It is very difficult to make time and psychological space to think with and about a child when there is no one to join in that process – when there is no one with whom to have a "meeting of the minds." I was in danger of succumbing to the pressure to act – of accepting the charge to "stabilize the placement," rather than thinking about what Christina needed from me and what I had to offer her. Stabilizing the placement really translates into asking children and foster parents to change behavior that is symptomatic of a difficulty in the relationship before there is time to understand the relationship or the difficulties it poses for each of them. When I was free to want Christina, and not to measure that desire by the number of hours I had for her or the speed with which I could calm the reverberations her behavior was sending through the system, I regained my capacity to think. Although it seems painfully obvious from this distance, at the time it was not so clear to me that "wanting" was at the core of the problems in the relationship between Christina and her foster mother. Christina did not want her; she wanted Maria who did not want her. Her new foster mother had initially wanted Christina, but her attachment to Christina was too tenuous to withstand Christina's not wanting her. With this in mind, I could help Christina and her foster mother think alone and together about what they wanted and the disappointments attendant to not being able to have what we often want so desperately that we believe we cannot live without it.

Conclusion

The placement was indeed stabilized – not because of any particular action, but because a shift in my understanding of my role restored my capacity to think and to bring my understanding of relationships to bear on this child and the adults in her life. At least temporarily, we prevented more disruptions in this child's life. I was able to help Christina and her foster mother find ways of wanting each other. However, they may still have to face disappointment and grief over losing what they now want. When they moved, the legally required search for potential adoptive parents among relatives had resumed. There was a remote possibility that it would succeed. Christina's father may recover enough from his addiction that he would prevail in an action to terminate his parental rights. Christina's foster mother may become her legal guardian – a tie that might not withstand the storms of adolescence. Christina's life is not easy, and probably never will be. She is impulsive and prone to hitting other children. It is exceedingly difficult for her to take any kind of responsibility for her actions. She has the kind of charm that pulls people in and then leaves them feeling angry and cheated at the shallowness of the connection that Christina offers. She is only seven – she has time. She is already seven – she does not have much time – I fully expect that Christina will spend the next 11 years of her life in foster care. I hope that she will be able to stay in the same foster home, and that she will have good and frequent contact with Jack and her father. I could hope that her father would relinquish his parental rights and allow for an open adoption, but at this juncture I am not prepared to face the disappointment that that particular hope would almost surely bring. I hope that Christina and I will find ways of staying in touch, and that she and I will both have the energy to keep our connection alive and enlivening. I hope that my wanting her helped her to want relationships with others who truly want her.

Note

1 On one occasion I explained to the patient following Christina that I was waiting for the driver to pick up a young child. She rolled her eyes in exasperation, "Really, they have to have the driver get the kid! Couldn't they at least have the nanny pick her up?" At that moment I was too distracted to muse on her comment, but often times since it has reminded me of how deeply cultural assumptions are embedded in our internal lives.

10

LEARNING TO SAY GOODBYE
The deaths of three fathers

In this chapter I explore the experience of parental death on child and therapist. It focuses primarily on a little boy's premature confrontation with the unexpected and untimely death of his father. However, in the background stand the death of two other fathers – one anticipated because of age and illness, the other unexpected but, perhaps, predictable from the history of what came before. Benjamin was only 27 months old when his father died; Ernie was 12, and I had reached middle age at the time of my father's death. Ernie's father's death resulted in his entry into foster care and eventual placement with relatives whom he had barely known. Benjamin remained with his mother and brother as they rebuilt their family. And I had my husband, children, and familiar routines to comfort me through mourning.

Ernie

Carol, Ernie's maternal aunt, sought therapy shortly after her 12-year-old nephew had joined her family following his mother's arrest for the fatal shooting of her husband, Ernie's father. She described her sister as having a long-standing drinking problem. She explained that the marriage was unstable, and the father periodically disappeared for weeks at a time. Carol believed that when the parents were together their lives were likely punctuated with mutual violence. She didn't believe that Ernie had been the victim of physical abuse, but felt that the atmosphere in the house was abusive. Although she had often felt guilty for not having more contact with Ernie, the physical and emotional distance made it hard for her to spend time with her sister's family. She also felt that she had to protect her own family and was reluctant to expose her husband and daughter, two years younger than Ernie, to what she described as the toxic atmosphere in her sister's home.

She stated that she knew little about what had transpired, except that when the police had responded to a call from the neighbors they found her sister sitting with a gun next to her dead husband and Ernie staring blankly into space in an adjoining room. When asked, Ernie had said that he didn't know what happened. While he watched, his mother was handcuffed and taken away in a police car and he was taken to a foster home in another police car. He remained in that home, where he was one of three foster children, for approximately three months while arrangements were made to have him moved to his aunt's home.

Carol described Ernie as keeping to himself and showing little interest in getting to know the family. He spoke when spoken to – but barely – and rarely initiated conversations. She was highly ambivalent about having Ernie in her home. She felt that she really had no choice but to bring her nephew into her family but resented the disruption. Theirs was a close-knit family that enjoyed outdoor weekend activities, which Ernie joined only reluctantly. His few spontaneous comments were complaints about having to leave home for these outings.

The school made similar observations about his behavior with teachers and other students. He seemed to have little interest in adults or peers. However, he turned in his homework assignments and did well on them and on tests. Reports from his previous school indicated that he had been a good student with few friends. In his free time at school and at home he drew elaborate scenes – landscapes, cityscapes, medieval towns, and castles were all beautifully rendered and strikingly devoid of people.

In the first session, when asked, Ernie told his therapist that he was in therapy because "my mother killed my father." It was over two years into therapy before he spoke of the incident again and then, only in passing mentioned that he liked being able to talk to his mother by phone and would like to visit her more often.

Although Ernie preferred drawing to talking, he was quite engaged in the therapy. He rarely missed sessions and often found ways of extending them a bit. When he did talk, it was usually about his drawings, sometimes about school, and rarely about his new family. Consistent with his aunt's description, he complained about having to participate in family activities, preferring to stay at home and draw.

Despite their best efforts to integrate Ernie into their family, his therapist felt that Ernie was determined to remain an outsider both at home and at school. At one point when Ernie was voicing his complaints about the expectation that he participate in dinner conversation, his therapist suggested that he might be worried that if he felt part of this new family, it would mean that his other family really was gone. Ernie shrugged and with a slight nod of assent, commented, "I don't need another family."

Ernie's story captures many of the painful issues facing children in foster care. By report, his life prior to his father's death had been characterized by chaos, unpredictability, and uncertainty. It seemed as if Ernie, like some children when faced with instability at home, had turned to school for structure. He could not control his environment, but he could create orderly worlds through his drawings. His therapist felt that this talent was probably the key to Ernie's being able to withstand the chaos and terror of his external world.

In contrast to the certainty of his father's death, the loss of his mother is ambiguous. A jury found some credence in the mother's claim of self-defense and the court sentenced her to six years for the death of her husband. Maybe she will be paroled and they will be reunited earlier. Maybe she will have overcome her drinking problem while in jail, or maybe she will relapse. Maybe, if Ernie is still in high school, she will want to move to the city so that he can live with her. Maybe she will want to return to the small town where they had lived together and will want him to move there. Maybe they will get along and maybe they won't. The uncertainties and potential trials are enough to make anyone's head spin, let alone that of a young child who appears to be trying to keep himself and his family intact by maintaining a physical and emotional distance from those who could care for him.

When Ernie lost his father to death and his mother to incarceration, he also lost his school and community. Although the move to his aunt's home somewhat improved his socioeconomic circumstances, he could not rely on the familiarity of the environment in which he was growing up to help ground him. He did not belong; he had to learn to fit in, first at the foster home and then with relatives with whom he had had only a passing acquaintance.

Ernie was not a child who could ask for or accept comfort. His aunt reported that he did not like being touched, let alone hugged. We can reasonably assume that his parents made neither physical nor emotional comfort readily available, and that Ernie learned early to care for himself as best he could. This, too, is sadly true of many children in foster care – the strategies that they developed to survive without parental care in their families of origin prevent them from seeking or receiving care when it does become available.

The experiences following the death of Ernie's father stand in stark contrast to those of Benjamin, who also lost his father to premature death. Although Benjamin's mother was temporarily psychically absent, she was always physically present. His father left a gaping hole, but, because he had learned that he would be well-cared for, Benjamin was able to accept what others offered, to help him fill that horrible void.

Benjamin

I was introduced to Benjamin through a phone call placed during the week I was out of town to attend memorial services for my father. Periodically, throughout the week – when time stretched too slowly, or when I felt the need to connect to the everyday life my father's death had interrupted, or when I wanted distance from the intensity and complexity of intergenerational family dynamics – I would check the messages on my answering machine, finding the disembodied voices oddly comforting. As I stood in my mother's kitchen, surrounded by the sounds and feelings of mourning, and listened to the voice of a colleague asking if I had time to see a two-year-old whose father had died without warning, I felt an unusually intense pang of sadness and empathy.

I am not ordinarily so vulnerable to magical thinking but, in this instance, I felt as if the coincidence of the shared loss of our fathers bound me to this little boy in some important, almost mystical way. From the beginning, even before I knew many of the details of this child's life, I was acutely aware of the likely similarities and very great differences in our experience of loss. I imagined that the quiet bustle of mourning filled his mother's kitchen, too. Friends and family, along with those strangers who belonged only to his parents' lives, and brought words and food for solace. While welcome, the unfamiliar smells and tastes also served as reminders that everything had changed.

Death had disrupted the predictable activities of our daily lives. However, I would soon return to the comforting familiarity of the routines of work and parenthood – to a life separated by years and miles from my father's daily activities. In contrast, Benjamin's entire world, both internal and external, would be transformed by his father's death; he would face the discomfort and disorientation of an unwilling adjustment to unfamiliar patterns and altered family rhythms.

My father's death occurred at an expectable time in the life cycle. He had moved from responsibilities of work and parenthood to the leisure of retirement and grandparenthood. With his family and friends, he had experienced the inevitable, normal confrontations with loss, aging, and illness (Loewald, 1979; Pine, 1989). He had had a long lifetime to prepare for death. And by midlife, I had navigated many conflicts and complex affects stirred by the losses associated with developmental growth and change. My siblings and I now stood by the far side of separation-individuation, early oedipal strivings, and adolescence. In addition to the normative, developmental preparations for death, the diagnosis of my father's terminal illness some months earlier had forced us most directly into conscious preparation for his decline and death.

In contrast, Benjamin's father's death came far too soon. Developmentally, Mr. M. had only reached the stage of generativity, with its expectations of expansion – building careers, friendships, and families (Erickson, 1959). By all reports, he had relished this stage of "bringing forth fruit," in both his professional and personal life. Mr. M.'s energy and his deceptive appearance of good health not only did not demand a conscious preparation for his death, but allowed for questions of mortality to be set aside – to be considered at a later time. The tumor that killed Benjamin's father had given no warning; it simply grew, asymptomatically, until its fatal infringement on his brain's capacity to regulate vital functions. Benjamin and his brother were just beginning to navigate the complexities of life when they were surprised by their father's premature death. At a little more than a two years old, Benjamin was still negotiating the losses inherent in the process of separation-individuation and solidifying object constancy, while his baby brother, Noah, just eight months old, had barely begun to grapple with the emotional import of separateness.

Because of the coincidence of our fathers' death I knew, in undertaking psychotherapy with this little boy, that my mourning would be affected by his and would, in turn, influence my work with him. I seriously considered referring Benjamin to someone who might have more emotional distance from the issues confronting him. However, I was also curious about the little boy's encounter with death, and it seemed to me that if we could find ways of thinking together about death we might develop an enlivening relationship. Eventually I decided that a therapist who had emotional affinity with his situation might serve him as well as, though differently from, one with distance (Harris, in press). The influences of my mourning process on Benjamin's treatment were, for the most part, very subtle; in the pages that follow I will highlight those moments that seemed most touched by the aspect of my intraspychic processes.

However, my primary concern here is to consider Benjamin's earliest use of me. First I will briefly describe Benjamin's first three therapy sessions. I will then touch on some important factors in young children's experience of parental loss, including the importance of holding a place for the physically absent but psychically present parent. Next, I will discuss the clinical material, with particular attention to the nature of Benjamin's relationship to me in these early sessions and his comments outside the therapy sessions that illustrate his view of the place I gradually came to hold in his object world. Finally, I will discuss my subsequent contacts with Benjamin.

The beginnings of Benjamin's therapy

Benjamin and I met face-to-face three weeks after his father's death. Thin, with white-blond hair and large, sunken eyes, he was most forlorn-looking little boy. His pacifier, bobbing wildly because of his continual, vehement sucking, almost obscured his expressions and facial features. He seemed to glide, ghostlike, down the hallway from the waiting room to my office, as if too fragile to touch the ground. Once in the office he stood quietly by his mother, sucking and looking in my direction. I told him that I knew that something very, very sad had happened to him and that I would try to help him understand all of the very big feelings he must be having. He looked and sucked. I said that I knew that his daddy had died. "Yes," he responded, as he moved to a large basket of Legos on the floor next to his mother's chair. He began removing them one by one, each time exclaiming, "Look at that! Look at that!" Near the end of the session he left his mother's side to explore the toy cabinet briefly. He found a small basket of marbles, which he took to a dollhouse. Quietly and methodically, with only an occasional "Look at that," he removed all of the furniture from the dollhouse, then spread the marbles through its empty rooms. He said that he was keeping them safe there. As the session ended, uncertain as to the meaning of his comment, I merely agreed that it might well be a good idea to leave the marbles in a safe place.[1]

Early in the second session Benjamin's mother commented that he had talked a great deal about the marbles over the last week. Indeed in this hour he spent most of his time pouring the marbles from one to another of the containers in the tea set. Toward the end of the session he again moved toward the dollhouse. As he approached it, I noted, to my chagrin, that a single doll had been left, lying face down in one of the rooms, in the wake of another child's therapy session. Naming it a "Daddy" doll, at first Benjamin casually tossed it aside. A few minutes later, in the course of his play, he came across this figure again and this time quite forcefully threw it away from him without comment.

In the third session Benjamin's heightened distress led to a pattern that sustained a new role for me, that of a "placeholder." As the hour began he stood frozen next to his mother, his pacifier bobbing even more forcefully than usual. She said that this had been a very hard morning. I asked Benjamin if he would like to tell me about it. When he didn't respond, I asked if his mommy could tell me about what had made him feel so bad that morning. He nodded agreement. His mother explained that she and Benjamin had been in the kitchen reading when they heard Noah crying upstairs. She asked Benjamin if he would like to go with her to get the baby or wait in the kitchen. He elected to wait, so she settled him with his book. Within the space of two or three minutes Benjamin was at the bottom of the stairs crying and screaming in terror. She said that Benjamin had seemed very, very frightened, had taken a long time to calm down, and didn't seem to have any words to explain his feelings.

I said that I could understand how scary that might have been, because when Daddy died he had gone upstairs with baby Noah and hadn't come back. Benjamin answered, "Yes." I continued that Mommy had come back down, but maybe it had made him remember when Daddy didn't come back down and died. Again, Benjamin replied, "Yes."

I then said to Benjamin, "I know it was a long time ago that Daddy died, but I wonder if you can remember what you and Daddy were doing on the day he died, right before he went to put Noah to nap." Without any hesitation, Benjamin responded, "Baking brownies." His mother shook her head slightly, indicating that this was not the case. I continued, "And Daddy asked you to wait, like Mommy asked you to wait."

"And daddies, too," he added.

I said mommies and daddies sometimes did ask big boys to wait while they took care of babies.

At this point Benjamin again removed the marbles from the toy cabinet along with a basket containing miniature vehicles. He somewhat listlessly began pouring the marbles from one truck to another, but became more animated by the discovery of a small garbage truck. I suggested we make a garbage dump. He smiled and dumped the load of marbles. As his affect brightened, I continued that we might need a very large dump where we could get rid of all the old trash. Benjamin continued this play with increasingly gleeful affect, narrating his happy dumping with "Get rid of that garbage." However, at a particularly intense moment, he stopped his play and quickly moved to the toy telephones, which he examined but would not use. His mother commented that previously he had very much liked talking to his daddy on the phone, but since his father's death he had refused to speak to anyone by telephone.

Young children's experiences of parental death

When a child loses a parent in the earliest years of childhood, as Benjamin did, he simply cannot grasp the finality of death (Furman, 1973; Piaget, 1979). Developmentally, a young child may be particularly vulnerable to a kind of "split" in the ego, which enables him to maintain the fantasy of a living parent while cognitively accepting the fact of parental death (Freud, 1927; Wolfenstein, 1966). Although the effects of parental death in childhood remain ambiguous (Schafer, 2009; Thompson et al.,1998; Tremblay & Israel, 1998) the persistence of such a split in ego functioning through latency, adolescence, and into adulthood may well result in serious impingements on reality testing and the capacity for relationships.

However, in a very young child such a split likely reflects the cognitive immaturity that allows contradictory facts (Sekaer & Katz, 1986) along with fact and fantasy, or real and pretend, a comfortable coexistence. In this enchanted realm of childhood, where the world is experienced as both internally created and externally imposed, all manner of things are possible. If the world is controlled by magic and mother is both me and not-me, why cannot father be both dead and not-dead?[2]

At the time of our first meeting, Benjamin's family included a physically absent but psychically present father. In contrast, his mother was physically present but because of the preoccupying demands of her own mourning, her psychic absence disturbed mother and child alike. Mr. M.'s death catapulted him into an unusually prominent space in the psychic lives of those who had lived with and loved him. His presence was particularly enhanced for his wife and children by their struggle to integrate the fact of his permanent absence. Benjamin's mother was well aware of the incongruity of her efforts to be especially attentive to her children while feeling that she barely had the psychic time and space for her own mourning.

The therapist as placeholder

Especially in the beginning weeks of psychotherapy, I believe Benjamin and his mother viewed me, first and foremost, as someone who could keep the family from collapsing in on itself while they struggled simultaneously to hold and to relinquish the father. In my position as "placeholder" I helped to fill the ugly, gaping space created by Benjamin's father's death. In the dyadic aspects of this role I stood in for the absent parent as Benjamin assimilated the loss of his beloved father. In relation to the family, my function as placeholder was of a triadic nature, as I both practically and emotionally helped Benjamin's mother establish and maintain her bearings in her efforts to raise her children without her husband.

As they worked to reconstruct their family, Benjamin's therapy provided a "transitional space" for the expression of playful symbolization of the actual, overwhelmingly painful loss – a psychic and physical place where affects could be both expressed and contained (Ogden, 1988, Winnicott, 1953). Literally, I kept a consistent space to which Benjamin could return week after week and, unlike most of the other important adults in his world, affectively I remained relatively stable and predictable.

In contrast to much of work with very young children, where we focus on improving or enhancing the parent–child relationship, this mother–child relationship mostly required holding until it could stabilize itself through the affective storm of mourning. Benjamin had enjoyed solid and loving relationships with both parents; now his father was permanently lost to him, while his mother was struggling, with remarkable success, to keep her bearings as a parent while mourning the loss of her spouse. She had lost not only her husband but the crucial "third" who provides ballast for the mother–child relationship in the transition from symbiotic union through separation-individuation to autonomy (Mahler, 1975).

When I began to write this account, I realized that in my first intervention with this family I had unknowingly stepped into the role of the father in relation to a symbiotic pair. Mr. M. had done substantial work at home on the computer and, in my first meeting with Benjamin's mother, she reported that Benjamin had taken some of the disks, which and previously been off-limits, from his father's desk and now carried them everywhere. I wondered whether Benjamin might be confused or upset if allowed to break his father's rules. Therefore, I suggested that his mother might offer a substitute for the disks, while promising to save them for him. This recommendation had aspects of both protecting the psychic presence of the father and standing in for him in his actual absence. Benjamin had regressed in response to Mr. M.'s death, and his mother, in attuning herself to Benjamin's affective state, had tolerated his regression to an earlier developmental phase with fewer external demands and a less differentiated use of objects, both animate and inanimate. In her appreciation of this child's need for comfort, she had allowed his symbolic merger with his father – Benjamin could own his father's desk and its contents as an infant owns his mother's body – but unwittingly had also permitted the use of a forbidden pleasure, with the potential for heightened anxiety and later guilt.

I think that in suggesting a change, I had unconsciously offered myself to Benjamin's mother as the missing "third," who could think with her about parenting and provide a counterpoint to the symbiotic pull to the desired safety of a seamless, unbreakable parent–child relationship. At the same time, perhaps in an identificatory attempt to keep my own father alive in some fashion, I spoke for the absent father, protesting the invasion of the psychic and physical space he had previously occupied. My giving voice to his role as a protector of limits and boundaries with "Don't let him get into my things" offered protection against Benjamin's erasing the actual rules and intrapsychic constraints his father had established for him. This may have represented the beginning of my role as a placeholder – as father-not-father.

Benjamin's therapy evolved in ways that promoted my role as father-not-father, a person who both interpersonally and intrapsychically provided comfort in the face of loss and offered a much needed base for mother and child in their struggle to reconstruct family relationships. Subjectively, my somewhat muted mood in the wake of my father's death quite likely promoted an emotional attunement with this family, allowing me more easily to join in their grief. Like our fathers, I was sometimes "not quite there." With Benjamin and his mother my slightly altered state of consciousness, which blurred the boundaries between present and absent, present and past, seemed to provide an affective fit, while in my other sessions it often had a notable disquieting effect on me, and sometimes disturbed my patients.

Effects of my mourning on Benjamin's psychotherapy

During the weeks following my father's death, while sitting with other patients, I often experienced thoughts of my absent father as unbidden and confusing intrusions into my working mind. However, in the sessions with Benjamin thoughts of my father did not feel intrusive – in these sessions I could open the door to my father's company, using what I had absorbed from him about fathering to guide me in creating a paternal presence in the room.

Our sessions together granted both Benjamin and me a forum to explore fathers of all sorts – present, absent, missed, loved, longed for, conscious, unconscious, remembered, forgotten, hated, ambivalently held, idealized, forsaken, created. Holding the place of his absent father allowed me the opportunity for identification with the most nurturing aspects of my own lost father. In the sessions with Benjamin I was free to move from fatherless child to "father" of a fatherless child and, in ways both conscious and unconscious, to offer Benjamin a more complex and nuanced concept of father than he, at the age of 27 months, could possibly know (Ogden, 1987). In this sense I could stand in for Mr. M. as a "fathered father"; I could maintain and convey a sense of fatherless (Chodorow, 1978) that extended well beyond Benjamin's developmentally primitive and sometimes enviably naïve conception of relationships.

Creation of the placeholding function

I believe the reasons for and importance of my role as a placeholder in the beginning of this psychotherapy were manifold and interconnected. First, I knew from my own mourning-induced exhaustion that Benjamin probably had little psychic energy for the effort involved in interpersonal relationships, particularly the demands of getting to know a new person. Consequently, I assumed that initially he would have very little curiosity about or interest in me. At the chronological age of 27 months and in the throes of loss-induced regression, I expected that Benjamin's internal object world was far too fluid and in too much disarray (Furman, 1974; Klein, 1940) to make a separate place for me, and so I didn't ask for one until he demonstrated some interest in me as a distinct person.

Second, I believe both Benjamin and his mother saw me as someone with whom they could create and hold a place for the lost father. Benjamin, like other children trying to manage the loss of a parent, did turn to others as substitute objects (Furman, 1973). In this arena, I was superfluous. He had the good fortune of having many relatives, family friends, and a devoted grandmotherly babysitter to whom he could and did turn for care, comfort, and companionship. As much as possible for a two-year-old, they always existed in Benjamin's "real" world.

In contrast, because I had not been part of this real world, I was available to be created and used by Benjamin and his mother. By allowing myself to be embedded in their relationship, I could hold a place for and with the lost father until Benjamin could begin to make a separate space for a relationship with me that could help him mourn his loss. In parallel fashion, by creating me as the "third" in relation to the mother–child dyad, Benjamin's mother gained a space for actively mourning the loss of their children's parent and her parenting partner. While my willingness to step into Benjamin's internal drama is fundamental to psychoanalytic treatment, I believe that some of the atypical aspects of this case influenced the initial creation of me as a father-not-father – a placeholder for the lost father. Specifically, I entered Benjamin's life at a time of stark unreality – what could possibly be real or true about a loving parent's simply leaving, never to return?

His mother, like the other people closest to him, was in the altered state of consciousness that premature and unexpected death brings. What is known to be true one moment can abruptly become too unbearable to hold, felt instead as a dreadful nightmare that must certainly end with wakefulness. Initially, death is both known to be real and believed to be a dream or a horrible untruth (Engel, 1961; Didion, 2006). Internally, the bereaved person moves from one unbearable reality to another, and Benjamin's actual journey to my office paralleled this intraspychic travel from one world to another. He and his mother began their weekly trips from their home in a suburban neighborhood and traveled some distance through the gray, haunting fog of San Francisco winters to my office in the city. These trips from the comfortable familiarity of home to the strange world of the city, from known to unknown, for a young child might well have conferred a sense of moving from real to unreal on these journeys. All of this, along with the usual sense that the therapeutic relationship is like no other, may have contributed to Benjamin's initial use of me as a placeholder – someone both father and not-father.

Third I realized from the beginning of my work with this little boy that one day Benjamin might want to know about his reactions to his father's death and our work together. He was certainly too young to remember this process and, if his mother successfully mourned the loss, she would inevitably forget its details. Therefore, the task of remembering was mine. It occurred to me that Benjamin might want to know more about the loss of his father as he approached fatherhood himself.

I calculated that at the time Benjamin might be beginning a family, I would likely be about my father's age at the time of his death. I greeted this intriguing bit of information with great ambivalence. On the one hand, the idea that our connection might be extended in this way pleased me. However, I hardly needed one more reminder of my own mortality, nor did I welcome the prospect of the kind of record-keeping this task would require. Thus, another aspect of my role as a placeholder was my deliberate awareness of holding Benjamin's father – his presence and his loss – in my mind so that I could write a story for Benjamin.

Discussion of the sessions with Benjamin

These first three sessions poignantly display the intensity of Benjamin's distress. At the point when we first met, by his mother's description, he was a veritable ghost of his former self. Previously an energetic, happy little boy, Benjamin appeared profoundly depressed in both affect and behavior. His facial expression, when it could be discerned behind the ever-present pacifier, was one of the abject misery. His movements about the office displayed purpose, but no pleasure. One of those children who had skipped the "baby-talk" stage and had begun speaking in complete and complex sentences, Benjamin was now reduced to simple, often repetitive verbalizations. Frequently, I could barely decipher these through the pacifier, which had become his constant companion since his father's death, though he had cast it aside several weeks before this loss. His mother reported that he had even learned to eat around it, and when, in the third session, I asked if he could take it out of his mouth so that I might better understand him, he could tolerate its absence for only a few seconds.

With pacifier in place, Benjamin's first words to me were, "Look at that." Although these words manifestly referred to the Legos he picked from the basket, in retrospect I think they were a direct response to my comments about his father's death. I believe that Benjamin used these words to evoke the presence of his father in the room. It was as if he, mother, and father were grouped in one corner, standing solidly against the harshness of my statement about his father's death. In essence he corrected my statement that his father had died by his comment, which meant to assert, "My Daddy is not dead. He is here with me." Through this identifcatory statement he thus conveyed both his profound wish and unspoken belief that his father could not possibly have left him.

While evoking the protective presence of the father who could steady him as he met me and my unwanted words, he also introduced me to his father – began to tell me something of the place his father occupied in his internal world. In Benjamin's repetitive phrase, "Look at that," we can hear the voice of a protective and encouraging father, inviting his child to explore the new toys and comforting him in this unfamiliar, unexplored territory. As illustration, a few months later I was asked to evaluate a boy of 20 months during the stress of an interrupted adoptive process. His adoptive father, with whom he had lived for most of his life, brought him to my office. The child was understandably wary of yet another new place and person. His father quickly moved to the basket of Legos, and helped one up for his son's inspection, repeatedly commenting "Look at that!"

Benjamin also showed me his sense of the enormous disruption of his internal and external world when he emptied the dollhouse of its normal contents. With this, perhaps, he demonstrated the barrenness of a fatherless universe. After he had gone I paused to consider the meaning of Benjamin's leaving the marbles in the safety of the house. I wondered if this play demonstrated his understanding and hope that this therapeutic space could be of help to him? I wondered if therapy would provide a space where his wildly careening feelings, like the marbles that scattered and rolled through the rooms of the dollhouse, might be safely contained. His talking about the marbles during the week between the sessions seems to confirm his recognition and acceptance of the offer both his mother and I made for him to use me, the room, and the therapeutic process as a means of knowing and containing his feelings. Together we could create a transitional space capable of holding him and his responses to the absent but present father.

Usually I am careful to see that toys are in their regular places before therapy sessions. The presence of the father figure in the dollhouse probably surprised me more than Benjamin, who could not yet distinguish regular from irregular happenings in my office. In one sense, the doll's being out of place reflected the distraction stemming from my own mourning process – I was not as attentive to such details as usual. Until Benjamin approached the dollhouse I did not see that, with the doll lying face down on the floor, I had unconsciously portrayed for Benjamin my image of his father lying dead as he put his baby brother to bed. The father doll's presence in the house also reflected a "slip of the mind" that silently announced the purpose of our relationship: coming to terms with the loss of a father. As is typical, this slip simultaneously represented both my wish that our fathers were home, where they belonged, and my recognition that our fathers, like this displaced figure, were not in their proper intrapsychic spaces.

We can only speculate about the meaning of Benjamin's response to this figure. He may have felt the doll as an invasion into his thoughts or plans for play. Perhaps his action shows the force with which he felt his father wrenched from him; perhaps he tossed it away out of anger at his father for leaving; maybe he protested being prodded to confront and come to terms with a death that he could not yet grasp.

The events on the morning of the next session seem to offer more insight into Benjamin's concerns about the cause of his father's death. His cozy, private moment in the kitchen with his mother is interrupted by his baby brother's cry. When his mother leaves to tend to Noah, Benjamin, in terror, moves to the bottom of the stairs but does not go up after her. This suggests that he fears not finding her upstairs – fears that she, like his father, has died and will never return. In Benjamin's reported memory he and his father had been baking brownies when his father left him to tend to his baby brother. Baking together had been one of their favorite shared activities; however, that day they had apparently been together in the kitchen while Benjamin's father prepared dinner. We might reasonably assume that Benjamin had been angry at this father for leaving him, especially during such a treasured moment. We might also reasonably assume that the egocentric world view (Piaget, 1954) and fluidity between thought and action that characterize this age might have led Benjamin to conclude that his angry thoughts had killed first his father and now his mother. He had expressed anger in the days following his father's death. Standing at the window waiting for his father to return from work, he had angrily insisted that his mother was wrong – his father was *not* dead and *would* come home. However, sadness had been his predominant affect.

Benjamin's play with the truck – involving trash and garbage, going to and fro, collecting and dumping – both made and contained a mess. His interest in the garbage truck offered me an opportunity to offer myself as a "dumping ground" for his difficult feelings. Here, he could leave his unneeded "trash" so that he could move forward in his life. Simultaneously, this play reflected Benjamin's separate developmental concerns. In this play he behaves like most two-year-olds who, alternating between love and disgust for their bodily products, are captivated by this kind of play.

Benjamin's response earlier that morning may have signaled his growing consciousness of me as a person who could help him. Knowing that he would be seeing me, he might have used, whether consciously or unconsciously, his mother's trip upstairs to show her what he needed me to know. In the preoccupation with his father's death, he had temporarily lost himself (Shane & Shane, 1990). In the first session his mother and I had articulated the reasons for his visits to me; perhaps he used this session to let us know *his* reasons for joining in this endeavor. With this accomplished, he could begin the work of psychotherapy. I believe his ease and pleasure later in the session during our dumping play represented his first steps toward recapturing his developmental self. This session is that of a two-year-old whose developmental concerns are properly with his own alive body, its contents and products.

Then something happened that made him turn from his play. It might have been that his enjoyment was more apparent than real and actually a hypomanic defense against an overwhelming sadness that eventually broke through. His mother had explained to Benjamin that his father's body had stopped working, that he didn't need it anymore; perhaps he suddenly felt that we were dumping his father's useless body. Maybe he also felt that in this play, which involved his ideas and developmental concerns and brought him into a playful closeness to me, he had momentarily lost the connection to his father. He left the interaction and went to the toy telephones but did not use them in play. Perhaps this reflected his wish to reconnect with his father along with the beginning of the recognition that he could not.

The development of the therapist as placeholder in subsequent sessions

The third session established a rhythm for Benjamin's sessions that persisted throughout the early months of his therapy and brought me into the life of the family. When Benjamin's distress made it impossible for him to talk, his mother described the event that had upset him so. In subsequent weeks, on the drive to my office, she would ask Benjamin what he wanted her to tell me about the week or offer suggestions about what she thought I should know. Our sessions, then, typically began with her recounting stories about Benjamin, including important events, difficult feelings, funny happenings, discussions about his daddy, or plans for the coming weeks. Although Benjamin would talk at length to his mother about what she should tell me, he sometimes did not want to tell me his thoughts directly. The importance of this talk between his mother and me became increasingly apparent. Sometimes Benjamin would chime in, sometimes he just listened very attentively, while at other times his quiet play made it unclear how carefully he was attending to us.

I began to think of these discussions as similar to the conversations Benjamin had been used to hearing between his parents as the family gathered at the end of the day. This was one of the rhythms of Benjamin's life that had been disrupted by his father's death. In the early weeks of therapy, there were still many people in and out of the house and, although all of the adults were every attentive to Benjamin and Noah, the familiar, idiosyncratic sounds of his family had disappeared.

It was very important to Benjamin that I know about his life between our sessions and that I learn about it in his presence. I think this may have held such significance for him because of the time of his father's death in relation to Benjamin's development. Although extremely verbally precocious, Benjamin was still too young to relate a complex, detailed story. Just as he needed the help of one parent to tell the other about his daily life, he needed to see and hear himself reflected back in his parents' looks and words in order to come to know himself, both as an individual and as a person in relationship to them. Benjamin's parents enjoyed each other, their work, and their children. Benjamin's mother described the conversations that constituted the fabric of Benjamin's family life as largely lighthearted and pleasant. Like all others, Benjamin's parents had had conflicts but they seemed to have had the good sense and self control to protect their children from discussion that would distress or confuse them. Thus, in Benjamin's life, talk between adults had generally provided a soothing backdrop of sounds which sometimes drew him close, but also offered him security as he moved through the house with the noise of his parents' voices in the background.

This process of Benjamin's mother and me talking to and about him at the beginning of therapy sessions not only provided a bridge between home and therapy, but between the old life with his father and the new one without him. I believe that through this we also promoted the creation of me as a placeholder for Benjamin's father. In this system I held the place of the returning parent who learned of the important events that had occurred in my absence. At the same time, through his mother's words I learned about Benjamin's father, who he had been, how each of them had held him in their internal worlds, and how they were struggling to reorder those worlds without him. In this way, I could make a place for Benjamin's father in my mind as well, so that I could come to hold him for and with them. Through this process Benjamin also could come to know something of the relationship between these two adults who cared for and about him and each other. When he began psychotherapy he did not have the developmental capacity to grasp the separateness of the adult relationship between his parents (Fonagy et al., 1991). However, I believe Benjamin's position as the participant observer in these conversations between his mother and me helped him to recapture his developmental momentum. My position as a placeholder for the lost father provided the needed third position that held open the door to his continued separation and autonomy. As the months of therapy progressed, his perspective from the third point of his triangle allowed him to participate in, while maintaining separateness from, the nuances of relationship between two adults devoted to his well-being. As oedipal themes later became more prominent in his behavior at home and in the office, he became less enamored of the conversations between his mother and me.

My place in Benjamin's internal world

As Benjamin settled into therapy the particulars of his representations of me became apparent. The immediate crisis imposed by his father's death left little room for me. As it gradually quieted, Benjamin could begin to make a place for me in both his internal and external world. While running errands with this mother, he would often suggest to her that they could stop to visit Dr. Heineman, even though they were actually miles from my office.

Benjamin's mother had initiated a bedtime activity of listing "people who love Benjamin" as a means of helping Benjamin cope with his father's death. Although he had lost someone who had loved him, together they could remember all the loving people still in his life. He spontaneously added me to this roster, perhaps filling a void that his father's ambiguous place left – for in a young child's mind loving and leaving do not go together.

He most clearly articulated his view of me one evening about two months after beginning therapy. During that period, his mother had felt particularly tearful and described Benjamin's mood as similar. He seemed to be in a state of continual whimpering although he empathically insisted that he was *not* sad – the doll was sad, the dog was sad, the baby was sad, but he decidedly was *not* sad. As she got him out of the bath one evening he leaned into her with a moan. She asked what was wrong. He replied that he was fine and asked if she was fine. She responded that she was not fine – she was healthy, fine in that way – but she was very, very, very sad. Benjamin asked if some juice would make her feel better. She said that juice probably would not help. He then asked if going to see Dr. Heineman would make her feel better. She thanked him for the idea, but said that Dr. Heineman was to help *him* feel better. Again, he insisted that perhaps playing with Dr. Heineman's toys would help her. She told him that she had someone to help her with her sad feelings but that she liked going with him to see Dr. Heineman.

This brief, poignant interaction offers us a peek into Benjamin's internal world. He has told his mother that he cannot bear to name or claim his sadness. Perhaps this was out of fear that voicing it will only worsen it, or perhaps from a wish that eliminating the feeling will eliminate the reason for being, or perhaps from a worry that his father's death has transformed his mother into a sad, scared, tired tot – just like himself.

We also see that Benjamin has internalized protective, nurturing images of adults: he offers to care for his mother as she cared for him. Kindly and firmly she helps him with reality testing, gently explaining that juice does not cure grief. He then suggests that relationships cure grief and she agrees, reminding him that she is not a tot who will benefit from playing with toys, but his mother who has provided this relationship for him in his father's absence.

Later phases of Benjamin's psychotherapy

I saw Benjamin in weekly psychotherapy for a little more than a year. During that time his play took many forms. Particularly in the early weeks of therapy it was often tempting to focus on the themes of loss in his play and to see him as primarily concerned with his preoccupation with his father's death. However, developmentally Benjamin was also involved in sorting out the feelings associated with separation, a growing sense of autonomy, and those feelings stemming from the day-to-day separations and reunions of normal family life. Gradually, in his relationships with me and with friends and family, he moved to more oedipal interests. His play with me shifted to more competitive themes; often through play with toy soldiers or an army of trucks, he worked to find ways of identifying with me as a strong figure who could help him and would not retaliate for his obvious pleasure in victory over me.

Without doubt, Benjamin's relationship with his mother, including her mental health and capacity to gather and use the support of family, friends, and professionals was the single most important factor in Benjamin's renewing a healthy course. Wisely, with each new developmental challenge, she pondered how to balance Benjamin's need for extra time or care because of his father's death with his need to meet and master the demands of growing up. So, for example, she delayed the beginning of toilet training, but then held firm in her quite realistic expectations that he could master this step toward bodily control and autonomy. When he greeted his entry into nursery school with regression and minimal excitement, she decided that he needed more time at home before tackling those demands. A year later, he flourished in a new preschool.

Benjamin had returned to his generally cheerful demeanor with expectable expressions of anger and aggression. He seemed able to manage the ups and downs of daily life, including turning to adults for help when he felt the need. Benjamin's mother had begun a relationship with a man with two small children. Benjamin reacted with anticipated admixtures of positive and negative feelings – pleasure, possessiveness, jealousy, relief, competition, love, joy, and a renewed sense of family. He could and did talk openly about his feelings, including a couple of tries at manipulation through references to his sadness about his father's death when other attempts to have things his way failed.

Based on these and similar observations, Benjamin's mother and I independently began considering termination shortly before the anniversary of his father's death. As we discussed this possibility, we realized that because of planned absences in both of our schedules there was a danger of Benjamin's therapy becoming somewhat diffuse over the next several weeks. It seemed essential that Benjamin have a chance to say a proper goodbye – that our separation neither come as a surprise nor drift by without notice.

I felt very strongly that we should continue beyond the anniversary of the death, particularly because of the meaning it would have for the important adults in Benjamin's life. I expected that their preoccupation and diminished emotional availability would evoke, though to a much lesser extent, the losses Benjamin had suffered the previous year. His mother readily agreed to this plan and, indeed, the feelings evoked by the anniversary were stronger than she had expected. When I saw Benjamin the day after the anniversary he informed me that he had been very sad the day before, but today he was not too sad and wanted to play. I introduced the idea of termination by commenting that when he had first come to see me when his daddy had died he had been too sad to play but that now he could have sad feelings and still play just fine. We then had several weeks to talk about the ending of our regular meetings.

Subsequent contact

In the following year, at Benjamin's request, he returned on three separate occasions. His mother initiated the first two visits in response to Benjamin's talking about feeling particularly sad and asking to see me. Although both his mother and I were agreeable to his coming in for a number of sessions, Benjamin seemed satisfied with a single meeting on these occasions. Just knowing that he could "check in" appeared to be the most salient aspect of our contact.

The third reunion, which occurred just about a year after termination, was far more affectively and interpersonally complicated. As usual, his mother brought him to the hour but as it drew to a close, Benjamin became increasingly anxious as he frantically tried to find time to return to all of the familiar and favorite toys and play themes. When I said that it seemed that he needed more time and that we could arrange for a return visit he relaxed and indicated his agreement with this plan. Unexpectedly his mother's work schedule made it impossible for her to bring him at the agreed upon time; instead his stepfather, whom I had met previously, but not with Benjamin, brought him to the session. As they approached my office, there was no doubt about Benjamin's intention that this father would accompany him.

While Mr. S. settled into a chair with some uncertainty about how we would proceed, I reminded Benjamin that often when his mother brought him, she and I would talk and then he and I would play. He responded "This time, no talk. Just play." With this comment, he moved toward the basket of building blocks and invited his father to join him. While Benjamin and his new father worked together to build an elaborate tower, playfully negotiating the tension between collaborative builders and adversarial destroyers of their shared construction, I watched from the sidelines, enjoying my vantage from a different point on the triangle.

My position as placeholder had gradually shifted over the year of treatment as Benjamin sifted through the issues of loss, separation-individuation, and oedipal strivings. I felt that with this session my role as placeholder had officially ended. My initial task had been to hold, rather than fill, potential space. Thus when Benjamin came to my office accompanied by his newly gained and very real, alive, and interested father, he no longer needed to sort through the old toys and games that had occupied us in our time and work together. Instead, he could in a new and different way, with his father by his side, invite me to "look at that."

Conclusion

I have emphasized the very beginning of his psychotherapy. One of the psychological consequences of early childhood loss is that the weight of years and positive experiences cannot alone offset the impact of that loss. We know from observations and clinical experience with bereaved children that in healthy development these children revisit and revise their understanding of death and its impact on their personal histories as their cognitive and affective capacities grow and change. At the time I first began writing Benjamin's story for him he was 4 and a half and had lived half of his life without his father. In his early adolescence he asked his mother if he could visit me when they next travelled to San Francisco. The visit never materialized but he asked his mother if he could read the story that he knew I had written for him. At last report, Benjamin was a flourishing young adult.

Perhaps the outcome of Benjamin's therapy would have been similar if he had seen a different therapist or come to me at a different point in my life. However, I believe the confluence of the events in our lives promoted the particular process that emerged in our work together. My father had been at his best with very young children. Benjamin's age and vulnerability certainly promoted my identification with the most nurturing aspects of my own father, allowing me then to offer my father-self to him. Like Benjamin's world, my internal world of object representations was also in disarray, making it easier for me to create a new father for and with him – a father who could stand with us as we struggled with the internal reorganizations demanded by a fatherless external world.

Notes

1 Benjamin's behavior in this session is a good illustration of a secure attachment. When meeting me, a stranger, he uses his mother as a home base. Initially, he stays close to her and, as he gradually feels more comfortable, moves away to explore a toy that captures his interest. A less securely attached child might have felt the need to cling to the parent, refusing to leave her lap, disregarded her presence altogether, or perhaps (too) quickly engaged me in his play.

2 Benjamin vividly illustrated this phenomenon at the time of his third birthday, about nine months into therapy. By then he could talk readily about how his Daddy wasn't coming home because he was dead. As he and his mother walked from the celebration to the car, he quietly commented, "I thought that dead Daddies would come to birthday parties."

Section V

BACK TO BASICS

When we started A Home Within it was with the fundamental belief in the vital place of stable, caring relationships in healthy development and the power of therapeutic relationships to heal. We understood that development could be derailed by traumatic interactions with adults and peers who hurt children rather than helping them to grow. We also understood that, with time and care, supportive relationships could help children manage and even overcome the damage that lack of care or abuse inflicts.

In the intervening years much has changed – whether for good or ill – and so the therapeutic landscape is different. Technology has given us a much more profound understanding of brain function, yet we still wonder about the relationship between the brain and the mind. We have a vast array of psychotropic medications that can often give swift symptomatic relief from anxiety and depression, frequently bringing with them complex unwanted side effects. Instant access to worlds of knowledge is, quite literally, at our fingertips, but can leave us impatient with processes that don't offer quick or easy solutions. And the reasonable search for evidence that what we offer does actually help to alleviate human suffering sometimes imposes incomprehensible constraints on therapeutic endeavors.

However, some things haven't changed. Relationships still matter. Over the years of our work through A Home Within, with change swirling around us, we have maintained our fundamental belief in the power of relationships to heal, and we have collected evidence to support our position. We have also refined our clinical approach, learning from our clients and each other what works and what doesn't. The final chapter of this volume summarizes and synthesizes the fundamental tenets of Relationship-Based Therapy, the approach that drives our work and, according to what we have learned, provides the most effective treatment for those who struggle to surmount the emotional consequences of foster care.

11

THE ESSENCE OF RELATIONSHIP-BASED THERAPY

I hope that this chapter illustrates the triumphs, failures, and complexities of providing mental health treatment to traumatized children and youth who spend time in the foster care system. The clinicians of these vulnerable clients center their work on the development and maintenance of healthy relationships. In this chapter I highlight the crucial elements of Relationship-Based Therapy (RBT), paired with examples of each element from the cases presented earlier. Rather than a comprehensive discussion, the summary is intended to provide an overview of all the significant factors that contribute to the success of this approach.

A paradox of RBT is that it is at the same time straightforward, drawing heavily on common sense, and also incredibly complex and nuanced. In this chapter we outline the eight essential elements of RBT: 1) Engagement: being fully present in the relationship; 2) Environment: appreciating the context surrounding the relationship; 3) Empathy: imagining the feelings of another; 4) Egocentrism: recognizing the unique make-up of every individual and relationship; 5) Enthusiasm: bringing optimism to difficult realities, 6) Evidence: relying on demonstratively effective approaches; 7) Endurance: remaining open and available; and 8) Extending: appreciating the continuity of relationships. Many of these divisions may seem arbitrary, misrepresenting the complexity of how these elements are intertwined. For example, engagement requires empathy and enthusiasm supports endurance and endurance requires enthusiasm and engagement. Moreover, emotion is infused in all elements. For example, empathy requires an awareness of, and response to, the emotions of another. Throughout, we provide examples of the connection between each element and emotion.

I hope that you will read the pages that follow with an eye to discovering the ways in which you already incorporate RBT into your work and generating ideas about how the eight elements can support your continued clinical efforts. This chapter refers to children and youth because this volume has focused primarily on work in the foster care system. However, RBT applies as well to adults and to clients who have not spent time in foster care. The elements described here are fundamental to the building of any therapeutic relationship.

Engagement

Clients with a history of hurtful or disappointing relationships often do not enter into new relationships easily. If, as in the case of most foster youth, they have suffered numerous unexpected and unexplained losses – of family members, caseworkers, foster parents, and therapists – they are understandably wary of starting with yet another new person. Some clients, particularly adolescents, may be quite vocal about their expectations of being left. It's not uncommon to hear, "Why should I talk to you? You're just going to leave like all the others." Successful therapeutic relationships require that the therapist be fully engaged in the process of getting to know the client. This includes acknowledging and accepting the client's anxieties about entering a new relationship since, for many, stepping through the door is the hardest part of the therapeutic process.

Engagement includes protecting the integrity of the therapeutic process

Too often, therapists face external factors that impede the therapeutic process. Challenges can include a ceiling on financial support, a crisis situation that demands immediate action, the revision of an agency policy from do "whatever it takes" for your client to "whatever it takes, so long as it's within our catchment area." In each of these situations, the therapist has a responsibility to make the restrictions clear to the client. The same holds true for interns and others who may only be available for a limited time because of training demands. These situations call for a simple, straightforward explanation of circumstances that may limit the length of the relationship, such as, "I will be at the clinic until next summer," or "We have ten weeks to work together." Conversely, therapists who are working without specific external constraints are in a position to say, "I can't make any promises, but my intention is to be here until our work together is finished."

When delivering information they believe may upset the client, especially if it will confirm a negative expectation, therapists are often tempted to move quickly to try to soften the news. For example, "I will be at the clinic until next summer. Let's think about what we can accomplish in that time." The addition of the second sentence short-circuits the client's chance to experience and process feelings such as anger and disappointment and, understandably, risks sending the message that the therapist really doesn't want to hear anything upsetting.

The over-arching goal of the therapy is to develop a healthy relationship that can provide the foundation for the client to move into other satisfying and growth-promoting relationships; simply accepting all of the emotions that the client brings into the session is the first step toward that goal. Often, sitting quietly and listening to what the client has to say – whether in words or behavior – is the most powerful demonstration of the therapist's engagement with the client in the therapeutic process. Engagement can be exceedingly confusing and difficult for the therapist, particularly, as we saw in Chapter three, with children like Louise who cannot tell their stories in a coherent narrative.

Being fully engaged means being attentive to what might be going on in the mind of the client

We only know each other by a "meeting of the minds," and the therapist must facilitate this process. Sometimes this can be as simple as asking "What's on your mind?" or if the therapist notices a change in facial expression or shift in posture, "What happened just then?" These simple questions show the client that you want to know what he or she is thinking, and that you care. Many youth who have been abused may not make this relational assumption and such a question can be reparative.

Engagement includes expression of the therapist's personal thoughts and feelings only when such disclosures directly benefit the client. Especially for foster youth, who have not had the experience of being kept in mind, it is often remarkable to them that the therapist thinks about them even when they are not in a therapy session. When working with clients who have not had a consistent, caring adult who keeps them in mind, it is very important for therapists to be explicit about the fact that they think about them. This can be a powerful statement, but it can also be simple. The therapist might say, "As I was driving here I was thinking about what we talked about last week and how surprised you were to learn that I think about you even when we're not together. It made me sad to think how lonely that must make you feel." In this context it is important to remember that the therapy is for the benefit of the client and that information about the therapist's thoughts and feelings should be offered only for the purpose of promoting the relationship in a way that will help the client. In the example above, the client's surprise and the therapist's response open the door to a different kind of relationship. The therapist's expression of sadness still relates to the client's experience. This is different from a comment such as, "I was so lonely yesterday and it made me remember how lonely you feel sometimes," which is a statement about the therapist, not the client.

Engagement requires anticipation of closure

Engagement also raises the issue of disengagement and bringing the session to a close. Unlike clients whose experiences and relationships have been relatively predictable, those who have spent time in foster care have often been surprised by people leaving suddenly and never returning. It is both kind and helpful for the therapist to give sufficient warning before the end of a session so that the client doesn't feel cut off or interrupted mid-sentence. Simply telling the client that the session will end in about ten minutes and then in five, allows therapist and client to bring things to an orderly close. Saying, "I know that we're in the middle of something important and I'm sorry to have to interrupt you, but we can talk about it again next week," also reminds the client that the therapist can keep the client in mind until the next session, and that there will indeed be a next session. When therapists mention that the session will be ending, some clients assume that they are just counting down the minutes until they can escape. However, a conversation about ending, and a clear act that indicates a desire to meet again – such as giving the client a business card with the time and date of the next appointment – can serve as a concrete symbol of the continuity of the relationship.

Engagement is a powerful therapeutic and critical tool. For those who have not experienced positive relationships, this process may require time, patience, boundaries, and empathy.

Environment

The success of the therapeutic relationship is, in large measure, influenced by its environment. Therefore, the therapist assesses the environment and, as much as possible, attunes the therapy to the surroundings. This requires an awareness of a vast array of factors, including the physical environment of the therapy room, family and peer support, and societal values pertaining to therapy.

The therapy room sets the stage for stability and consistency

Therapists often decorate offices with the goal of creating a pleasant place for clients and themselves. They hang pictures that are soothing, arrange chairs comfortably, and look for ways to ensure warmth and relaxation. One thing many therapists don't realize is the importance of maintaining the environment for clients, not as a place to visit, but as a shared space that also belongs to them. Children may want to leave a toy in a special place, or create a Lego structure that they hope the therapist will save, or find ways to transform and control the physical space. When they return to the stable environment, where things remain the same, the knowledge that their trace does not vanish, and that they remain a part of the therapist's world can help provide a sense of security.

When therapists change the environment, clients notice. This is not to say that change is not acceptable or sometimes appropriate. Many clinicians must provide therapy in a different office each week, or in different community settings. Consequently, the critical principle is to look for ways to ensure environmental stability – be it a consistent meeting place, a seating arrangement, or the presence of a favorite toy. When there is change, the therapist needs to acknowledge it and hold space for the client to express his or her feelings about the change. We know that, too often, foster youth are asked to change without consideration of their feelings. They are sometimes even expected to behave as if the change hadn't happened or was of no consequence. It is our responsibility to help them learn how change can be integrated into their lives in healthy ways.

It is important to keep in mind the inherent power imbalance in the therapeutic relationship

Part of the environment created by the therapist and client involves acknowledgment of power differentials that exist in the relationship. In therapy it is simple: the client is asking for help and the therapist is there to provide it. Unfortunately, embedded in

ESSENCE OF RELATIONSHIP-BASED THERAPY

this implicit agreement may be the assumption that something is wrong with the client and the therapist can fix it. For foster youth, this assumption may confirm their belief that they are "broken," leaving them feeling that they have to protect themselves against someone who they fear will see them as damaged or flawed.

Therapists will also see the repercussions of the chronic disempowering of foster youth. Many youth have never had the choice to attend a meeting, to move homes, or to change schools. Rather, they have simply been told what to do, often without input or preparation. When they enter therapy, they are resistant to another adult who will tell them what to do and who will have power over their choices. Providing clients with choices when appropriate is critical to empowering them to be a part of the therapeutic process.

It is the responsibility of the therapist to be aware of ethical issues related to power, including the many small and seemingly inconsequential ways in which therapists can exploit clients. One common example of this is through timeliness. Many therapists may think that being five minutes late to a session is acceptable. However, therapists who frequently arrive late to sessions announce, by their behavior, that they don't take their clients' time seriously. This is an example of behavior that, at first glance, may seem unimportant, but is actually quite meaningful and, therefore, entirely unacceptable.

Clinicians working with clients who have been abused or mistreated may sometimes feel as if they are the ones being exploited in the therapeutic relationship. Clients come late, or just don't show up; they disparage the therapist's comments and suggestions; they hurl insults or fall asleep in the session. Or they taunt the therapist by withholding themselves and sometimes, like Jimmy in Chapter seven, food. At these times the clinician must understand that this is the only way that many clients can introduce therapists to their experience and their environment. They may have no other way to tell us about what it is like to feel as if no one cares enough to show up on time, or discounts all of their opinions, or seems not to hear anything they have to say. Therapists who attend to their own feelings of being disregarded, discounted, or exploited will learn something very important about the emotional lives of their clients. Moreover, therapists who are able to use this information to connect with the youth may also develop a deeper understanding of their clients' experiences. For example, if a client consistently arrives late to sessions, the therapist might offer something like, "Maybe without even knowing it, you wanted me to know what it feels like to be waiting and wondering if anyone's going to show up." Rather than telling clients that they need to change their behavior, comments such as this invite them to reflect on their actions in the context of the relationship.

The adults who care for children and adolescents are the single most important aspect of their environment

It is essential that the therapist meet with caregivers to understand their expectations for the therapy, including the extent to which they will lend their support. Support from caregivers includes getting the child to and from sessions on time, keeping the therapist informed of changes in the child's life – including moods and behavior – and meeting with the therapist periodically to collaborate on behalf of the child. This support is imperative, not only for acquiring adequate assessment information, but for generalizing treatment gains beyond the therapy.

When meeting with parents, we must recognize their perceptions of, and experiences with, therapy. If caregivers have been told by a teacher or a caseworker that their child needs to go to therapy and have thus been made to feel as if they are not good parents, the clinician might reasonably expect them to be wary and wanting to keep a distance from the therapist, lest they be judged negatively or be asked to do more when they are already overwhelmed. On the other hand, if a child is referred for treatment by caregivers who have themselves had good experiences with therapy, the clinician can reasonably expect that the parents will have some understanding of the process and will be supportive of the relationship. Many foster parents are instructed to take a child to therapy without adequate explanation of the process, desired outcomes, or their role. Therapists must offer information and support if they expect cooperation and collaboration.

It is incumbent upon therapists to assess societal expectations of therapy that influence the client

In some communities psychotherapy is commonplace, while in others people believe that "only crazy people see a shrink." Whether directly or indirectly, attitudes such as these will influence the therapeutic relationship and affect the child's turning toward or away from the therapist as an ally. Especially for adolescents and young adults, their peer relationships will be decisively influence the therapeutic relationship. This is particularly true for groups that are easily marginalized and/or mistreated. For example, many foster youth have been traumatized through no fault of their own. However, many of them have also been labeled with behavioral and psychological problems that can imply that they have caused their own difficulties. When referred for therapy, these youth may be unwilling participants and instead, turn to peer groups for affection and acceptance they missed from their families. When assessing environmental influences, keep in mind that we are all part of many, often intertwined, communities, leaving marginalized populations at risk of being stigmatized by different systems simultaneously and repeatedly. A young Hispanic lesbian may face racial prejudice from the larger community and also be ostracized by her devoutly Catholic family who cannot reconcile her homosexuality with their religious beliefs. In situations such as these, the cumulative effect of multiple environmental impingements must be taken into account.

A careful consideration of the therapist's own biases must be part of the environmental assessment

In any therapeutic relationship, it is necessary that clinicians attend to issues of gender, race, ethnicity, culture, sexual preference, disability, class, religion, and socioeconomic status. When treating clients from the foster care system it is particularly important to keep in mind cultural differences between those who have grown up in a relatively stable family and those whose childhood relationships were characterized by instability and repeated loss. Too often, in this situation, as in others, those from the majority culture assume that those in the minority share their perceptions and values. Assumptions may also be made that those in the majority culture can understand the other person's experience by "putting themselves in his or her shoes." While this is a first step, we must realize that increasing empathy and perspective still does not ensure that we understand in any way the true vantage point of that other person. We need to recognize that cultural competence and understanding is a process. It is not something we can ever completely achieve, but rather something that we must continually strive to attain. We also need to keep in mind that the best way to learn is from the clients themselves.

Empathy

The capacity to perceive accurately the feelings of another is a cornerstone of RBT. Empathy, which may emerge from observations or imagination, involves simply comprehending how someone else is feeling in a given situation. For example, while you are walking you see a man across the street being attacked by a dog, you will almost certainly be able to imagine how the victim feels, not only intellectually, but by your own fear response. The more you learn about this person, including his history and experiences, the better you can imagine what this experience was like for him. Empathy involves a deep understanding – an imagining of what it would be like to be the client, with his/her background and experiences and beliefs. As Dr. Brown's work with Ruby described in Chapter four illustrates, it is also important to approach caregivers and other important adults in a child's life with empathy in order to develop an enhanced understanding of their attitudes and behavior.

Empathy demonstrates the human capacity to construct a "theory of mind."

The ability to identify and experience the feelings of another allows therapists to have a much fuller understanding of their clients' experiences than if they relied on cognitive or intellectual capacities alone. A therapist, hearing a young adult describe being punished as a child by being shut in a dark closet, may find herself shuddering, her heart pounding, and palms sweating. She need not have had the experience of being locked in a closet in order to imagine what that must have felt like to a young child. However, the more she gets to know her client and her experiences, the more she can envision the particulars of how the client felt during that experience. This requires that the therapist attempt to see the event not from her own reactions, but the client's. Maybe the therapist would have been scared, but maybe the client was numbed because being locked in the closet was a recurring event. To acknowledge this, the therapist could say, "I think that you had been scared so many times that you no longer felt anything when that happened."

Empathic comments allow the client a glimpse into the therapist's mind. They demonstrate that client and therapist have had a "meeting of the minds," acknowledging that the client has successfully conveyed what is in her mind, and that the therapist has thought about what she has said and allowed herself to imagine the experience. Suppose that the therapist had the misfortune of also being locked in a closet as a child and responded, "I know exactly how you felt." Even though this gives the information that therapist and client have a shared experience, this is not an empathic comment because it is about the therapist, not about the client. It is a statement that the therapist was not actually listening to the client. Instead, the story caused the therapist to attend to the memories stored in her own mind, rather than those of her client, resulting in an empathic failure.

Children who have been mistreated often behave as if they have limited capacity for empathy

To many observers, this behavior is counterintuitive. People often assume that those who have been mistreated will be more sensitive as a result. In fact, though we are hard-wired to be empathically attuned, all neural structures and activity are enhanced or impaired by experience. The child whose parents correctly read and respond to his signals – of excitement, hunger, sadness, or joy – will become increasingly adept at identifying his internal state and, as the neural connections are strengthened, will be able to send progressively clearer and more precise messages about his needs and desires. In turn, he will mirror the attunement of his parents, smiling when they smile at him or joining them in their distress. However, if caregivers are consistently misattuned to a child's signals or respond harshly and without empathy to his distress, the child will mirror their responses. Over time he will do unto others what was done to him – he may become indifferent to or respond cruelly to others' distress. He may greet sadness with laughter rather than a show of sympathy.

Clients who have been mistreated do not expect to be well treated

For those who have been mistreated, a comment such as, "You must have had a hard day," can be heard as an insult, or a suggestion that the client isn't tough enough to manage. It is essential that therapists remember that victims of maltreatment have lived much of their lives in a traumatized state and are often made anxious by the efforts of those who want to help them. Moreover, this trauma is held in the body, as well as the mind. They may have had little time or space for relaxation or calm reflection. They are used to hearing voices that hurt, rather than help, and words that blame or punish rather than soothe or inspire. In these situations, therapists need to mold the pace of the process to the client's comfort and, in some cases, incorporate relaxation techniques to still their minds to triggers of trauma. Moreover, therapists need to learn to choose their words carefully and be quick to apologize if they have misunderstood or misspoken, since empathy allows us to imagine, but not to know for certain, what it feels like to be standing in another's shoes.

Egocentrism

Although egocentrism has negative connotations, referring to people who think primarily of themselves, in the context of RBT we use it in two different ways. First, egocentrism refers to the importance of tailoring the therapy to the unique needs of every client, putting the client at the center of the therapy. It also refers to the fact that trauma results in people living in very self-absorbed, egocentric worlds.

The experience of trauma requires egocentrism

One of the unfortunate consequences of trauma is a preoccupation with the traumatic events. Sometimes clients ruminate about their traumatic histories, with stories and pictures running endlessly and repetitively through their minds. They often feel completely unable to stop these tormenting images. Understandably, those whose minds are filled with images from the past have difficulty in attending to people and events in their present lives, often giving the impression that they have no interest beyond their internal worlds. While they may act as if they are the center of the world, it is often because they are swirling in the inescapable vortex of their traumatic past.

Sadly, abuse, neglect, and repeated abandonment are common among foster youth, often leading to their living in a state of constant, heightened anxiety and egocentrism. Unfortunately, many foster children and youth have endured multiple forms of abandonment, neglect, and abuse – sometimes from a single person and sometimes from many people. The attuned therapist will keep this in mind, perhaps offering comments such as, "I think that sometimes you worry that people will hurt you and sometimes you worry that they will leave you. And sometimes you're not sure which is more frightening."

The attuned therapist will examine what underlies egocentrism rather than making its undoing a treatment goal in and of itself. For example, when individuals attend only to their own experiences, with a concomitant lack of awareness of others, the focus of treatment can quickly turn to decreasing this self-focus and increasing social skills and empathy. However, for those working with traumatized individuals, egocentrism must be seen as a coping skill and something that serves a clear and important purpose in their lives.

Egocentrism can challenge rapport building

Consideration of the multiple adverse experiences in the lives of foster youth should make clear the necessity of therapy that is tailored to meet the unique needs of each individual. In addition to abuse and abandonment, so many foster youth have also suffered neglect – their needs have simply not been recognized or met. Why, then, would they expect interest or help from a therapist?

This puts therapists who are attempting to form relationships with their clients in an understandably difficult position. They want to engage someone who expects, based on past experiences, that relationships do not meet their needs, are hurtful, and disappear without reason or warning. Why exactly should they take a chance on what we have to offer? Assessing and keeping in mind the needs of the individual client, the therapist is in a position to craft an approach that is "egocentric," that is tailored to the unique needs of the other person in the room, including that person's understandable need to be distrustful for awhile. As Angie's story in Chapter eight so painfully illustrates, when the particulars of the circumstances that brought a child, teen, or young adult to treatment are not taken into account, the consequences can be dire and far-reaching.

Therapists must also simultaneously draw on the resources they have developed from being in healthy, sustaining, satisfying relationships. Even therapists who have had more than their share of unhealthy or hurtful relationships must be able to hold the knowledge that relationships can be sources of pleasure and sustenance. It is necessary that they do this while clients gradually come to know that for themselves. This situation is not so different from that of an adult facing a teenager who feels as if the world is coming to an end because of the breakup of a romance; the adult must fully understand the depth and truth of the teen's feelings, while holding the knowledge that the feelings will pass and that the world will not end.

RBT is not a quick or easy solution to overcoming the pain inflicted before or during foster care. It is not a straightforward, linear process. Like development, the building of a relationship can often move two steps forward and then one step back. There is no simple formula, but there are solid guidelines. To state the obvious, no two people are alike and no two relationships, therapeutic or otherwise, will be identical. The therapist is there to offer help and the client is there to receive it. Even though the relationship is not equal, for it to succeed both parties must engage in the process with the shared purpose of improving and enriching the life of the client.

Enthusiasm

RBT is hard work, but it is also extremely satisfying work. Human beings are hard-wired to tell stories, and every story is unique. If we are willing to listen genuinely and respectfully we will have the privilege of hearing the amazing stories our clients bring to us. Those working with foster children, youth, and young adults will also hear horrific stories of mistreatment, often leaving them wondering how the person sitting in the room has survived. Regardless, it is our job to show our interest and our enthusiastic desire to hear and appreciate the stories that have shaped our clients into the people that sit in the room with us.

It is difficult to hear stories that tear at our hearts day after day

It is not surprising that therapists get discouraged when they hear tragic stories of abuse and trauma on a regular basis. It is also hard to remain enthusiastic when things seem to move slowly or the client who seemed to be making progress suddenly disappears. Even when the therapist knows that building trust goes slowly and that clients who have been abandoned often leave without warning, feelings of hopelessness and helplessness can and do emerge. Our work is challenging; at times it feels impossible to be present, let alone enthusiastic, especially if like Dr. R in Chapter seven, the therapist is worried that the therapy itself will add to a child's disappointment.

New clinicians who approach their work with eager excitement are particularly vulnerable to feeling as if their enthusiasm is slowly being drowned in a sea of woe, changing regulations, unreturned phone calls, endless paperwork, and little time to think or reflect on all that has come their way. They may find themselves questioning their choice of professions. They may feel more tired than usual, as if they have been overtaken by some low-grade virus that never becomes acute but never disappears. They may complain to colleagues that their supervisors are overly critical and their clients less than appreciative. Or they may find themselves trying to avoid clients who seem to have little interest in actually engaging in the therapeutic process.

And then something shifts

A child who has been withdrawn and emotionally distant tentatively offers to draw a picture and signs it with "love." An adolescent who has shown little interest in school announces that he worked really hard and got a good grade on an exam. A young adult who has been too depressed to do much of anything announces that she has begun a friendship with someone at work. Of course, these changes could be the result of environmental influences, but the therapists might also take them as evidence that the therapeutic relationship is beginning to have positive effects.

Interactions such as these – no matter how small – can renew enthusiasm and remind therapists what initially drew them to the mental health profession. They can bolster a fading sense of competence. However, placing undue reliance on clients' successes or progress poses dangers for therapist and client alike. It leaves therapists vulnerable to losing their confidence when things aren't going so well. Clients, particularly those who, like many foster children, have had to assume responsibility for shoring up fragile parents or caregivers, may quickly surmise that they need "to get better" in order to please their therapist. Success for the sake of the therapist runs counter to the tenets of RBT because it has shifted the focus of the therapy from the emotional life of the client to that of the therapist.

This is not to suggest that Relationship-Based Therapists do not appreciate and enjoy the positive steps in their clients' lives. But they do not look to their clients to sustain them and they do not focus on successes and strengths to the extent that they overlook the real pain and struggles in their clients' lives. Everyone has strengths and weaknesses; the latter are often more difficult to talk about. Many parents don't like to confess that they wanted to – or actually did – hit their child. Children are humiliated when they lose control of bowel or bladder and announce, "I don't want to talk about it." Teens may be embarrassed by their difficulties in understanding their emerging sexuality and bring up their questions and feelings only hesitantly. It is important that there be time and space for quiet reflection so that difficult topics can be raised in the client's own time. Therapists who focus primarily on building a safe and trusting relationship with their clients have both the freedom and responsibility to attend to changes in the therapeutic relationship as the primary means of assessing the effectiveness of the therapy.

Curiosity is a powerful tool for therapists

Curiosity helps the therapist to maintain an enthusiastic interest in what the client brings to the sessions. It also compels the therapist to attend to all of what the client brings – both positive and negative – as well as noting what is missing from the narrative. The therapist's curiosity can also help to spur clients' interest in the workings of their own minds, helping them to build essential self-observational skills. For example, a therapist might comment, "You know, it seems to me that you rarely talk about positive things about yourself, yet you have friends, and people come to you for advice. I wonder what they see in you that you don't talk about." The client might respond with something like, "I thought therapy was only to talk about problems." This gives the therapist an opportunity to extend the conversation into the client's expectations of relationships – in this example, as in the case of many foster kids, that you can only command attention by having problems or being needy, or that resilience doesn't count.

Enthusiasm and curiosity are steadfast therapeutic partners. The mind of the enthusiastic clinician has boundless curiosity and the therapist's curious mind is alive and interested in all that clients bring to the relationship. The therapist's openness to exploration invites a "meeting of the minds" with the client. For clients who have had very few relationships with people genuinely interested in their thoughts and feelings, the therapist's true interest in them can be both terrifying and liberating. The clinician must remember that RBT always offers the possibility of both.

Evidence

Over the last two decades, clinical researchers have provided us with an ever-growing body of evidence supporting the efficacy of different approaches to psychotherapy. This research has spawned attention from policy makers, clinicians, administrators, and insurance companies alike. And it appears that, in many ways, evidence-based practices are the current future of psychotherapy research. However, although these tools have merit, at present they are limited.

There is a need for more research with foster youth

The use of evidence-based practices with current and former foster youth has profound limitations. Many evidence-based practices have not been tested with foster youth; consequently, we remain unsure whether we can generalize treatments for at-risk and delinquent youth to foster youth – a vulnerable and unique population. Moreover, of the evidence-based practices available, a limited number focus on the therapeutic relationship, despite an understanding that therapeutic rapport is imperative to successful treatment. Rather, these practices allot limited time (e.g., one–three sessions) to "rapport building" without further note of relationship impasses or maintenance. Obviously, we need specific research on evidence-based practices with foster youth, a population for whom, understandably, trust and relationship-building are part of a long and enduring process.

The research-informed clinician

Therapists have a professional and ethical responsibility to remain abreast of advances in their fields and to carefully assess new information as it becomes available. This can be a daunting task, particularly for clinicians working in community-based settings with high demands for client care. Clinicians may also work in sites that require that all staff adhere to a particular theoretical orientation or rely only on interventions that are clearly and succinctly outlined and supported by traditional experimental outcome research. In situations such as these, clinicians may feel that their individual responsibility is irrelevant. This is a dangerous position because it assumes that what is happening in the mind of the clinician during the therapy session is of limited value – that the therapist's main challenge is to understand and deliver what other professionals have developed, what clinical researchers have demonstrated to be effective, or what their agency dictates. In other words, the therapist is merely a messenger, or even a pawn. It is also dangerous because it assumes that what is happening in the mind of the client is of equally little consequence except to confirm that the message has been received. Clinicians who thoughtlessly implement manualized interventions and procedures effectively remove themselves from the therapeutic relationship and deprive their clients of the most important thing they have to offer – the willingness to know their client's mind.

The link between research and RBT

As noted many times over in this volume, evidenced in massive amounts of research on child development, and supported by common sense – caring, stable relationships with adults are vital to healthy development. Moreover, client–therapist rapport is a key mechanism of change. Thus, clinicians who are able to enter into a therapeutic relationship with those whose childhoods lacked continuity and guidance from an adult who cared for and about them, have an enormously important opportunity to demonstrate that relationships can have a positive influence on life. Good relationships help our moods; they offer a chance for give and take; they let us learn about ourselves and others; they let us laugh and cry together; they are the cornerstone to healing; they allow us to lay the foundation on which other healthy relationships can be built. They actually allow us to live, not only healthier and happier, but longer.

RBT does not preclude the therapist using other modalities when indicated. Rather, RBT can act as an underlying assumption that can be melded beautifully with evidence-based techniques. For example, a therapist may rely on play to assist a child who has trouble verbalizing. He might help another client create cognitive strategies for managing depressing thoughts. With another he might suggest tactics for controlling anxiety in an upcoming job interview. Skilled clinicians acquire many therapeutic tools and, with practice, they learn which are most effective with particular clients or in particular situations. Over time, they also learn which are the best fit for who they are and how they approach their work.

The truth of the evidence we gather is not always immediately or easily demonstrated. We form hypotheses and test them. Rather than asserting our ideas and insisting on the final word, we help our clients learn the power of wondering and considering different possibilities. We do this in order to keep both parties engaged in the therapeutic process. Peggy's therapy described in Chapter four vividly demonstrates the importance of attending to the evidence the client bring to the therapy about his or her changing state of mind and need for distance or engagement. This allows for a meeting of the minds.

We must never forget that the most important evidence available to the clinician working in Relationship-Based Therapy is the relationship itself. We notice the way in which the client enters the room and begins the session. We listen to the verbal content – attending not only to what is said but also to what remains unspoken. At the appropriate moment, we tell the client what is in our mind about what is transpiring in the session and/or the relationship. We monitor our own thoughts and feelings because they offer another lens into what is happening in the consulting room. Sharing our observations and the sense we make of them opens a window into our minds for our clients and gives them an opportunity to expand their ways of knowing themselves. The process of continually testing, expanding, and refining concepts makes for lively and enlivening discussion, which lies at the heart of the therapeutic relationship.

Endurance

RBT is not a sprint; it's a cross-country race and you can't know in advance exactly what you'll see along the way. Like long-distance runners, therapists must be well prepared and physically, emotionally, mentally fit to build lasting relationships with clients. Nonetheless, therapists too often become so concerned with meeting the needs of their clients that they don't take care of themselves. They forget – or ignore – the basic tenets of good health. They ignore the reality that we cannot do good work when we are emotionally, intellectually, or physically depleted. We need to demonstrate to our clients what it means to take good care of one's self. Our clients learn as much – or more – from our actions as they do from our words.

ESSENCE OF RELATIONSHIP-BASED THERAPY

A number of difficulties can arise from therapists' sense that their work must rise to the heroic

The most obvious difficulty that arises from unrealistic therapist self-expectation is that they will inevitably fail and disappoint both their clients and themselves. There is no theoretical orientation or practice that can guarantee success in every situation, even in the hands of the most skilled clinicians or in the most supportive environment as we saw in Chapter four as people trying to help Marcus repeatedly failed despite their best and determined efforts. Particularly when working with multiply traumatized clients, we must be aware of our therapeutic limits. We cannot undo the fact of trauma and we do our clients a disservice if we lead them to believe that neglect, abuse, and abandonment do not leave scars. We must balance this knowledge with an optimistic understanding that strength can and does emerge from adversity and that satisfying and productive lives are possible, even in the wake of tragic childhoods.

The hardships that our clients have endured will inevitably make their way into the therapeutic relationship

It is human nature to treat others as we have been treated. Clients who have been mistreated will mistreat others, including their therapists. The healing power of the therapeutic relationship arises from the therapist's capacity to understand this behavior as having to do with past relationships and to respond with compassion rather than with anger or despair. The therapist is in a unique position to break the cycle of mistreatment, but not by meeting anger with anger or withdrawing in response to the client's emotional distance. As shown by so many of the therapists in this book, the therapist must demonstrate a different way of being in a relationship. When the behavior of foster youth is hurtful, too often they are met with a response meant to let them "see how it feels." They already know how it feels to be mistreated! Retaliation for their misbehavior only confirms their belief that people cannot be trusted and relationships offer nothing good.

Another pattern that is common in treatment is that clients don't show up, and yet they keep coming back. Many foster youth will not come to their sessions week after week, or come late, and yet they continue to schedule and show up now and again. For example, a client will not come for the regular Thursday meeting for three weeks, only to show up the fourth week with the expectation that the time is still available. Being able to hold this spot open for a client can be a great show of commitment and promoting trust. It is when we show our clients that we don't give up on them as so many others have, that they can begin to realize that maybe we can be different and maybe, they can look to us for a sustained connection.

163

Withstanding the feelings that traumatized clients bring to the therapy is not easy

Therapists understandably want to withdraw from anger and hurt. This can lead, for example, to their shutting down or acting out their feelings by cancelling or changing sessions for little more than their own convenience. Clinicians need help in managing their feelings in a way that promotes the growth and well-being of their clients. They need to take care of themselves and maintain healthy balance so they are available in a therapeutic way for whatever their clients bring into the room – week after week.

Therapists who work extensively with traumatized clients are particularly vulnerable to secondary trauma and may find that they develop symptoms that mimic those of their clients: difficulty sleeping, heightened anxiety, emotional numbness, and preoccupation with the clients' stories, for example. It is important for therapists to remind both themselves and their clients that trauma is held in the body, as well as the mind. In some cases, relaxation techniques can and should be incorporated into the sessions; in other cases, clients may benefit from a reminder that sometimes walking – whether around the block or up and down the stairs of the clinic – can help to still their minds.

The consultation groups that are an integral part of A Home Within can and should be replicated in other settings

Therapists working with traumatized populations need the support and understanding of consultants and colleagues. We cannot do this work alone – it is just too hard. All clinicians working in a relationship-based model should have access to a group of like-minded colleagues who can help them endure and understand the complex feelings and behavior their clients bring to the therapy. Without the support of consultants and colleagues, therapists can too easily become overwhelmed, making it impossible for them to think. Sometimes the group is called upon to think when the therapist cannot. For example, one therapist complained to her consultation group that her client repeatedly cancelled sessions at the last minute. She was angry and discouraged, feeling that her time was being wasted; she wondered if it was even worth continuing. The group was sympathetic to the therapist's feelings and also noted that calling at the last minute was a way of finding out if the therapist was actually there. The therapist then remembered that this client had been locked out of her home many times as a child. With this in mind, she decided that she would call the client the day before their session and remind her that she was planning to see her the next day. The client began attending sessions more regularly and, when she needed to cancel or change an appointment, calling in advance. This was the first step toward her being able to recognize this pattern in her relationships.

This example demonstrates how the capacity to think can be obscured by feeling mistreated and how it can be restored by feeling understood. With the help of the group, the therapist was able to use her feelings creatively to help her client. This closely parallels the process by which parents of young children help them manage feelings that threaten to overwhelm them. For example, when a toddler panics at the sight of a scratch on his knee, the reasonable parent neither rushes him off to the emergency room nor ignores his distress. Instead she sympathetically reassures him that it's a small scratch, cleans it and finds a bandage – sometimes two or three, if that's what it takes to bring the panic under control.

Instances such as this are repeated thousands of times over in healthy parent–child relationships. Through them children learn that they can count on adults to help them and that life's hurts can often – though not always – be soothed. They learn to distinguish between small and large injuries – both physical and emotional – and to respond appropriately. Those who have not had these comforting childhood experiences can easily be confounded and respond to an inadvertent slight as if it were an insult and appear to barely notice a truly aggressive comment. And, like the patient parent, the therapist will soon learn that interventions will need to be repeated many times over to be truly helpful.

Effective therapy demands endurance – both the capacity to withstand difficult thoughts and feelings in the moment and the willingness to withstand them over and over and over again until the therapy draws to a natural close. We usually know that we cannot care well for others unless we take good care of ourselves, but we sometimes forget. What we need to remember is that taking care of ourselves is part of our commitment to our clients.

Extending

The interpersonal aspect of the therapeutic relationship will, inevitably, draw to a close. At some point therapist and client will stop meeting. For those who have spent time in foster care and lived through so many relationships that ended unexpectedly and abruptly, it is exceedingly important that the conclusion of therapy, if at all possible, be planned and include input from the client about how and when the sessions will stop. While there are many ways that therapy can end badly, there is no single right way to manage the final stage of therapy.

In an ideal world, the therapeutic work continues until client and therapist agree that it is time for it to end

However, we live in an imperfect world and there are external factors that often determine the length of the therapy as is amply illustrated by Christina's story in Chapter nine. As noted at the beginning of this chapter, therapy may be limited for financial reasons, insurance limits, or agency policies requiring a predetermined number of sessions. Clients seeing interns will usually only have access to their therapist for the training period, though sometimes therapy can be continued in a different setting as the intern moves toward licensure. When this isn't possible or when insurance or finances limit the length of treatment, therapy should include a planned termination.

Unplanned endings call for creative thinking

The most painful endings are those that replicate earlier losses and come without warning as, for example, when a parent or other caregiver suddenly decides that the therapy must end. Even when the therapist is able to argue for a few additional sessions, the decision is rarely revocable. When it becomes clear that the end has come despite the therapist's best efforts, he should assist with a transfer to a new therapist, if appropriate. If it is impossible to have even a few termination sessions, at the very least, the therapist should make every effort to bring closure by sending a note along with a small memento of the time spent together. In one instance a teenager was suddenly moved from one foster home to another about 50 miles distant with no one willing to provide transportation so that she could say a proper "goodbye." Her therapist copied and laminated one of the collages they had worked on together and sent it to her with a note that she would keep the original in her office as her reminder of the time they had spent together. Phone calls and/or emails can also help to bring closure, when face-to-face meetings aren't possible.

Sometimes therapy ends in fits and starts

One young man kept regular appointments for about a year before his attendance became sporadic. He would leave a message saying that he wanted to set up an appointment, sometimes changing his mind when the therapist returned his call and sometimes attending a session. This continued for several months. In one phone call the therapist commented, "It seems like you're sometimes not sure if you want to come in or not." He replied, "I think I don't need to come in any more, but I don't want any session to be the last one." The therapist reminded him that he had an open-door policy and the client could always return. "Okay, then why don't I come next week and it will be the next-to-last session. We just won't schedule the last one," was his response. The therapist agreed to this plan, pleased that the client could move on, comforted by carrying the possibility of one (or more) sessions with him.

In the example above, the client was able to explain his behavior. Sometimes clients disappear without explanation. In those cases the therapist can only speculate about the reasons. We know that some clients can't imagine that someone would notice their absence, let alone miss them, while others stay away because they can't imagine anything other than a painful separation. These endings are often very difficult for therapists, who understand that bringing closure to activities and relationships can be satisfying and make the transition to life's next chapter easier.

Foster youth often have little experience with smooth transitions. Children are often expected to say "hello" to a new foster home before they have had time to say "goodbye" to the last. This is especially important to keep in mind if therapists are beginning work with clients who have been transferred from another clinician. Therapists are often so eager to begin building a relationship with new clients that

ESSENCE OF RELATIONSHIP-BASED THERAPY

they overlook their need to mourn the loss of the previous therapist. Particularly in settings staffed by interns, loss will be at the center of the therapeutic relationship. The client who has been left by one therapist will have trouble embracing the second and may not even try with the third. However, there is no chance of forming a meaningful relationship unless the therapist acknowledges the pain of these losses and tries to help the client bear the grief.

One of the ways we manage grief is by carrying those we have loved and lost with us

Whether we lose someone to death or through the vagaries of life, the internalized relationship does not end, unless it has been so brief or inconsequential that we have not taken it in. A successful therapeutic relationship, like the gains made as a result, will extend well beyond the interpersonal interactions on which it was built. A young child needs to be in proximity to her mother to feel her comfort, but as she grows she can call on the soothing maternal presence she carries within her. Clients in a new relationship with a therapist require frequent and regular contact in order to be able to draw on the therapist's strength. It is only over time that they can internalize that strength and make it their own. At the beginning of a therapy that stretched over several years a young woman called her therapist several times a week in a state of panic. Brief phone contact usually calmed her, but did not sustain her for more than a few days. After some time, if the therapist didn't reach her when returning a call and left a message, those calls would sometimes not be returned. The client explained that hearing the message was enough. Still later, the client described that in states of anxiety she would sometimes listen to the therapist's outgoing message to calm herself. Finally, although her anxiety had diminished significantly, in those moments when she felt it building she was able to simply think about her therapist in order to restore calm.

One of the most important pieces of work in the final phase of therapy is helping clients recognize the ways in which the relationship and therapeutic gains now belong to them. They can get along without us precisely because they have us with them. We live in A Home Within them.

Summary

"What good are you? What I need is a mother!" That was the opening salvo of an adolescent meeting her therapist for the first time. Whether spoken or unspoken, this is the fundamental question that therapists working with parentless children must continually grapple with; we cannot afford to forget it. We need to keep in mind, hard as it is, that our connection to our clients cannot ever fill the void created by parental absence. We must also never forget that the therapist's task is not to fill the void, but to help the children, teens, and young adults who come to us for help, recognize their losses, and mourn them as best they can.

Those who have spent time in foster care have every reason to be sad and angry. We are charged with knowing that for and with them. If we are to work effectively, we must acknowledge that trauma cannot be undone, but can be overcome. As we have repeatedly heard in the stories in this volume, the traumatic histories that foster youth bring to treatment tempt both clients and therapists to turn away from the pain of the past – to move quickly toward the present and the future. If we give in to this temptation then we doom our clients to repeating their pasts in their future relationships. If they have been abused or abandoned, they risk becoming embroiled in abusive and unstable relationships. Neglected children, as adults, will find themselves unable to care fully for themselves or others. Therapists cannot replace parents, nor should they try. However, they can offer a turning point through a relationship that refuses to repeat the past and holds a vision for a different future. Through a healthy, caring, lasting therapeutic relationship foster youth can come to know that relationships hold the possibility for growth, pleasure, respect, and love.

REFERENCES

Albus, K. E., & Dozier, M. (1999). Indiscriminate friendliness and terror of strangers in infancy: Contributions from the study of infants in foster care. *Infant Mental Health Journal 20 (1),* 30–41.

Altman, N. (1995). *The analyst in the inner city: Race, class, and culture through a psychoanalytic lens.* Relational perspectives book series, Vol. 3. Hillsdale, NJ: Analytic Press, Inc.

Alvarez, A. (1992). *Live company: Psychoanalytic psychotherapy with autistic, borderline, deprived and abused children.* New York: Routledge.

Aron, L. (1991). The patient's experience of the analyst's subjectivity. *Psychoanalytic Dialogues: The International Journal of Relational Perspectives 1 (1),* 29–51.

Bernstein, N. (2000). *A rage to do better.* San Francisco: Pacific News Service.

Bernstein, N. & Foster, L. K. (2008). *Voices from the Street: A survey of homeless youth by their peers.* Sacramento: California Research Bureau. www.library.ca.gov/crb/08/08-004.pdf

Biederman, J., Wozniak, J., Martelon, M., Spencer, T. J., Woodworth, Y., Joshi, G., & Faraone, S. V. (2013). Can pediatric bipolar-i disorder be diagnosed in the context of posttraumatic stress disorder? A familial risk analysis. *Psychiatry Research 208 (3),* 215–224.

Birch M. (1994, April). Rock-a-bye baby: Ordinary maternal hate. Paper presented at the annual meeting of the American Psychological Association, Washington, DC.

Birch, M. (2000). Love in the countertransference. Presented at the spring meeting of the Division of Psychoanalysis. American Psychological Association. San Francisco, CA.

Birch, M., & Zorrah, Q. (2012). Containment, trauma, and coherence: A case presentation and discussion. *Journal of Infant, Child, and Adolescent Psychotherapy 11 (4),* 316–341.

Blatt, S. J., & Levy, K. N. (2003). Attachment theory, psychoanalysis, personality development, and psychopathology. *Psychoanalytic Inquiry 23(1),* 102–150.

Bosma, H. A., & Kunnen, E. S. (2001). Determinants and mechanisms in ego identity development: a review and synthesis. *Developmental Review 21 (1),* 39–66.

Bowlby, J. (1975a). *Attachment and loss, Vol.1 — Attachment.* New York: Basic Books.

Bowlby, J. (1975b). *Attachment and loss, Vol.2 — Separation: Anxiety and anger.* New York: Basic Books.

REFERENCES

Bromberg, P. (1998). *Standing in the spaces: Clinical process, trauma, and dissociation.* Hillsdale, NJ: Analytic Press, Inc.

Bromberg, P. (2000). Bringing in the dreamer: Some reflections on dreamwork, surprise and the analytic process. *Contemporary Psychoanalysis 36 (4)*, 685–706.

Caper, R. (1996). Play, experimentation, and creativity. *International Journal of Psychoanalysis 77 (5)*, 859–869.

Chandler Warner, G. (1989). *The boxcar children.* Morton Grove: Albert and Whitman Company.

Chodorow, N. (1978). *The reproduction of mothering: Psychoanalysis and the sociology of gender.* Berkeley, CA: University of California Press.

Chused, J. (1991). The evocative power of enactments. *Journal of the American Psychoanalytic Association 39*, 615–639.

Cicchetti, D., & Cummings, E.M. (1993). *Attachment in the preschool years: Theory, research and intervention.* Chicago: University of Chicago Press.

Cicchetti, D., Rogosch, F.A., & Toth, S.L. (2006). Fostering secure attachment in infants in maltreating families through preventive interventions. *Development and Psychopathology 18 (3)*, 623–649.

Clausen, J.M., Aguilar, R.M., & Ludwig, M.E. (2012). Fostering healthy attachment between substance dependent parents and their infant children. *Journal of Infant, Child, and Adolescent Psychotherapy 11 (4)*, 376–386.

Cohen, Y. (1988). The "Golden Fantasy" and countertransference: Residential treatment of the abused child. *Psychoanalytic Study of the Child 43*, 337–350.

Conley, D. (1999). *Being black, living in the red: Race, wealth, and social policy in America.* Berkeley, CA: University Press.

Dervin, D. (1983). A dialectical view of creativity. *Psychoanalytic Review 70 (4)*, 463–491.

Deutsch, R. (Ed.) (In press). *Traumatic ruptures: Abandonment and betrayal in the analytic relationship.* New York: Analytic Press.

Didion, J. (2006). *The year of magical thinking.* New York: Random House.

Douglas, M. (1986). *How institutions think: The Frank W. Abrams lectures.* Syracuse, NY: Syracuse University Press.

Ehrensaft, D. (2007, April). A child is being eaten. Paper presented at the Division 39 meeting of the American Psychological Association, Toronto, Ontario, Canada.

Engel, G. (1961). Is grief a disease? In R. Frankiel (Ed.), *Essential papers on object loss* (pp. 10–16). New York: New York University Press, 1994.

Erikson, E.H. (1980). *Identity and the life cycle.* New York: Norton.

Esman, A.H. (1987). Rescue fantasies. *Psychoanalytic Quarterly 56 (2)*, 263–270.

Fitzgerald, F.S. (1925). *The great Gatsby.* New York: Charles Scribner's Sons.

Fonagy, P. (1998). Prevention, the appropriate target of infant psychotherapy. *Infant Mental Health Journal 19 (2)*, 124–150.

Fonagy, P., Steele, M., Steele, H., Moran, G.S. & Higgitt, A.C. (1991). The capacity for understanding mental states: The reflective self in parent and child and its significance for security of attachment. *Infant Mental Health Journal 12 (3)*, 201–218.

Fraiberg, S., Adelson, E., & Shapiro, V. (1975). Ghosts in the nursery: A psychoanalytic approach to impaired infant-mother relationships. *Journal of American Academy of Child Psychiatry 14 (3)*, 1387–1422.

Frankiel, R.V. (1985). The stolen child: A fantasy, a wish, a source of countertransference. *International Review of Psycho-analysis 12 (4)*, 417–430.

REFERENCES

Freud, S. (1909). Family Romances. *Standard edition of the complete psychological works of Sigmund Freud. Vol. IX* (pp. 237–241). London: Hogarth Press.

Freud, S. (1927). Fetishism. *Standard edition of the complete psychological works of Sigmund Freud: Vol. XI.* London: Hogarth Press.

Freud, S. (1930). Civilization and Its Discontents. *Standard edition of the complete psychological works of Sigmund Freud. Vol. XXI.* London: Hogarth Press.

Frosch, J. (1909). Transference derivatives of the family romance. *Journal of the American Psychoanalytic Association 7,* 503–522.

Furman, E. (1973). A child's capacity for mourning. In R. Frankiel (Ed.), *Essential papers on object loss* (pp. 376–381). New York: New York University Press, 1994.

——— (1974). A child's parent dies: Studies in childhood bereavement. New Haven, CT: Yale University Press.

Gediman, H. K. (1974). Narcissistic trauma, object loss, and the family romance. *Psychoanalytic Review 61 (2),* 203–215.

Gillman, R. D. (1992). Rescue fantasies and the secret benefactor. *Psychoanalytic Study of the Child 47,* 279–298.

Glenn, J. (1974). The adoption theme in Edward Albee's *Tiny Alice* and *The American Dream. The Psychoanalytic Study of the Child 29,* 413–429.

Greenacre, P. (1958). The family romance of the artist. *The Psychoanalytic Study of the Child 13,* 9–43.

Greenberg, J., & Mitchell, S. (1983). *Object relations in psychoanalytic theory.* Cambridge, MA: Harvard University Press.

Hanly, C. (1909). Metaphysics and innateness: A psychoanalytic perspective. *International Journal of Psychoanalyis 69,* 389–399.

Harris, A. (In press). Psychoanalytic process in the shadow of rupture: Clinical encounters with death, dead mothers, and deadly mothers. In R. Deutsch (Ed.), *Traumatic ruptures: Abandonment and betrayal in the analytic relationship* (pp. 15–47). New York: Analytic Press.

Harris, A., & Sinsheimer, K. (2008). The analyst's vulnerability: Preserving and fine-tuning analytic bodies. In F. S. Anderson (Ed.), *Bodies in treatment: The unspoken dimension* (pp. 255–273). New York: Analytic Press.

Hart, C. (2012). The "Dead Mother Syndrome" and the child in care: A framework for reflecting on why some children experience multiple placement breakdowns. *Journal of Infant, Child, and Adolescent Psychotherapy 11 (4),* 342–355.

Heineman, T. (1999). In search of the romantic family: Unconscious contributions to problems in foster and adoptive placement. *Journal for the Psychoanalysis of Culture and Society 4 (2),* 250–264.

Heineman, T. V. (1998). *The abused child: Psychodynamic understanding and treatment.* New York: Guilford Press.

Heineman, T. V. (2001). Hunger pangs: Transference and countertransference in the treatment of foster children. *Journal of Applied Psychoanalytic Studies 3(1),* 5–16.

Heineman, T. V., Clausen, J. M. & Ruff, S. C. (Eds.) (2013). *Treating trauma: relationship-based psychotherapy with children, adolescents, and young adults.* Lanham, MD: Jason Aronson.

Heineman, T. V., & Ehrensaft, D. (Eds.) (2005). *Building a home within: Meeting the emotional needs of children and youth in foster care.* Baltimore: Paul Brookes Publishing.

Hewitt, J. W. (1993). Moving from the language of action to the language of words. In L. B. Boyer and P. Giovacchini (Eds.), *Master clinicians – On treating the regressed patient* (pp. 259–277). New York: Jason Aronson.

REFERENCES

Hewitt, S. K. (1994). Preverbal sexual abuse: What two children report in later years. *Child Abuse and Neglect 19(7)*, 855–863.

Horner, T. M., & Rosenberg, E. B. (1974). The family romance: A developmental-historical perspective. *Psychoanalytic Psychology 8 (2)*, 131–148.

Ippen, C. G., Harris, W., Van Horn, P. & Lieberman, A. (2011). Traumatic and stressful events in early childhood: Can treatment help those at highest risk? *Child Abuse and Neglect 35 (7)*, 504–513.

Jackson, J., & Stricker, G. (1989). Supervision and the problem of grandiosity in novice therapists. *Psychotherapy Patient 5 (3–4)*, 113–124.

Joubert, D., Webster, L. & Hackett, R. (2012). Unresolved attachment status and trauma-related symptomatology in maltreated adolescents: An examination of cognitive mediators. *Child Psychiatry and Human Development 43 (3)*, 471–483.

Kaplan, L. J. (1974). The concept of the family romance. *Psychoanalytic Review 61 (2)*, 169–202.

Kay, C., & Green, J. (2013). Reactive attachment disorder following early maltreatment: Systematic evidence beyond the institution. *Journal of Abnormal Child Psychology 41 (4)*, 571–581.

Keenan-Miller, D., & Miklowitz, D. J. (2011). Interpersonal functioning in pediatric bipolar disorder. *Clinical Psychology: Science and Practice 18(4)*, 342–356.

Kingsolver, B. (1999). *The poisonwood bible*. New York: Harper Perennial.

Klein, M. (1940). Mourning and its relation to manic-depressive states. In R. Frankiel (Ed.), *Essential papers on object loss* (pp. 95–122). New York: New York University Press.

Lehrman, P. R. (1927). The phantasy of not belonging to one's family. *Archives of Neurology and Psychiatry 18 (6)*, 1015–1023.

Lemma, A., & Fonagy, P. (2013). Feasibility study of a psychodynamic online group intervention for depression. *Psychoanalytic Psychology 30 (3)*, 367–380.

Lieberman, A. F. (1993). *The emotional life of the toddler*. New York: Free Press.

Loewald, H. W. (1979). The waning of the Oedipus complex. In *Papers on psychoanalysis* (pp. 384–404). New Haven, CT: Yale University Press.

Lyons-Ruth, K., Bureau, J. F., Riley, C. D. & Atlas-Corbett, A. F. (2009). Socially indiscriminate behavior in the Strange Situation: Convergent and discriminate validity in relation to caregiving risk, later behavior problems, and attachment insecurity. *Development and Psychopathology 21 (2)*, 355–372.

Lyons-Ruth, K., Dutra, L., Schuder, M. R. & Bianchi, I. (2006). From infant attachment disorganization to adult dissociation: Relational adaptions or traumatic experiences? *Psychiatric Clinics of North America 29 (1)*, 63–86.

Mahler, M. (1975). On human symbiosis and the vicissitudes of individuation. *Journal of the American Psychoanalytic Association 23*, 327–333.

Main, M. & Hesse, E. (1990). Parents' unresolved traumatic experiences are related to infant disorganized attachment status: Is frightened and/or frightening parental behavior the linking mechanism? In M. Greenberg, D. Cicchetti, and E. M. Cummings (Eds.), *Attachment in the preschool years: Theory, research, and intervention,* (pp. 161–182). Chicago: University of Chicago Press.

Main, M., Kaplan, N. & Cassidy, J. (1985). Security in infancy, childhood and adulthood: A move to the level of representation. In I. Bretherton and E. Waters (Eds.), *Growing points of attachment theory and research (Monographs of the Society for Research in Child Development)*. Chicago: University of Chicago Press.

REFERENCES

Malawista, K. L. (2004). Rescue fantasies in child therapy: Countertransference/transference enactments. *Child and Adolescent Social Work Journal 21 (4)*, 373–386. London: Springer.

McQueen, D., Itzin, C., Kennedy, R., Sinason, V. & Maxted, F. (Eds.) (2008). *Psychoanalytic psychotherapy after child abuse: The treatment of adults and children who have experienced sexual abuse, violence, and neglect in childhood.* London: Karnac Books.

Mulkerns, H. & Owen, C. (2008). Identity development in emancipated young adults following foster care. *Smith College Studies in Social Work 78(4)*, 427–449.

Newman, K. (1999). *No shame in my game: The working poor in the inner city.* New York: Alfred A. Knopf.

Ogden, T. H. (1987). The transitional oedipal relationship in female development. *International Journal of Psycho-Analysis 68 (4)*, 485–498.

——— (1988). On the Dialectical Structure of Experience – Some Clinical and Theoretical Implications. *Contemporary Psychoanalysis*, 24:17–45.

——— (1997). *Reverie and Interpretation: Sensing Something Human.* Northvale, NJ: Jason Aronson.

Oyen, A., Landy, S. & Hilburn-Cobb, C. (2000). Maternal attachment and sensitivity in an at-risk sample. *Attachment & Human Development 2 (2)*, 203–217.

Papoušek, M. (2011). Resilience, strengths, and regulatory capacities: Hidden resources in developmental disorders of infant mental health. *Infant Mental Health Journal 32 (1)*, 29–46.

Pavuluri, M. N., Henry, D. B., Nadimpalli, S. S., O'Connor, M. & Sweeney, J. A. (2006). Biological risk factors in pediatric Bipolar Disorder. *Biological Psychiatry 60 (9)*, 936–941.

Pawl, J. (1995). The therapeutic relationship as human connectedness: Being held in another's mind. *Zero to Three Journal 15 (4)*, 1–5.

Piaget, J. (1954). *The construction of reality in the child.* New York: Basic Books.

——— (1979). *The child's conception of the world.* Totowa, NJ: Littlefield, Adams & Co.

Pine, F. (1989). The place of object loss in normal development. In D. R. Deitrich and P. C. Shabad (Eds.), *The problem of loss and mourning* (pp. 159–173). Madison, CT: International Universities Press.

Rachman, A. W., & Mattick, P. (2012). The confusion of tongues in the psychoanalytic relationship. *Psychoanalytic Social Work 19(1–2)*, 167–190.

Raphael-Leff, J. (2012). "Terrible Two's" and "Terrible Teens": The importance of play. *Journal of Infant, Child, and Adolescent Psychotherapy 11(4)*, 299–315. New York: Analytic Press.

Rucklidge, J. J. (2006). Psychosocial functioning of adolescents with and without paediatric bipolar disorder. *Journal of Affective Disorders 91(2–3)*, 181–188.

Sander, L. (1975). Infant and care-giving environment: Investigation and conceptualization of adaptive behavior in a system of increasing complexity. In E. J. Anthony (Ed.), *Explorations in child psychiatry* (pp. 129–166). New York: Plenum Press.

Schafer, M. H. (2009). Parental death and subjective age: Indelible imprints from early in the life course. *Sociological Inquiry 79(1)*, 75–97.

Schenkel, L. S., West, A. E., Harral, E. M., Patel, N. B. & Pavuluri, M. N. (2008). Parent-child interactions in pediatric bipolar disorder. *Journal of Clinical Psychology 64 (4)*, 422–437.

Sekaer, C., & Katz, S. (1986). On the concept of mourning in childhood: Reactions of a 2½-year-old girl to the death of her father. *Psychoanalytic Study of the Child 41*, 287–314.

REFERENCES

Shane, E., & Shane, M. (1990). Object loss and self-object loss: A consideration of self psychology's contribution to understanding mourning and the failure to mourn. *Annual of Psychoanalysis 18*, 115–131. Hillsdale, NJ: Analytic Press.

Shapiro, S. L., & Carlson, L. E. (2009). *The art and science of mindfulness: Integrating mindfulness into psychology and the helping professions.* Washington, DC: American Psychological Association.

Sidel, R. (1999). Hearts of iron: Readings. *A Journal of Reviews and Commentary in Mental Health 2*, 14–18.

Siegel, L. (2011). A mother learns to enjoy her baby: Parent-infant psychotherapy and art therapy in the treatment of intergenerational separation-individuation struggles. *Infant Observation 14 (1)*, 61–74.

Singer, P. (1993). *How are we to live? Ethics in an age of self-interest.* Melbourne, Australia: Text Publishing Company.

Slade, A. (1999). Attachment theory and research: Implications for the theory and practice of individual psychotherapy with adults. In J. Cassidy and P. Shaver (Eds.), *Handbook of attachment: Theory, research, and clinical applications* (pp. 575–594). New York: Guilford Press.

Smith, W. B. (2011). *Youth leaving foster care: A developmental, relationship-based approach to practice.* London: Oxford University Press.

Stolorow, R. (1999). The phenomenology of trauma and the absolutisms of everyday life: A personal journey. *Psychoanalytic Psychology 16 (3)*, 464–468.

Sudol, T. (2009). Information packet: Workforce issues in child welfare. National Resources Center for Family-Centered Practice and Permanency. New York: Hunter School of Social Work.

Tabin, J. K. (1998). The family romance: Attention to the unconscious basis for a conscious fantasy. *Psychoanalytic Psychology 15 (2)*, 287–293.

Thompson, M. P., Kaslow, N. J., Kingree, J. B., King, M., Bryant, L. R. & Rey, M. (1998). Psychological symptomatology following parental death in a predominantly minority sample of children and adolescents. *Journal of Clinical Child Psychology 27(4)*, 434–441.

Tremblay, G. C., & Israel, A. C. (1998). Children's adjustment to parental death. *Clinical Psychology: Science and Practice 5(4)*, 424–438.

Tucker, D. J., & MacKenzie, M. J. (2012). Attachment theory and change processes in foster care. *Children and Youth Services Review 34*, 2208–2219.

Tuters, E., Doulis, S. & Yabsley, S. (2011). Challenges working with infants and their families: Symptoms and meanings – two approaches of infant–parent psychotherapy. *Infant Mental Health Journal 32(6)*, 632–649.

Waterman, A. S. (1982). Identity development from adolescence to adulthood: An extension of theory and a review of research. *Developmental Psychology 18 (3)*, 341–358.

Watters, T. A. (1956). Forms of the family romance. *Psychoanalytic Review 43*, 204–213.

Weston, R. B. (2006). In search of the fuzzy green pillow: Fragmented selves, fragmented institutions. In T. V. Heineman and D. Ehrensaft (Eds.), *Building a home within: Meeting the emotional needs of children and youth in foster care.* Baltimore, MD: Paul H. Brookes Publishing Co.

Widzer, M. E. (1977). The comic-book superhero: A study of the family romance fantasy. *Psychoanalytic Study of the Child 32*, 565–603.

Wieder, H. (1977). The family romance fantasies of adopted children. *Psychoanalytic Quarterly 46 (2)*, 185–200.

REFERENCES

Winnicott, D. W. (1953). Transitional objects and transitional phenomena – A study of the first "not-me" possession. *International Journal of Psycho-Analysis 34*, 89–97.

Wolfenstein, M. (1966). How is mourning possible? *Psychoanalytic Study of the Child 21*, 93–123. New York: International Universities Press.

Zeanah, C., Scheering, M., Boris, N., Heller, S., Smyke, A., & Trapani, J. (2004). Reactive attachment disorder in maltreated toddlers. *Child Abuse & Neglect 28 (8)*, 877–888.

Zukowsky, N. (2006), Doctor forever: Acute loss in the context of chronic loss. In T. V. Heineman and D. Ehrensaft (Eds.), *Building A Home Within: Meeting the emotional needs of children and youth in foster care* (pp. 95–110). Baltimore, MD: Paul H. Brookes Publishing Co.

INDEX

abandonment: early experiences of 29; effects of 157, 163; emotional 65; fear of 65; as precipitating event 101; reasons for 65, 72

abuse: difficulty in describing 32–5, 37–40, 44n1; history of 66, 67; lasting effects of 39–40; as precipitating event 101; *see also* abused children; sexual abuse; substance abuse; violence

abused children: attempts to help 46–57; demands on therapists 53–7; as difficult to love 51–2; lack of empathy in 156; physically aggressive 49–51, 57; psychotherapy with 37–8, 46; *see also* abuse

abused children, case studies: "Barbara" 36; "Corrine" 40; "Joey" 35; "Louise" 38–9; "Marcus" 46–8; "Michelle" 41–3; "Peggy" 53–6; "Ruby" 49–52

abusers, as "bad guys" 45–6

actions, ambiguity of 34–5

adolescence: emotional turbulence in 107, 128; support during 10, 17, 29, 30

adoptive placements 2, 8, 19, 59, 72, 76, 78, 80, 99, 116, 126, 139; fantasy in 62, 65–8

adults: fantasies of 3; as most important aspect of child's environment 153–4; *see also* foster parents; parents

A Home Within 147; beginnings of 4–6; as network for clinicians 9–13

anxiety: and bipolar disorder 108; among caseworkers 88; in children with attachment problems 20; among foster children 50, 54, 63, 64, 69, 75, 89, 157; among homeless youth 28; medication for 10, 147; in parents 47, 74; in patients 20, 167; resulting from trauma 164; in therapists and interns 5, 9, 95

attachment: ambivalent 20–1, 23, 88; anxious preoccupied 20, 23; avoidant 19–20, 23; of children in foster care 60; difficulties of homeless youth 21–4, 25–6; disorganized 21, 23, 67–9; insecure 19–21, 23; needs of homeless youth 29–31; secure 18–19, 29, 118, 146n1

attachment theory: defined 18–21; and the importance of relationships 84; and programs for homeless youth 26–9; value of 17–18; *see also* attachment

attorneys 2, 3, 11, 37, 48, 53, 59, 66, 67, 70, 72–4, 76, 80, 97, 100, 116

Being Black, Living in the Red: Race, Wealth, and Social Policy in America (Conley) 100

bipolar disorder (BD) 105, 107–8, 113–14; *see also* pediatric bipolar disorder

Bowlby, John 17

caregivers: children's attachment to 18; involvement of in therapy 153–4; *see also* foster parents; parents

caseworkers 2, 3, 40, 59, 60, 83, 88, 103, 111–13, 115–16, 127, 150

change: adjusting to 1; in behavior 21, 121, 127, 153–4; in environment 81, 89, 152; in the lives of foster children 2, 82–6, 88–9, 97, 132, 153; in parent-child relationships 75; in placement status 60, 90, 97, 111; positive 159; possibility of 4, 8, 30; in rules 97, 101; in therapeutic relationship 160–1

character disorders 115

childhood patterns 85–6

children: abusive behavior of 57, 78; and the creation of self 81–3; as creatures

INDEX

of habituation 1–2, 84–5; emotional development of 105–7, 108–9; emotionally disturbed 107; grieving 133–46; idealization of 72; mythical parentless 61; relationships with parents 35–6, 37 (*see also* attachment); sexualized behavior of 120; structures in which they are embedded 3; transformational power of 75–80; *see also* abused children; foster children; homeless youth

"Children's Psychotherapy Project, The" 5–6; *see also* A Home Within

Clinical Chapters 7

clinicians *see* therapists

closure 151, 166

community: influence of 3, 10; sense of 7

Conley, Dalton 100

Consultation Groups 6, 7, 11–13, 164–5

continuity 2, 21, 59, 82, 86, 97, 107, 149, 152, 161

countertransference 99

court appointed special advocate (CASA) 116, 119

curfews 28, 30

curiosity 160

death: coping with 1; of fathers 117, 129, 131–2; of mothers 12; of parents 134–5; *see also* loss

decompensation 69

depression 77, 105, 108–10, 112–13, 115, 147

disorganization, affective 41–3

dissociation 34, 87

divorce 1, 3, 10, 82

Douglas, Mary 96

drug abuse *see* substance abuse

drugs, *in utero* exposure to 108, 112

drug treatment programs 5, 72, 115, 122

educational organizations, influence of 3, 10

egocentrism, in RBT 157–8

ego functioning, split in 135

emotional abandonment 65

emotional development 105–7, 108–9

emotional distress 21

emotional reserves 100–1

empathy, in RBT 155–6

endurance, in RBT 162–5

engagement, in RBT 150–2

enthusiasm, in RBT 158–60

environment, in RBT 152–2

evidence, in RBT 160–2

extending, in RBT 165–7

family(ies): abusive 28, 40, 84; adapting to 85; child's desire for 96–101; extended 1, 10, 15, 49–50, 101, 111; influence of 3, 18, 21–3, 27, 82–3, 92, 100; loss of 108, 141–2, 144, 150; of origin 3, 84; rebuilding 129, 135–6; romantic (*see* family romance[s]); rules of 30; stable vs. unstable 2, 9, 99, 155; support from 9–11, 152; withdrawal from 130–1; *see also* foster families; parents; siblings

family issues, case studies: "Bobby" 73–5; "Christina" 119–128 ; "Deanna" 72–3"; "Nicholas" 69–72; "Sally" 76–80; "Vera and Barbara" 67–9

family romance(s) 62–4, 80n2; and the belief in an ideal parent 67–71; as externalization 69, 70; fantasies about 62–4, 67–71; and the transformational power of the child 75–80; unresolved 80, 80n1

"Family Romances" (Freud) 62

fantasies: of involved adults 3; about the romantic family 62–4, 67–71; shared 99, 101

food, significance of 93–4, 97–8, 101–2

foster care 2–3; children's experience of 90–2; emotional economics of 100–1; failed placements 84, 124; instability of 2; losses created by 2, 59–60; moving children from one placement to another 2, 60, 81, 83–6, 89, 97; siblings in 5, 40, 68, 116, 119; uncertainty in 2; *see also* foster placement

foster care, case studies: "John" part one 83; "John" part two 87–90;

foster children: arranging therapy for 103–4; disempowering of 153; internet postings 90–1; interviews 90; needs of 6, 13; networks surrounding 10–11; relationship with a single therapist 9; treatment plans for 113

foster families 2, 59, 60, 83, 88, 90, 94, 101, 111–12, 125

foster parents 10–11

foster placement, 65, 80n1, 111

INDEX

Freud, Sigmund 62, 63
friends, as support group 7, 25

grief management 129, 165; *see also* mourning
grief management, case studies: "Benjamin" 131–46; "Ernie" 129–31

habituation 1–2, 84–5
homeless youth 17–18; attachment needs of 29–31; complaints regarding shelters 26–9; individual needs of 31; interviews with 22–5, 28, 82–3; premature self-reliance of 24; reasons for homelessness 21–4
Home Within, A 147; beginnings of 4–6; as network for clinicians 9–13
hope 3–4

identity formation 60, 81–3, 86, 89, 90
imbalance 152–3
infant-parent psychotherapy 115–16; beyond 124–28; joys of 116–18; pains of 119–24
instability 59, 70, 82, 97, 130, 155; *see also* stability

judges 11

Kingsolver, Barbara 101
knowing, burden of 7

language, inadequacy of 37–40, 43
loss: chronic 3–4, 7; coping with 1, 112, 145–6; experienced in foster care 2, 59–60; of fathers 117, 129, 131–2; of mothers 12; of parents 134–5

mental illness 3, 19, 21, 23, 27, 105, 108, 112, 114
mentors, relationships with 7
mood disorders 108
mourning: of children 138–41; of therapists 137; *see also* death; grief management; loss

narrative: inadequacy of 35–6; life 3; of self 33; use of in psychotherapy 34
neediness 20
neighborhood, influence of 3, 10
networks: absence of 24–6; of family and community 9–10; social 9–10

obsessive-compulsive disorder 113
Oedipal development 62, 65

parents: children without 61–2; choosing between 66; death of 134–5; emotional abandonment by 65; fantasies about 62–4; homosexual 80n1; imprisonment of 76, 101, 130; reunification with 2, 70–5, 115, 130
Pawl, Jeree 31
pediatric bipolar disorder 105; among children in foster care 107–9; case studies, "Angie" 109–14; diagnosing 107, 109, 113
peer relationships 7, 25
personal history 90, 113
Piaget, Jean 84
placement(s): failed 84, 124; stabilization of 127–8
Poisonwood Bible, The (Kingsolver) 101
post-traumatic stress disorder 107
poverty 82, 94, 97, 107, 108
power, ethical issues related to 153
psychic numbing 56
psychoactive drugs 107–8
psychosis 47, 115
psychotherapy: with abused children 46; as creative process 33; and the mourning therapist 137; *see also* infant-parent psychotherapy; therapy
purpose, shared 7, 158

rapport building 157–8
RBT *see* Relationship-Based Therapy
Reactive Attachment Disorder 19, 107
reality 36, 51–2, 75, 100, 110–11; denial of 122; distortions of 115; of patients 36, 122; preservation of 119; testing 64, 71–2, 105, 135, 143
Relationship-Based Therapy (RBT): application of 4, 147; egocentrism 157–8; empathy 155–6; endurance 162–5; engagement 150–2; enthusiasm 158–60; environment 152–5; essential elements of 149; evidence 160–2; extending 165–7; research in 161–2
relationships: building 5, 29–30, 157–8; effect of early attachment on 18; harmful 3; importance of 8, 15, 90, 106–7, 147; parent-child 35–7, 75, 165; with peers and mentors 7, 25; stable and lasting 6–7; supportive 7; therapeutic 150–3, 160–1

179

INDEX

relative visits 116
religious organizations, influence of 3, 10
rescue fantasies 46
research, in RBT 161–2
reunification with parent(s) 2, 70–5, 115, 130
routines 1–2, 84–5
runaways *see* homeless youth

Samuels, Bryan 89
self: narratives of 33; sense of 81
self-regulation 30
self-reliance 24
self-soothing 87
sexual abuse 3, 15, 32, 41, 66, 121
shared purpose 7, 158
siblings, in foster care 5, 40, 68, 116, 119
social networks 9–10
social workers 11, 49, 66, 67, 72–8, 80, 87–9, 97, 100, 101, 120–3
splitting 49, 52, 66
stability 2, 21, 59, 69, 77, 81, 94, 105, 107, 108, 114, 119, 152; *see also* instability
substance abuse 3, 21, 27, 50, 65, 66, 72, 76, 119, 122

theory of mind 155–6
therapeutic relationships 150–3, 160–1
therapist(s): biases of 154–5; challenges of 158–60, 163–4; emotional involvement with children 100; gifts from 94–6;

mourning 137; networks of 6, 11–13; place in child's network 1–11; as placeholder 135–8, 141–2; relationship with parents of clients 103; research-informed 161–2
therapy: external influences on 150; for grieving child 133–46; narrative 34; social expectations of 154; termination of 165–7; *see also* psychotherapy
therapy room 152
transference 57n, 99
transference issues, case studies: "David" 94–6; "Jimmy" 97–9, 101–2
trauma: of chronic loss 3–4, 7; and egocentrism 157; exposure to 5, 108, 114, 149, 154, 156, 158, 163–4; history of 107–8, 168; impact of 29–30; retraumatization 53, 57; secondary 164; treatment of 15–16; unresolved 118; *see also* violence

violence: child's exposure to 107, 108; by the child 57, 78; domestic 129; *see also* trauma
Voices from the Street: A Survey of Homeless Youth by Their Peers 21–5, 27–30, 90

youth, homeless *see* homeless youth

Zukowsky, Norman 12